Ibo Politics

The Role of Ethnic Unions
in Eastern Nigeria

Ibo Politics

The Role of Ethnic Unions
in Eastern Nigeria

Audrey C. Smock

Harvard University Press
Cambridge, Massachusetts
1971

© 1971 by the President and Fellows of Harvard College
Distributed in Great Britain by Oxford University Press, London
Printed in the United States of America
Library of Congress Catalog Card Number 70-134328
SBN 674-44025-0

To David and Erica

Contents

Tables

Map

Preface

In 1965 when I decided to undertake field work on Ibo ethnic unions in Eastern Nigeria, the first Nigerian Federal Republic was still frequently cited as the showcase for democracy in Africa, despite its many crises and the known perversions of a democratic political process. On the eve of my departure for Nigeria, a group of dissident junior and middle grade officers launched an abortive coup, which managed to topple the civilian political edifice. By January 16, 1966, one day after the attempted takeover, General J. T. U. Aguiyi Ironsi, to whom most of the army remained loyal, had gained control of the situation. A rump of the Federal Council of Ministers was convened and invited the army to assume power. The Ironsi regime itself became the casualty of a countercoup on July 31 of that year.

My stay in Eastern Nigeria coincided with the duration of the Ironsi administration. It proved to be an excellent period in which to do research. People in the East had no premonition that the military takeover would precipitate a tragedy. Quite the contrary, members of the military government were viewed as saviors from the corrupt civilian political order. Most people were confident that the Ironsi regime would initiate a new era of national unity and progress. Doubtless the sense of optimism derived in part from the fact that Ironsi and a majority of the army officers were Easterners, while the Northern People's party had dominated the civilian federal government. The educated elite, illiterate traders and farmers, and even some former politicians talked freely about the inadequacies of the civilian regime and stressed their hopes for the future.

My experience in Eastern Nigeria reaffirmed the assessment of others that for research purposes Eastern Nigerians were among the most open, honest, and cooperative people in Africa, or for that matter anywhere in the world. The vitality of the local ethnic unions and the pride that they instilled in their members greatly facilitated my research. Some ethnic unions curtailed their activities during this period in order to avoid attracting the attention of the military government, but the vast majority continued functioning. Although the ethnic unions representing inclusive nationality groupings, such as the Ibo State Union and the Ibibio Union, were dissolved by decree in May, the local ethnic unions were not discredited by their former involvement in politics. My ability to complete the research project in so short a period resulted from the unfailing cooperation and assistance of the people of Abiriba and Mbaise. Officers of ethnic unions in both communities granted me access to correspondence, minute books, and other records. I was invited to meetings of the various ethnic unions, some of which were conducted in English for my benefit. Officers and members of the ethnic unions allowed me to interview them extensively on a wide variety of matters. My inquiries concerning their history and activities sparked an independent search for information by members of several ethnic unions.

No one familiar with Eastern Nigeria can remain untouched by the tragedy which has befallen that region. During most of my writing the war still raged, and each day newspaper accounts revived concern that the optimistic and confident people I had known from Abiriba and Mbaise might become war casualties. The old order in Eastern Nigeria has been irrevocably shattered by the combined force of bullets, bombs, and starvation. Yet I still feel compelled to tell the story of Abiriba and Mbaise, both to preserve their contributions and to facilitate an understanding of the Ibo people. It is also my belief that ethnic unions can and probably will be mobilized to make an indispensable contribution to the reconstruction effort.

It is impossible to list all those in Abiriba and Mbaise who contributed their time and efforts, but I would particularly like to thank Kalu and Igwe Ogba, Ejim Akuma, O. O. Otisi, and Ina Obasi from Abiriba, the officers of the Mbaise Youth Movement branch in Port Harcourt, and D. N. Abii from Mbaise. Two friends, Richard Henderson of Yale University and Howard Wolpe of Western Michigan University, helped to plan the research strategy and select the two communities for study. My advisers at Columbia University, L. Gray Cowan and Dankwart

Rustow, provided considerable assistance in the initial conception of the project and the original presentation of the data. I owe an intellectual debt to Gabriel Almond, Samuel Huntington, and Robert Dahl. The work of David Smock on the Ibos influenced my initial approach, and later, after we had met and married, he contributed significantly to the revision of the manuscript.

A.C.S.

Accra, Ghana
March 1970

Ibo Politics

The Role of Ethnic Unions
in Eastern Nigeria

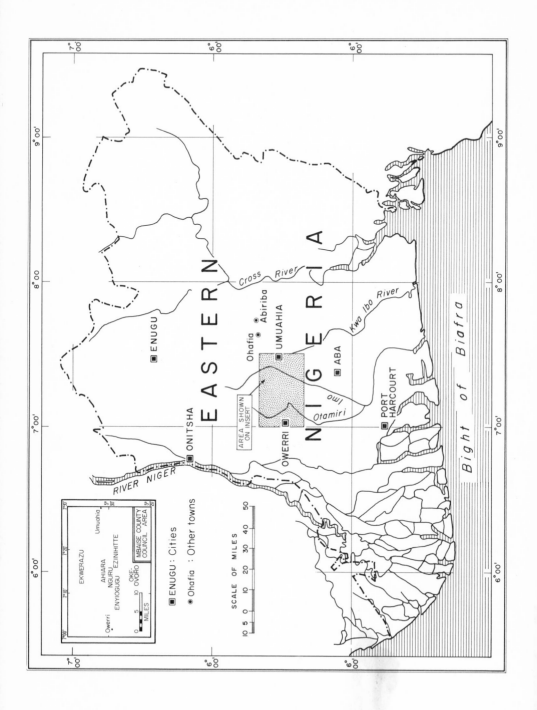

Introduction: Ethnic Identity
and Associations

The secession of Eastern Nigeria on May 30, 1967, and the resulting war with its tragic consequences, precipitated world-wide concern for that area. In 1966, only seven years after gaining independence, the Federal Republic of Nigeria disintegrated, though once widely heralded as the model for democracy and development in Africa. Ironically and sadly, the ethnic group whose members had most strongly advocated a united country, the Ibos, ultimately dismembered the Federation by leading the movement to create Biafra. Scholars, diplomats, and political leaders attempting to comprehend the dimensions of this tragedy are therefore confronted with the need to know more about the Ibo people and the dynamics of their politics.

In studying the politics of the Ibo, the predominant ethnic group in Biafra, one might be tempted to draw conclusions from a national Nigerian or regional perspective, since these broad frameworks would facilitate data collection and interpretation. However, such an approach would distort the analysis, because it would lead to generalizations about local communities on the basis of insufficient data. Moreover, the Nigerian Federation consisted of four relatively autonomous regional units which together determined the outcome of national political affairs. The Nigerian Constitution assigned most functions of government to the regions and therefore awarded a preponderance of revenue to them. According to the Constitution, the federal parliament could make all laws relating to currency, defense, external affairs, armed forces, communications, and exchange controls. All unlisted or residual powers, such as those concerned with agriculture, health, education, and public works, which brought government into contact with the

1

population were left for the regions. The institutional framework of the Eastern Region also resembled central Nigerian structures. The region had a premier, a council of ministers exercising authority, an appointed governor as ceremonial head, and a bicameral legislature, the latter consisting of an elected House of Assembly and an appointed ceremonial House of Chiefs. These were the counterparts of the federal prime minister, council of ministers, president, and House of Representatives and Senate. Eastern Region politics in turn comprised a series of compromises between alliances involving representatives of local communities. Hence, the path to discovering and interpreting the substance of Ibo politics and the dynamics of political development lies in a thorough study of local communities.

Though each local community is in some ways unique, so that in a sense there is no typical community, an investigation of a micropolitical system can serve as a reliable testing ground for hypotheses. Moreover, micropolitical entities provide the most meaningful vantage point from which to study the process of political development. Political development refers to the various phases in the process of nation-building during which a state becomes a more viable and self-directed political entity. The concept of political development subsumes three major components: institutionalization of the administrative and political structures, political integration, and modernization of cultural attitudes toward the political system. Political institutionalization refers to the process by which institutions and procedures become regularized and effective. Political integration alludes to the process by which identification with a more general community gradually supersedes parochial commitments. Cultural modernization implies the assumption of attitudes, values, and orientations that foster political development. The complexity ˉof the process of political development favors studying it in depth in either a single institution or a limited geographic area, for each aspect of the process depends on an array of variables that are difficult to measure and require a significant amount of data for analysis.

In most African states at least 80 percent of the people still live in rural areas. Obviously, then, if economic and political development is to be effected, it must take place in the countryside. The creation of effective political institutions, the promotion of a national identity, and the transformation of political attitudes must occur at the most primary and immediate level of the political system, where it has the greatest contact with the population. Hence, the competence of a national

planning commission, the cohesiveness of national leadership, the origi-
nality of a party's ideology, and all the other national concerns on which
political scientists tend to focus will be of no avail unless they penetrate
to the villages in which the people live. Pronouncements made in the
capital by the government or the party do not automatically filter down
to local communities. Quite the contrary, they are not translated into
effective policies unless a considerable amount of human and material
resources is allocated over a long period of time to building effective
political institutions. At this stage of African development, only empirical research can determine the ability of any national or regional
government to reach out into particular communities. Models and paper
constitutions, whether they are for administrative institutions or for
political parties, often bear no resemblance to the actual order of things
in the country.

Accordingly, this study concentrates on the political systems of two
Ibo communities in Eastern Nigeria: Abiriba, a large village-group or
town in Bende Division, and Mbaise, a populous county council area
in Owerri Division, during the period from 1941 until 1966. Particular
emphasis is placed on the role that ethnic unions played in these
micropolitical systems and their effect on local political development.
The form of organization in which many ethnic groups confront the
political systems of Asia and Africa is the ethnic association, which
combines the modern structure and functions of a voluntary organization with an ascriptive membership base. The most complete and
complex proliferation of such ethnic associations seems to have taken
place in Eastern Nigeria, where they constituted the most common
and significant indigenously established organization. Their formation
in most communities preceded the attempts of political parties to
organize in the countryside and the efforts of the colonial administration
to introduce a modern system of local government. In addition, ethnic
associations contributed greatly to the rapid economic and educational
development of the Ibo people.

This is not the first micropolitical study of rural or urban African
communities. Recently other scholars have called attention to the need
for such research and analysis. A number of anthropologists and political scientists have aptly assessed political development and modernization through the perspective of rural communities.[1] As a consequence
of this change in perspective, scholars have begun to reevaluate and
discard some of the models and conclusions reached by earlier re-

searchers, who generalized on the basis of data collected primarily in capital cities.

From the vantage point of Abiriba and Mbaise before 1967, as well as of the communities of immigrants from those areas established in Port Harcourt, the industrial center of Eastern Nigeria, many of the explanations currently offered for the disintegration of Nigeria do not appear sound. The popularity of the facile and simplistic notion that tribalism is the most significant factor impeding political development in Africa has led some analysts to cite Ibo tribalism as the catalyst for the breakdown of the Federation of Nigeria. However, contrary to widely assumed notions about the negative influence of tribalism or ethnicity in general and of ethnic unions (sometimes referred to as tribal unions) in particular, ethnicity does not necessarily impede political development. Ethnic identity, as it operated through the ethnic unions in Abiriba, Mbaise, and Port Harcourt, tended to promote the positive evolution of the Eastern Nigerian political system. Moreover, Ibo identity as such did not constitute the salient referent for Ibo-speaking peoples before the federation began to disintegrate. In fact, Ibo unity rarely existed on any political issue. Consequently, unless the definition of tribalism is severely qualified, it becomes difficult to attribute Biafran secession to Ibo ethnicity.

ETHNIC IDENTITY

The term "ethnic group" is here defined as an association of people bound together by felt ties of kinship or contiguity. Ethnicity or ethnic affiliation refers to the identification of members with the group. Ethnicity constitutes one of the most common expressions of what Clifford Geertz called "primordial attachments" stemming from the "givens" of social existence that seem to have "an ineffable, and at times overpowering, coerciveness in and of themselves."[2] The definition of ethnic group used here, indicating that the ties are conscious or felt, purposely emphasizes the subjective nature of ethnic affiliation. Attempts to delineate objective characteristics of ethnic groups, like common descent or cultural or linguistic homogeneity, limit the application of the term. Moreover, not all ethnic groups share similar objective characteristics, because the phrase "ethnic group" encompasses many different types of association, ranging from a small patrilineage of less than one hundred persons to a people or nationality, like the Ibos, of several million members.[3]

The relative nature of such concepts as common descent and cultural and linguistic similarity also militates against an attempt to impute specific characteristics to ethnic groups. Ethnic affiliation is self-defined in the sense that members of the group rather than outsiders draw its boundaries. Certain characteristics, like a common dialect, may be shared by two communities, which perceive themselves to be members of separate ethnic groups, while in another situation linguistic factors may determine the boundaries of ethnic affiliation. Slight differences in dialect or culture between two contiguous communities may or may not prevent them from joining together to form one ethnic group. Thus, the objective existence of minor variations in dialect or culture cannot by itself indicate whether communities will perceive these differences as establishing an ethnic boundary.

Not only are the boundaries between ethnic groups somewhat arbitrary, they are also mutable. When social or cultural transformations occur, two communities may begin to stress the bonds they hold in common rather than the factors that formerly divided them. Under the stimulus of changed conditions, cultural patterns in two communities may alter and in the process narrow the gap between them. Although in the past such changes probably took place gradually over long periods, Paul Mercier suggested that important modifications of ethnic frontiers can be accomplished in relatively short intervals of time in response to radically new conditions.[4]

The existence of different types of ethnic groups at varying levels of inclusiveness allows individuals and entire communities to maintain multiple affiliations. Which affiliation the members stress depends on the particular situation. The patrilineage, which may be relevant for ceremonial purposes, is superseded for other common activities, such as building shrines or irrigation ditches. In turn, a wider sphere of several communities becomes the focus for purposes of defense or trade. When only two communities oppose one another, the situation provokes an accentuation of the particular differences between them. But these same differences become irrelevant when the two unite to pursue another type of activity vis-à-vis a third group.

The impact of colonial rule in Africa provided the stimulus for a change in the boundaries and attitudes of many ethnic groups. The concept of social change originally held by many colonial administrators and some scholars, which sharply distinguished between the traditional and the modern, led them to believe that thoroughgoing contact with the forces of modernity would fundamentally transform the social landscape by eroding commitments to existing ethnic groups. Somewhat ironically, however, initial contacts with modernity seem to have strengthened rather than weakened ethnic affiliation. In the precolonial political systems most persons spent their lives within the confines of their immediate group. Even when a political superstructure existed linking a number of different communities over a wider geographic area, contact with the outside world tended to be mediated by the village headman or another representative. In this situation of relative isolation, any identification with an ethnic group, while automatic, rarely became explicit. By bringing communities into a wider range of contact with other groups, of both a similar and a dissimilar nature, the colonial administration precipitated transformations in the nature of ethnic identity.

First, ethnic identity assumed new dimensions as an explicit referent through which members of a community could distinguish themselves from outsiders, with whom they now had more frequent contact. By its very nature, therefore, ethnic awareness intensified in situations of intergroup contact. Moreover, during the colonial period some ethnic communities began to compete openly for the benefits distributed by the administration and to vie for status. Differing responses of these various groups to the new opportunities for advancement also generated stronger ethnic allegiance as a defensive reaction.

At the same time, ethnic communities often became redefined as more inclusive and even nontraditional entities. The small scale of many traditional ethnic groups made them inappropriate as reference units in certain situations. For example, only a few members of a village would emigrate to a specific urban center, or the original groups would be too small to be effective in the new enlarged political arenas. Given these changed conditions and needs, individuals began to identify with larger, more amorphous communities, only a few of which had traditional counterparts. In the Nigerian context the emergence of the Ibo people under the stimulus of colonization exemplifies this process of changing levels of identity. The Mongo people in the Congo, the Kru people in Liberia, the Sukuma people in Tanzania, and the Teso people in Uganda provide other examples of cultural clusters that awakened to self-consciousness despite their lack of a traditional central political structure.

UNIFICATION OF THE IBOS

Before colonization there were no Ibo people. In the forested hinterland of what was to become Eastern Nigeria and along the west bank of the Niger River in what later became the Mid West Region of Nigeria, there were several hundred village communities, each of which usually consisted of no more than eight thousand people.[5] Because each village community constituted a separate political unit and a socially endogamous grouping, its inhabitants had little concern with the outside world. They and their ancestors had spent their lives within the confines of the village, interrupting their isolation only to trade or to fight with neighboring villages. Although relations among Ibo villages somewhat resembled Hobbes' state of nature, religious diviners, medicine men, and some traders did travel through the area. Oracles and their agents, particularly the one located at Aro Chuku, also extended their influence over large parts of Ibo territory. However, there was no sense of a common identity among these separate and inward-oriented villages.[6]

The awakening of the Ibos to their common identity owed more to the forces of modernity unleashed by the colonial administration than to any conscious efforts by the Ibos. Karl Deutsch suggested that a people consists of a large group of persons linked by complementary habits and facilities for communication. By complementary habits he meant the "ability to communicate more effectively, and over a wider range of subjects, with members of one group than with outsiders."[7] Before the establishment of colonial rule the Ibos did not fulfill these criteria. Without channels of communication, the separate village groups did not become conscious of their widespread cultural or linguistic similarities. Moreover, differences in dialect and customs existed from village to village.[8] Groups first encountering one another probably perceived these slight variations as insurmountable barriers. While prolonged interaction among groups was instrumental in making the culture and language somewhat more uniform over time, even more important was the enlarged frame of reference resulting from contact with the non-Ibo peoples in the Eastern Region and the federation, which reduced the significance of these discrepancies among the Ibo-speaking people.

Inclusion in a more comprehensive colonial administrative unit initially pierced the shell of village autonomy. The mobility made possible by the Pax Britannica also sparked increased contacts, as traders traveled greater distances more frequently. Cities, the melting pots of civilization, incubated new forms of ethnic identity in Nigeria. Especially in the early years of urbanization, when few persons from any one local area were likely to emigrate to a city, an individual's range of contacts, both during work and recreation, included a more diversified group of people than in the village. At this time the ability to communicate in one's own language was an important source of identity. As a result of their high population density—parts of the Ibo-speaking territory have been among the most heavily populated rural areas in the world—Ibos flocked to the new towns in large numbers.

Another factor fostering assimilation to the Ibo identity was the perception of similarity by outsiders. In consequence of its initial administrative problems in governing Eastern Nigeria, the colonial government sponsored several anthropological surveys to discover more about the nature of the traditional sociopolitical units. These surveys and later research undertaken by missionaries and scholars emphasized the linguistic and cultural uniformities in the area. In the cities many foreigners and members of other ethnic groups, having more sophisticated traditional sociopolitical systems or experiencing earlier contact with missionaries, regarded the Ibo-speaking groups with contempt because of the simplicity of their culture and their lack of education.

The process of assimilation took place very gradually. In the mid-1930's many groups, especially those of Onitsha, Aro Chuku, and Oguta, rejected the name Ibo as applying to themselves. When the administrative secretary of the Ibo State Union toured the rural hinterland of the Eastern Region in the late 1940's, he found that the concept of "all the Ibos" was still incomprehensible to most of the villagers. By 1930, educated Ibo-speaking people associated themselves as a linguistic unit. A common acceptance of the wider frame of reference probably occurred only in the 1950's. Even then, however, the more primary ethnic identities remained stronger and more salient than the inclusive Ibo grouping. Furthermore, the absence of clearcut linguistic boundaries between various communities in parts of the Eastern Region, as in the area around Port Harcourt known as the Rivers territory, sometimes fostered a tenuous sense of Ibo identity among groups speaking marginal dialects.

ETHNIC ASSOCIATIONS

Ethnic associations in Asia and Africa represent an attempt to attain some form of accommodation with modernity. Caste associations in India, for example, first appeared in the middle of the nineteenth century, and their proliferation in the twentieth century paralleled the increasing penetration of the colonial administration and the greater opportunities for political participation.[9] In Africa, ethnic unions originated in the urban centers during the twentieth century to provide a sense of security for the new immigrant. These ethnic unions and the "old boys" alumni clubs of secondary school graduates were usually the first specifically African voluntary associations to be established without sponsorship from either the colonial administration or a church.[10] Today in most transitional political systems in Africa a whole panoply of voluntary associations exists. Despite this organizational competition, ethnic associations have generally maintained an important social and political role, for the processes of social differentiation and economic specialization usually have not advanced sufficiently to provide an adequate foundation for functional interest groups.

Ethnic associations in Africa resemble other modern voluntary organizations in many ways. For example, they model their structure and procedures on typical voluntary organizations by electing officers, forming committees, scheduling meetings, and keeping minutes. Frequently officers of African ethnic associations pattern their objectives and tactics after the other voluntary associations with which they are familiar, including political parties. Unlike such organizations, however, the ethnic associations confine their membership to groups defined by ascriptive boundaries—usually a village, clan, or geographic unit. Although ethnic associations are based on communities of origin rather than interest or occupation, membership is usually voluntary. Associations do not automatically confer membership on all persons in the community but, like other voluntary organizations, require an explicit commitment to join. Furthermore, many of the groups that have inspired the formation of these ethnic associations did not exist prior to the establishment of colonial rule. In Africa, ethnic associations promote the interest of villagers, clans, administrative divisions, and entire peoples, although only the village necessarily corresponds to a precolonial grouping. Moreover, the multiplication of ethnic associations representing communities of varying levels of inclusiveness sometimes presents individuals with a choice between membership in two or more of them. Ethnic associations in Africa are commonly called tribal unions. The usage is unfortunate, since it obscures the specific character of the associations and has negative connotations. African ethnic associations evolved on almost every level of the political system and thus represent a variety of communities, many of which do not fit any commonly accepted definition of a tribe.

References to ethnic associations appear in the literature on many African political systems.[11] In Sierra Leone the Mende Tribal Committee and the Temne Tribal Union evolved as by-products of the system of tribal headmen employed in Freetown beginning in 1905. In other parts of Africa they formed more spontaneously without direct encouragement from the colonial administration. In the Congo immigrants living in Leopoldville (now Kinshasa) organized the Federation Kasienne in 1916 and the Federation Kwangolaise about nine years later. The first known ethnic associations in Katanga date from the late 1920's. In Nigeria ethnic associations began to multiply in the late 1920's. The Kikuyu Association, the first of many ethnic unions in Kenya, was formed in 1919. One major phenomenon in the new towns of French West Africa in the interwar period, when political organizations were specifically prohibited, was the rise of *associations d'originaire*. Similar ethnic unions have originated in Uganda, Tanzania, Zambia, and Ghana.

The proliferation of ethnic unions after World War II, when the rate of urbanization sharply increased in many African territories, underscores the nature of these organizations as adaptations to new social conditions. Despite their early origin, ethnic associations in Freetown only grew strong during the postwar period. Most ethnic associations in the Belgian Congo sprang up in the early 1950's as a result of the postwar influx of new immigrants into urban centers; by 1956, eighty-five associations had registered in Leopoldville alone. In Freetown the newer ethnic associations reflected the more thoroughgoing penetration of modernizing influences. The political processes within the earlier Mende Tribal Committee and Temne Tribal Union remained in some ways traditional, centering more on the ascriptive position of the headman than on elected officers in the association. In contrast with the Temne Union, the Temne young men's companies, organized after the war, more closely copied the structure and practices of the voluntary associations based on European models. Like most ethnic associations originating in this period, the Temne young men's companies selected educated, capable leaders instead of relying on traditional elders. In Elisabethville (now Lubumbashi) the ethnic associations founded before the war also remained limited in membership and retained more traditionally oriented leadership than did those formed after 1945.

As an expression of the search for solidarity and identity in a new environment, many ethnic associations have undertaken cultural activities. Usually these cultural activities have amounted to nothing more than providing a forum in which persons from the same rural home area could gather, so as to preserve a link with their community of origin. Other associations, however, have had more ambitious programs. For example, the Abako Union, probably the strongest and most important ethnic association in the Belgian Congo prior to independence, claimed as its immediate objective the need "to unify, preserve, and spread the Kikongo language." This objective arose not from cultural pride but in reaction to the employment of Lingala rather than Kikongo as the language of administration and education in Leopoldville.

Most ethnic associations have engaged predominantly in modern activities. In Freetown the colonial administration employed ethnic associations to perform administrative tasks, such as registering births, deaths, and the arrival of new immigrants. But in most cities the ethnic associations first and foremost provided some form of mutual assistance. Whether this aid was extended as financial payments at times of crisis or on ceremonial occasions, or as assistance in locating living quarters and a job, it was the only form of welfare available to the new immigrant, because the colonial administration and later the independent government could not afford social security. The steady wage paid to the urban workers allowed the ethnic associations to levy dues. Sometimes ethnic associations then employed their accumulated resources to sponsor development projects.

Ethnic associations have also attempted to maximize their members' share of the welfare, educational, and economic resources distributed by the political system. To achieve this objective, associations often adopted various pressure group techniques and promoted the nomination of members for elective office. During the colonial period in both Nigeria and the Congo, ethnic associations often agitated in favor of specific social, economic, and political reforms before political parties had become effective vehicles of protest. One ethnic association in the Congo, the Abako, spearheaded the drive for independence prior to

1960. In several territories in Africa political parties utilized the existing network of ethnic associations as their basis for organization. In their haste to extend the party organization during their early years, leaders of the Sierra Leone People's party, the Parti Democratique de Cote d'Ivoire, the Tanganyika African National Union, and the National Council of Nigeria and the Cameroons (NCNC, after independence the National Convention of Nigerian Citizens), among others, absorbed ethnic associations as the nuclei for party branches. Sometimes this relationship between local ethnic associations and a political party persisted despite decisions of party leaders to substitute individual for institutional membership.

Prior to the January 1966 military coup in Nigeria, most of the country's major political parties were intimately connected with ethnic unions. Until 1952 membership in the NCNC remained confined to associations, of which ethnic unions were then one of the most common types. An ethnic organization, the Egbe Omo Oduduwa (Society of the Descendants of Oduduwa, the mythical progenitor and cultural hero of the Yoruba people), inaugurated in 1948 by Obafemi Awolowo, provided the core of support for a political party in the Western Region, the Action Group. Even the Nigerian National Democratic Party heralded its formation in March 1964 with the prior establishment of a new pan-Yoruba association, the Egbe Omo Olofin (Society of the Descendants of Olofin, another name of Oduduwa). Of the major political parties holding power in Nigeria, only the Northern People's Congress lacked ethnic affiliates, since the common Islamic faith of most of its adherents apparently constituted an alternate source of solidarity. Few of these ethnic associations, however, had an independent base of political support that allowed them to exert influence on the relevant political party. Political parties promoted a close relationship with ethnic associations in Nigeria merely to reinforce their own legitimacy in the eyes of the more traditionally oriented elements of the electorate. Hence, when the nationality associations linked to political parties, such as the Egbe Omo Oduduwa, assumed a political role, they usually acted as the agent of the political party.[12] Although Ibo village, clan, and divisional unions did have a significant independent political role in the Eastern Nigerian political system, the inclusive Ibo nationality association, the Ibo State Union, which many people identified with the NCNC, could not manage its own members, let alone control the NCNC.

IBO ETHNIC UNIONS

Many ethnic groups in Africa responded to the stresses and inse-curities of urban life by forming mutual aid societies with an ethnic base. Ethnic unions among the Ibo differed from these mutual aid associations in several ways. Many Ibo ethnic unions attained a greater organizational complexity than did their counterparts in other African political systems. Mergers were often effected of several Ibo ethnic unions based on the same home community but operating in different cities to which the members had emigrated. In order to tap all potential resources, the branches coordinated their activities by holding annual or semiannual meetings at home, to which they sent representatives. At these meetings, elections were held for central officers, who were authorized to direct and coordinate the activities of the branches in accordance with the goals and priorities accepted by the delegates. Al-though the structure and activities of many Ibo unions were similar, communities autonomously launched ethnic unions in response to local initiatives, needs, and motives. Ethnic unions acquired a similar organi-zational structure through copying the institutions of other Ibo unions.

In contrast to the somewhat random and sporadic manner with which other ethnic groups established associations, a high proportion of Ibo-speaking communities of varying levels of inclusiveness sponsored the formation of ethnic unions. Provincial and divisional unions were often among the first ethnic unions organized by Ibo-speaking immi-grants in urban centers. When immigrant populations were small, only an expansive grouping incorporated enough people to sustain a union. Eventually unions began to represent villages, clans, and occasionally counties. In some localities, as in Mbaise, individuals could potentially belong to several unions. The existence of Ibo ethnic unions of different degrees of inclusiveness has led some people to assume incorrectly that these unions constituted a linked hierarchy.[13] The truth is that the more inclusive unions performed different functions from those of the parochial unions. Furthermore, the more parochial unions were often better institutionalized and executed more significant functions. Many of the unions that encompassed several primary communities, such as the Mbaise Federal Union and the Ibo State Union, symbolized the unity of the wider group but accomplished little else. In addition, the more comprehensive unions had no control over lower level unions.

Unlike virtually all other ethnic associations, Ibo ethnic unions became rurally oriented by linking immigrants from the same community in urban centers throughout Nigeria, and sometimes West Africa, for the purpose of developing their home communities. While associations among other ethnic groups occasionally undertook development projects, these projects were often for the urban immigrants. Moreover, the scope and number of community development activities completed by Ibo unions exceeded those of other ethnic groups.[14] Most of the Ibo unions believed that education held the key to advancement and therefore concentrated their efforts and resources on building schools and endowing scholarships. In consequence, a substantial portion of the schools opened in the Eastern Region in the period between 1930 and 1957, when the Eastern government inaugurated a primary education program, owe their existence to the efforts of these ethnic improvement unions. During the 1930's when Ibo unions were beginning to form, educational facilities expanded at a faster rate in the Eastern Region than elsewhere in Nigeria. The efforts of the ethnic unions thus sparked the massive self-help drive of the Ibo-speaking communities through which they caught up with the groups who had experienced earlier contact with missionary education.

The viable institutional structure and strong rural base of many of the Ibo ethnic unions allowed them to assume substantial political roles. In some rural communities the ethnic unions attempted to recruit candidates for political office and to secure patronage in the form of development amenities for their members. Ibo divisional and provincial unions also came to be political forces in urban electoral contests.

A number of factors seem to have contributed to the singular evolution of ethnic unions among Ibo-speaking communities. Because of the high population density, Ibos probably emigrated to modern urban centers during the colonial period at a faster rate than most other groups. Hence, members of many different Ibo communities were exposed to unfamiliar types of organization. The Ibos' feeling of inferiority, promoted by Europeans and other Africans, and their predilection for modern ways, deriving from their precolonial cultural patterns, might have inspired the decision to modernize their home communities and thus elevate their status and foster self-respect. Since the small scale and simplicity of traditional institutions made them unsuitable for this bold venture, Ibo communities embraced ethnic unions as the organizational vehicle for the task. The traditional Ibo sociopolitical system and culture in part explain their choice.

The precolonial Ibo political system, lacked a differentiated administrative structure and permanent elective or hereditary offices—with certain local exceptions, such as the Onitsha kingship. Although several villages were often related in village groups through recognition of a common ancestor, political and social institutions usually operated on the level of the single village. Moreover, while all members of a village recognized a common ancestor, the founder of the village, the effective kinship organization emphasized divisions within the community. The basic social unit was usually the patrilineage, a kinship group consisting of all the descendants in the male line of a particular individual. To a great extent, the patrilineage was self-contained and handled its own affairs. A horizontal organization of the village into age sets existed, to supplement and compensate for the vertical division of the community into patrilineages. Male age groups, constituted in many places by the children born within a three-year period, and larger groupings formed by cooperation among several age groups, performed much of the communal work, especially among the Northern Ibo. Title societies, consisting of any member of the village who could pay a prescribed fee, also cut across the patrilineages and thus helped integrate the village.

A general assembly or council intermittently exercised political authority for the village. When the village council met, each man could attend and speak. After the preliminary discussion, the elders of the village retired to make a decision. The decision, announced to the assemblage by a spokesman for the elders, was then either ratified or rejected. However, the elders only theoretically exercised political leadership as their conciliar prerogative. Instead, men whom G. I. Jones called "natural leaders" covertly determined policy behind the facade of the conciliar consultations of the elders. Like an American political boss, this natural leader manipulated the political system through his special knowledge and skills. His most valuable asset was the ability to arbitrate the incessant disputes inherent in a segmentary society. His influence depended on how many clients he could attach to his "machine," that is, the number of persons accepting his authority because of the services he performed for them. However, most Ibo villages lacked centralized leadership, because a single man could rarely resolve disputes successfully for all factions over a prolonged period.[15]

Despite the usual classification of the Ibo political system as "primitive,"[16] the Ibo culture embodied many of the characteristics considered to inhere in modernity. One significant value permeating Ibo institutions was equality of opportunity. Children did not inherit their parents' social status, political position, or career. Individual initiative and achievement determined the position each person assumed within the system. Following from and giving meaning to this equality was a spirit of competition in every sphere of life. Individuals and groups seeking power, status, and prestige were respected for their ambition. Through an emphasis on achievement, individual choice, and alternate paths, the underlying world view of the Ibos emphasized the very essence of an open system—change. In contradistinction to the static universe of eternal verities presented by most traditional cultures, Ibos perceived a dynamic world in which all things underwent change, even man's relationship with the spiritual order. Along with this acceptance of change, the Ibos incorporated a willingness to innovate.

Also in contrast to most traditional societies, the Ibos emphasized material accomplishments rather than other-wordly preoccupations. The amassing of wealth, formalized by membership in one of the title societies, was the prerequisite for status and generally for leadership as well. In order to acquire prestige, the successful man employed part of his wealth to assist his village. Hence, a strong corporate identity and loyalty somewhat offset the predisposition toward individualism.

The Ibo attitude embodied a pragmatic orientation toward life. They perceived the world as a marketplace, with everything in it subject to negotiation and manipulation. Political leadership followed from the ability to bargain and conciliate, two characteristics of the pragmatist. Each new dispute presented the political leader with a challenge to verify his prowess and thus maintain his following.[17]

Traditional Ibo institutions were inappropriate vehicles for the task of development, both because of the small scale of the precolonial political units and because political authority was dispersed rather than centralized. Moreover, as a consequence of the Ibos' strongly engrained sense of their right to participate in the formulation of decisions affecting them, many Ibo communities resisted the imposition of colonial administrative institutions. Because of this special difficulty, the Ibo hinterland was one of the last areas of Nigeria to be pacified by the British. For this reason, too, missionary activity began somewhat later among the Ibos than among other ethnic groups. When the British did regularize administration in Ibo areas, neither the original system, based on appointing individuals by warrant to serve as chiefs and employing the district commissioner as the presiding official of the native courts, nor the revised system, based on native authority councils, succeeded in providing effective local political units.

In contrast, precolonial Ibo cultural patterns prepared individuals and communities to take advantage of the new horizons opened by the colonial era. For the Ibo, development and modernization primarily entailed the application of usual patterns of response to new opportunities, rather than the transformation of their existing network of values. Perhaps the very "primitiveness" of their traditional political institutions in conjunction with the modern orientation of their culture propelled the Ibo toward embracing more modern organizational forms. Thus, a will to modernize along with organizational inventiveness and skill seem to account, at least partially, for the incidence of effective ethnic unions among the Ibo.

THE IBO STATE UNION

The Ibo State Union theoretically consisted of representatives of all branches of Ibo village, clan, divisional, and provincial unions but actually included only a small proportion of them. As the self-appointed spokesman, defender, and arbiter of the Ibo people, the Ibo State Union claimed wide powers. Moreover, opponents of the NCNC, the dominant party in the Eastern Region, often concurred in this evaluation, describing the Ibo State Union as the all-powerful, directing agent of a monolithic, organized Ibo people. According to this analysis, the Ibo State Union worked through the NCNC, which was mythologized to be its political deputy. The NCNC was thus claimed to be an Ibo political party, intent on gaining Ibo hegemony in Nigeria. In order to provide the correct setting for an analysis of the dynamics of ethnic unions in Eastern Nigeria, it is important to dispel these myths surrounding the Ibo State Union.[18]

Despite its grandiose self-image, the Ibo State Union never effectively coordinated the activities of other Ibo ethnic unions and never exerted appreciable influence on the NCNC. The weakness of the Ibo State Union as an organization partially derived from its structure and operation. Only a small proportion of the units eligible for membership ever bothered to register and pay the annual contribution necessary to participate actively in the activities of the union. Although the impetus for Ibo unions usually derived from the more educated men living in

urban centers, the Ibo State Union came to be dominated by predominantly uneducated businessmen from two cities, Port Harcourt and
Aba. Officers elected by the general conferences frequently disagreed
about the distribution of power among themselves and about the objectives that should be pursued. For all but five years of its organizational life from 1947 to 1966 the Ibo State Union had one president,
Z. C. Obi, a Port Harcourt businessman.[19] When personality and policy
differences caused B. O. N. Eluwa, the original organizer of the Ibo
State Union, to resign in 1954, Obi was free to transform the union into
his personal instrument. He diminished the role of the Executive Committee by coopting a large number of illiterates and by refusing to call
it into regular session. He also kept the minute books and records at
his home rather than at the secretariat. A rivalry between Obi and
his principal lieutenant, V. C. I. Anene, who objected to Obi's per-
sonalization of the union, further weakened the organization between
1954 and 1965, when Anene was replaced by Dr. J. I. J. Otuka as
secretary.

Although the inauguration of the Ibo State Union preceded the
establishment of most of the rural ethnic unions in the Eastern Region,
the Ibo State Union did not call forth a sudden proliferation of these
associations. The formation of all of the unions about which information
is available occurred in response to specific needs or goals of the
community, not as a result of the organizational activities of the Ibo
State Union or its predecessors. Consequently, the local ethnic unions
remained autonomous and resisted the superficial efforts of the Ibo
State Union to coordinate their undertakings. In fact, the very success
of the parochial ethnic unions made superfluous most of the planned
programs of the Ibo State Union. The projected Ibo National Bank,
for instance, which was to finance the construction of schools, never
opened. Only one Ibo national high school was built by the Ibo State
Union, because local ethnic unions preempted its role in promoting
education.

The salience of primary identities within the Eastern political system
also diminished the potential significance of the Ibo State Union.
Neither the colonial nor the postcolonial political systems fostered the
evolution of a strong federal or regional government with extensive
control over local communities. Rather, the configuration of power
within these political systems sustained the relative autonomy and integrity of primary ethnic groups. Within the Eastern political system

there were no regional constituencies or interest alignments. The recruitment and election of candidates for political office, the formulation of demands and competition for amenities, and the communication of messages between politicians and the populace reinforced the local constituency boundaries within which they took place. On the regional level, representatives of the local communities competed to attain personal and constituency objectives through forming loose alliances, which often reflected divisional and provincial boundaries. These alliances frequently brought Ibo politicians together with representatives from other ethnic groups. Since the Ibo people constituted approximately two-thirds of the population of the Eastern Region prior to secession, the dynamics of the political process engendered competition among Ibo subgroups.

The Ibo State Union has been variously portrayed as the director and handmaiden of the NCNC—particularly by the Northern People's Congress, the dominant political party in the Northern Region and thus in the Nigerian Federation, and by the Nigerian National Democratic party or NNDP, the dominant party in the Western Region after 1963. In fact, the Ibo State Union was basically a cultural body whose origin, role, and source of support was independent from the NCNC. It did not significantly influence the NCNC, both because it could not mobilize the Ibo masses or even its affiliated ethnic unions, and because the NCNC received the support of the vast majority of the Ibo people without its assistance. Moreover, the leaders of the NCNC usually embraced a national orientation rather than an exclusively regional or ethnic perspective, and the NCNC itself had a base of political support among other ethnic groups within the East as well as in sections of other regions. After the creation of the Mid West Region in 1964, the NCNC became the only political party to control more than one regional government. Hence, leaders of the NCNC were hesitant to associate the party with the Ibo State Union since they had nothing to gain politically and potentially had something to lose.

The closest connection between the Ibo State Union and the NCNC occurred during the period when Nnamdi Azikiwe, one of the founders of the NCNC and the leading Ibo politician, was president of the union, from December 1948 to 1952. Other leading members of the NCNC were also elected to or coopted by the union's Executive Committee. This recruitment of politicians to offices in the Ibo State Union came at the initiative of its first organizer and secretary, Eluwa, who hoped that the presence of political notables would enhance the status of the union. However, his overt role as leader of a cultural organization representing the Ibo people embarrassed Azikiwe and caused him to resign from the union in 1952. Although Azikiwe was concerned with the progress of his own ethnic group, he was also a sincere proponent of Nigerian unity. When a dispute arose within the NCNC in 1953 over continued participation in the colonial political system established under the Macpherson reforms, both sides canvassed for support within the union. As an organization, the Ibo State Union remained officially neutral, but unofficially it was loyal to the Azikiwe faction, which favored withdrawal. In the aftermath of the incident, virtually all politicians withdrew from active participation in the Ibo State Union, and the dissident faction within the NCNC opposed to Azikiwe formed an opposition party, the United National Independence party (UNIP).[20]

The Ibo State Union became involved peripherally in several other political issues. After K. O. Mbadiwe had unsuccessfully attempted to wrest control of the NCNC from Azikiwe in 1958, the Ibo State Union attempted to reconcile the two political leaders, but both factions refused its offer to mediate. In 1958 the Ibo State Union was one of the many ethnic associations presenting testimony to the commission appointed by the British government to investigate the fears of minorities in Nigeria and to propose means of quieting them.[21] Following the rejection of the 1963 census by the NCNC because of alleged gross irregularities, especially in the North, a wave of anti-Ibo reaction erupted in both the North and the West among supporters of the NNDP. In the budget session of March 1964, Northern legislators made a series of derogatory speeches about the Ibo, calling them "black imperialists, apes and monkeys." They demanded that all Ibos working for the public services in the North be repatriated to the East immediately and that the houses and property belonging to them be confiscated. Two newspapers, the pro-NNDP *Daily Sketch* and the federally owned *Morning Post,* regularly published articles lambasting the Ibo State Union, claiming that it controlled the NCNC and that Ibos monopolized federal posts. These attacks, which were directed primarily at the Ibo people rather than the NCNC, prompted the Ibo State Union to release rebuttals to the press and in 1964 to publish at least nominally two pamphlets, "Nigerian Disunity: The Guilty Ones" and "One North or One Nigeria."[22] A reliable source, directly involved in the production of the pamphlets, claimed that the NCNC did most of the work assembling the material to refute the Northern and Western charges and then gave it to the Ibo State Union to publish under the union's name. When harassment and discrimination against the Ibos continued in the North and the West, the Ibo State Union requested and received an interview with the prime minister Sir Abubakar Tafewa Balewa in an attempt to rectify the situation.

Shortly after forming the first military government in Nigeria, Major-General J. T. U. Aguiyi Ironsi decided in May 1966 to suspend all organizations that he believed might be working against Nigerian unity. His decree suspended not only all existing political parties but the twenty-six apex associations embracing entire peoples, including the Ibo state Union.[23] Ironically, the Ironsi regime did not prohibit operation of the local ethnic unions, so long as they did not engage in manifestly political activities. It was these local town and clan unions, however, not the Ibo State Union, that consistently became involved in politics, as demonstrated by the operations of the ethnic unions in Abiriba and Mbaise.

ABIRIBA AND MBAISE

Abiriba was a town in the Bende Division of Eastern Nigeria about thirty miles from Umuahia. The inhabitants of Abiriba regarded themselves as descendants of a common ancestor, so that all Abiribans considered themselves kinsmen. Most of the adult males in the community became traders and thus spent much of their time away from Abiriba in the cities or towns of Nigeria. At any one time, over half of the adult males in the community of approximately forty thousand might have been away from Abiriba. Before the war, Abiribans were reputed to be one of the wealthiest Ibo communities. The Abiriba Communal Improvement Union (ACIU) protected the unity of the Abiribans and undertook community improvement projects. By harnessing the wealth of the community, the ACIU was able to sponsor many significant projects.

In contrast with Abiriba, Mbaise was a county council area, located in the Owerri Division about thirty miles from Umuahia in another direction. It was, furthermore, a colonial creation embracing several different clans. Although an artificial unit, Mbaise developed a certain cohesion and identity. Approximately 225,000 people lived in Mbaise before the war. Unlike Abiriba, Mbaise was a densely populated, poor, and somewhat bleak area. Its complex ethnic composition gave rise to the formation of a multiplicity of village, clan, and county unions. Rather than concentrating on community development, as did the ACIU, the clan unions in Mbaise focused on political activities.

Obviously Abiriba and Mbaise were not comparable units, since they differed in size, ethnic composition, and number and types of ethnic unions. Their dissimilarity was significant in that it revealed the operation of ethnic unions under different circumstances. Branches of both of these ethnic unions were maintained in Port Harcourt, the largest city and the industrial center of the Eastern Region. Since Ibo ethnic unions typically consisted of several urban branches connected with the home community through a general conference, to which they all sent representatives, a description of the branches is essential for an accurate analysis of the ethnic unions' nature, activities, and impact.

Prior to the colonial period there were over six hundred separate groups among the people now called Ibos, so that extensive variations must have existed among the communities. Before secession the Eastern Region had some nine hundred local and one hundred county council areas for a population of approximately twelve million, two-thirds of whom were Ibo speaking. Obviously, when such diversity and numbers are involved, it is very difficult to ascertain features that are representative or typical. Moreover, the relative wealth of Abiriba and the large size of Mbaise made them somewhat exceptional, while at the same time giving them political importance. In terms of size of population and level of development, however, the constituent villages and local council areas in Mbaise approximated the conditions in many other Ibo communities. Though the ACIU completed more projects than most other ethnic unions and the clan unions in Mbaise maneuvered politically to a greater extent than many other Ibo unions, they provide significant examples of typical involvements of the ethnic unions.

The role of ethnic unions in the micropolitical systems of Abiriba, Mbaise, and Port Harcourt, and the characteristics of their leadership, deserve special stress. The role of the ethnic unions refers to the functions they performed. Following Robert Dahl's approach in his study of New Haven, the sections on Abiriba and Mbaise concentrate on certain key issues and analyze the participants, both individually and collectively, who made and carried out the decisions.[24] The key issues selected by Dahl for New Haven were urban renewal, public education, and nominations for political office. For Abiriba and Mbaise, three comparably significant issue areas were community development, education, and nominations for political office.

The empirical findings on these micropolitical systems are then evaluated for their impact on the larger Eastern Region political system. Because the Federation of Nigeria was a decentralized political system with most of the functions of government inhering in the four separate regions, the region appeared as the more relevant political arena from the perspective of local political actors. The impact of the ethnic unions is assessed in terms of the three dimensions of political development: institutionalization, integration, and cultural modernization. More specifically, an attempt is made to determine whether the ethnic unions prevented the NCNC and the local government councils from becoming more effective political institutions or facilitated their functioning. Analysis is offered of the degree to which the activities of the ethnic unions may have inhibited the evolution of more inclusive levels of identity. Finally, the question is examined as to whether the ethnic unions contributed to the further modernization of the Ibo political culture. Although the precolonial Ibos already held many political attitudes, values, and orientations that are considered modern or secular, they confined their social and political interactions to the village-group, so that in order to ascertain whether the political culture adapted to the requirements of the colonial and postcolonial political systems, one must determine whether the Ibo transferred their traditional orientations to the larger and more differentiated regional political arena.

For anyone familiar with Eastern Nigeria before the war, it is painful to reflect on what has happened. Both Abiriba and Mbaise remained under Biafran control until the final stages of the civil war. Mbaise, previously one of the most densely populated parts of the Eastern Region, had its population further swelled with the influx of refugees from other parts of Biafran territory. Consequently, the area was particularly stricken by starvation.

But even under today's fundamentally changed conditions, this study of Ibo ethnic unions has continued relevance. The conclusions reached contradict many of the stereotypes about ethnicity and ethnic unions. The proportions of the Nigerian tragedy and its significance for the future of Africa call for accurate and unbiased knowledge about the political dynamics of the Ibo people in order to comprehend more thoroughly what prompted the secession of the Eastern Region. This study cannot determine the specific causes of the final disintegration of Nigeria, because its scope is limited, but it should help to dispel some of the myths already gaining credence.

Secession and war led to the dissolution of the NCNC and the dislocation of official government bodies. Of all the institutions existing before the war, the ethnic unions had best survived the turmoil. They had assisted in the relocation of the almost two million Eastern Nigerian refugees from other parts of Nigeria who fled back to the East in 1966 after the massacres. On the eve of secession they began to organize local militia and civilian defense units.

Now that the war is over, ethnic unions may be one of the major instruments for reconstruction. As people return to their homes and attempt to resurrect their former lives, ethnic unions in most of the communities will probably resume functioning. As the expression of the unity and aspirations of the local community, ethnic unions should escape both the taint of defeat and the recriminations of the Nigerian government. Even before the establishment of a new political order in the East Central State, ethnic unions can provide organizational direction and inspiration for reconstruction in the rural areas. And someday, when competitive politics revives, ethnic unions will surely be there to structure political involvements. In short, no understanding of the past, present, or future condition of the Ibo people can be complete without a knowledge of their ethnic unions.

Part One | Ethnic Unions in a Rural Environment

I | The Evolution and Role of the Abiriba Communal Improvement Union

Ibo ethnic-improvement unions have played an important role in shaping political and economic developments in Eastern Nigeria. Although the Ibo State Union, an apex association, comprised a number of Ibo village, clan and division organizations, it did not directly control the affairs of its member units. Those units, and of course the great number of unaffiliated unions, remained autonomous agents. Consequently, one must study the local unions in order to understand the manner in which ethnic associations affected development in Eastern Nigeria.

The Abiriba Communal Improvement Union (ACIU) was one such association. Founded in 1941, the ACIU underwent several stages of development. Its well-articulated structure resembled the model followed by many other unions. Since the Abiriban community was one of the wealthiest in Eastern Nigeria, the ACIU was able to raise enough resources to undertake many different types of community improvement projects.

THE COMMUNITY OF ABIRIBA

Abiriba, a town of approximately forty thousand, formed part of the Owuwa Anyanwu County Council area in the northern part of Bende Division.[1] It typified many Ibo communities in that its members constituted an ethnic unit, the clan being supposedly descended from the same ancestor. They were thus united by bonds of sentiment and communal solidarity as well as by common interests. The three territorial divisions of Abiriba—Ameke, Amaogudu, and Agbaji—furnished only secondary sources of geographic identification, which did not threaten

27

the unity of the larger community.[2] According to tradition, Abiribans migrated to their present location from a point somewhere to the north. Versions of the legend differed considerably in the area designated as the point of origin, with variations including Libya and Egypt, but all mentioned the crossing of a river and described extensive fighting to occupy the territory. Abiribans displayed a paddle considered to have been used in crossing the river. In addition, a monument in Amaeke, the largest and most important of the three territorial divisions, exhibited wooden figures of warriors and various artifacts of booty commemorating victories over neighboring groups. Smaller halls with similar relics existed in the two other territorial divisions.

Another symbol of unity in which the Abiribans displayed pride was the *eze*, the title given to the man regarded as the head of the town by virtue of his direct descent from the founder. The chief of Amaeke, a hereditary position filled by the oldest male member of one of the two families that alternately held the office, also served as the eze or paramount chief of Abiriba. All available records and oral histories described the eze as merely the titular head of the community, with political policy, to the extent that it existed, resulting from the decisions of the village council, in which the senior age groups predominated. The eze merely announced the decisions made by the council in judicial and administrative matters. Traditionally he symbolized the unity of Abiriba by presiding over the sacrifice to Ale, the common goddess of the town.[3] In 1966 the eze, along with the chiefs of Agbaji and Amaogudu, still enacted certain laws on ceremonial matters once a year. The ACIU also sought his concurrence to legitimize their decisions. For several years the ACIU, in order to increase the prestige of Abiriba, mounted a campaign to have the Eastern government recognize the eze as a first-class chief with a seat in the Eastern House of Chiefs, the ceremonial body established in 1959 as a compliment to the elected House of Assembly.[4]

Unlike most other Ibo areas, in which the age organization degenerated, in Abiriba it continued to play a role in the sociopolitical system. Abiribans displayed considerable pride in the distinctiveness of their system, consisting of many competitive age sets forming three larger divisions called age groups. Age sets or grades formed every three years, with the young men first meeting formally together at sixteen in order to begin raising money to perform the *ekpe* festival. Formerly, the ekpe festival indicated the coming of manhood and marked entrance into the young men's age group. It entailed the assumption of guard and military duties and the provision of labor for community projects. The second festival, the *egwamang,* performed by age sets at about thirty-five, manifested the attainment of full maturity and initiated the participants into membership in the middle age group. It was unusual to marry before performing the egwamang ceremony. After the third festival, the *uche,* performed at about fifty-five, all military obligations were withdrawn. As the elders, the men in this group exercised the most influence in arriving at decisions at the town meeting. All age sets competed against one another in finding ways to celebrate the three festivals.

These traditional duties receded into the background with the coming of order and peace under the British administration. In 1912, in one of the first known attempts at community improvement initiated by the indigenous community under British rule, three Abiriban age groups dredged the Igwu Creek from the mouth to Okopedi-Itu in order to make it navigable for canoes in all seasons.[5] After the ACIU had fostered the concept of community improvement, the age groups began to compete in the completion of projects, usually undertaking them in conjunction with the performance of the egwamang festival.

Their heritage of trading provided another source of identification for Abiribans. Ejim Akuma, the administrative secretary of the ACIU, in his history attributed the early rise of trade to the skill of the Abiriban people as blacksmiths, whose wares were requested first by the Aros and then throughout the Ibo territory.[6] By 1927 a large proportion of the men were engaged in trade in the towns, and Abiribans had settled in the major trading centers of the Eastern Region. The district officer in charge of Bende Division at that time considered the Abiribans to be one of the most enterprising and wealthiest communities in the division.[7] A rough census taken by the ACIU in 1941 showed that 1,381 Abiribans had left Abiriba to trade and to seek jobs in towns throughout the Eastern Region and in Lagos.[8] Abiribans maintained their reputation of being among the most enterprising and affluent of Ibo communities. Before 1966 their traders resided in all the trading centers of Nigeria. One Abiriban estimated that four times as many members of the community traded abroad as those who remained at home to farm. (When Abiribans used the word "abroad," they meant another town or city in Nigeria.)

Abiribans admired commercial success and the qualities that contribute to it. "To be ambitious therefore is one of the characteristics of

Abiriba man and woman from the cradle to the grave," according to Akuma. "This pattern and ambitious spirit of Abiriba people is hereditary, and is due to the original stock of their ancestors who were not of this division in origin."[9] Religion, education, and cultural activities were of secondary concern to commercial success. The poverty of the first educated men, who were teachers, contrasting with the financial success of the illiterate traders, resulted in a disdain for education, which was later overcome only when the monetary value of education had been demonstrated. Even then Abiribans valued education primarily for its instrumental uses, and respected the wealthy trader as much as the graduate with a school certificate or university degree. If the graduate did not receive a lucrative position, Abiribans considered his education a waste. Education by itself did not confer prestige.

Each group of traders retained the old pattern of organization and had its own officials and a council. The oldest man in each community abroad became the head of a trading house and regulated its affairs in conjunction with a council of all the members. Formerly Abiribans sent their children to one of these communities and apprenticed them to a master at the age of twelve. The various trading communities were organized into two groups, the maritime or water people (referred to as the Umon group), who settled along the Cross River with Calabar as the center, and the railway or land people (called the Bende group), with Port Harcourt generally acknowledged as the leading community.

ESTABLISHMENT AND DEVELOPMENT OF THE ACIU

Associations of Abiribans, based on a British model, first appeared after the introduction of Christianity. The first missionaries reached Abiriba in 1911 and built a school the following year. Chief Agwu Otisi, the eze of Abiriba, along with his family, was baptized in 1916 and subsequently was elected the first church elder. Gradually most of the community converted to Christianity, at least nominally.

In 1918 missionaries asked Abiriban Christians living abroad to contribute nine shillings each toward the erection of a church. One year later these traders formed the Abiriba Youngmen Christian Association.[10] Between 1919 and 1935 meetings of the various branches were held in Okopedi Itu and Umuahia. Attempts to reform the society culminated in a meeting in 1935 at Calabar, then one of the two most important trading centers—the other being Umuahia—at which the members of the Abiriba Youngmen Christian Association adopted the name Abiriba Youngmen Society, in order to include pagans. The following year the Abiriban Youngmen Society became the Abiriba Youth League.

The society had few concrete achievements. It purchased some band instruments and banners. In 1932 it assisted two youths in their training as a sanitary inspector and a drug dispenser. Few records exist on which to base an analysis of the role of the society in fostering social change. While Akuma attributed considerable influence to it, he lacked perspective as a participant and never revealed the criteria on which he based his estimation.[11] Membership in the society was confined to Christians trading outside of Abiriba; branch organization remained haphazard, and central coordination almost nonexistent.

After a group of students, the Abiriba Homestars, had tried unsuccessfully in 1935 to inaugurate an improvement union encompassing all Abiribans, they turned to several leading traders for assistance, one of whom was L. E. Ifendu.[12] During litigation between the Abiriban traders at Umuahia and the people of Owerri in 1937, Ifendu, a trader with a few years of elementary education, was impressed by the unity demonstrated by Abiriba's opponents. He convinced the Abiriban traders at Umuahia to contribute a penny a week to establish a fund for emergencies. The Abiriba Youth League also adopted this policy in 1939. At a meeting held at Ifiayong in 1941, the Abiriban Youth League with the concurrence of Ifendu and other traders transformed itself into the Abiriba Improvement Union, renamed the Abiriba Communal Improvement Union in 1944.[13] The officers elected at that meeting were all traders residing in Calabar, Umuahia, or Port Harcourt. The majority of them had no education, although two—Ejim Akuma, the general secretary, and J. O. Udeagha, the assistant general secretary—had the equivalent of a primary school education, the standard six certificate. Several of the men present at the inaugural meeting, including Ifendu, Akuma, P. O. Iboko, E. K. Onuma, S. U. Agwu, and O. M. Agbagha, later were frequently elected as officers of the ACIU. Akuma remained active as the permanent, paid administrative secretary.

The ACIU was thus begun by members of the community living away from Abiriba. The recognized need of the settlers to join together for mutual assistance furnished the immediate impetus for its establishment. The motto of the ACIU, "Self-help is the sure path to success," provided the inspiration for its activities. According to the constitution, the aims and objectives of the ACIU included the following:

(1) To cater for the welfare of the Abiriban people wherever they may be;

(2) To promote and preserve the aspects of Abiriban culture and tradition which are in keeping with modern times;

(3) To promote and encourage community development in Abiriba;

(4) To promote the economic well-being of the Abiriban people;

(5) To encourage the education of our people at all levels. To this end, the Union may establish Education Institutes in Nigeria, establish Education Committees to advise on matters relating to education policy, offer scholarships to deserving sons and daughters of Abiriba and other citizens of Nigeria as far as Education Policy of the Union shall permit.

(6) To promote peace, unity and harmony among Abiriban people at home and abroad and between Abiriba and other clans of Nigeria.[14]

From its inception the ACIU successfully mobilized the symbols and authority of tradition without becoming subservient to them. The ACIU made the eze and the chiefs of Agbaji and Amaogudu its patrons, thus conferring on them an honorary position and enhancing the legitimacy of the union, while rendering the chiefs impotent to influence its affairs. The three traditional festivals of ekpe, egwamang, and uche had disappeared after the introduction of Christianity. In order to raise funds to finance its programs, the ACIU resuscitated these festivals, but substituted the payment of money for the traditional pagan ceremonies in order to make the festivals acceptable to Christians.[15] An agreement between the ACIU and the chiefs in 1945 conferred automatic membership in the union on all residents of Abiriba at twenty-one years of age.[16]

Following its initial phase, the ACIU passed through two stages. During the first stage, which terminated with the formal opening of Enuda College in 1954, the union concentrated its resources almost entirely on educational projects, especially the staffing and building of the secondary school. Virtually all community improvement projects undertaken during this period in Abiriba were initiated, financed, and directed by the union. When the ACIU assessed dues and special education levies, it collected them with relatively little difficulty.

A few months after the opening of Enuda College, for the first time an age set undertook a project to benefit the community, when the Okezie age set built a town hall to commemorate its ekpe or initiation festival. This event inaugurated a competition among the age sets to construct facilities for the community. While the ACIU continued to direct community development, during the second stage age sets volunteered to construct projects suggested by the union and upon completion presented them to the union to operate on behalf of the community. In this way Abiriba acquired a post office, a hospital, and a second secondary school. During this stage the ACIU relied on government assistance for providing piped water and electricity, as well as tarring the main road. As the number and diversity of its responsibilities increased, the ACIU simultaneously found it more difficult to collect regular dues and almost impossible to impose special levies. As a consequence, the ACIU was continually limited by financial considerations in embarking on new activities.

The need for improved educational facilities monopolized the attention of the ACIU during the early years. At its first meeting in 1941 the members gave £200 to the manager of the Ohafia District School to keep as a school fund for them.[17] The idea of building a secondary school in Abiriba appears to have been the goal of the union from its inception and may even have been a contributing factor in its establishment. From 1942 through 1946 the union spent £260 to finance free primary education for the three initial grades in the Church of Scotland Mission School in Abiriba. Between 1944 and 1946 the union gave two students limited assistance, a combined total of £64, to complete their secondary education. In order to provide staff for the secondary school, the union awarded five scholarships for higher education. They enabled two students to attend Edinburgh University in 1946, one to attend University College, Ibadan, in 1948, and two to attend Howard University in 1948. Three of the students received more than one advanced degree, and one completed a doctorate. Up to November 1956, when all but one student had returned, the union spent a total of £11,835 on these scholarships.[18] In 1948 the ACIU donated £200 to the Church of Scotland Mission School for extension of the primary department.[19]

Enuda College stands as the most important monument to the ACIU's accomplishments. The government granted permission to the ACIU in 1948 to build, equip, and maintain a secondary school.[20] Enuda College formally opened in March 1954, although construction continued through 1962. Even after most buildings were completed, educational policy and the management of the school continued to preoccupy the union. In addition to managing Enuda College, the ACIU assumed control, at a cost of £3,000, of the First Century Gospel School in January 1961, when its former proprietor could no longer operate it.[21] A girls' secondary school, built by the Egwuena age grade, opened in March 1963. Hence, today the ACIU operates three schools: Enuda Primary School, Enuda College, and Egwuena Girls' Secondary School.

In addition to these projects, which were undertaken by either an age set or the government in conjunction with the ACIU, the union opened a rubber plantation in 1963 in order to provide further employment in Abiriba and to bolster its financial position. By the end of 1965, 107 acres of the envisaged 2,000 had been planted. In April 1966 the union decided to negotiate a £10,000 loan from the Fund for Agricultural and Industrial Development of the Eastern Region to use in an extension of the rubber plantation.[22]

THE ORGANIZATION OF THE ACIU

The model of organization embodied in the ACIU typified that of many other Ibo improvement unions. This model linked branches in the home area and the urban centers through annual conferences to which delegates were sent. Officers elected at these conferences formed a central executive, which coordinated the activities of the various branches. Atypical structural characteristics of the ACIU included the appointment of a full-time, paid administrative secretary and the frequency of general meetings. Also, the centralization of power in the central executive achieved by the ACIU remained only an aspiration for most other unions.

Prior to the mass exodus of Ibos back to the East, branches of the ACIU existed at Abiriba, Port Harcourt, Calabar, Aba, Umuahia, Enugu, Onitsha, Ifiayong, Ekori, and Okopedi Itu in the Eastern Region; at Zaria, Kano, Kaduna, Jos, and Imboku in the Northern Region; and at Lagos and in the Cameroons. Other branches organized at Umon, Itumbauzo, Ikomodu, and Uzuakoli had ceased to operate or had merged owing to dwindling membership. Each branch was autonomous, meeting separately, usually twice a month. The union held two general meetings or conferences each year—during the last week in August or the first week in September, and during late December or early January at Abiriba—to which each branch and the auxiliary women and youth organizations sent from two to four delegates. In addition, at least one extraordinary or emergency conference of the ACIU met each year, usually in April.

In theory every Abiriban automatically became a member of both the ACIU and an age grade when attaining a certain age. Male age grades or sets formed every three years. Women's age grades, which also were constituted every three years, rarely performed any role, despite the tendency for Abiribans to marry within the clan. Active membership in the ACIU, that is, the obligation to attend meetings and contribute dues, began at one's twenty-first birthday. As with the women's age grades, a fairly permissive attitude was maintained about nonmembership for women. From time to time various branches abroad attempted to form women's auxiliaries under the tutelage of the parent male body, with little noticeable success.

Before the war, the ability to compel Abiribans resident in cities to attend meetings and contribute their dues differed from area to area. However, on the whole, the compulsion to participate had declined since the period during which Enuda College was built. According to Akuma, the administrative secretary of the ACIU, there were only about 1,000 dues-paying members in 1965.[23] Even if half of the population of 40,000 was under twenty-one, and of the remaining 20,000, half were women, a potential membership of 10,000 adult males would have existed. Hence, the "compulsory" membership extended to only one-tenth of those eligible. This decline probably reflected the lack of enthusiasm for paying dues and attending meetings after twenty-five years of such solicitations.

The extensive powers of the officers elected yearly at the general meeting enabled them to control the affairs of the ACIU. The central officers directed the secretariat and the paid administrative secretary. In order to establish a new branch or merge existing branches, groups first obtained permission from the central executive. The central executive determined the level of financial contributions in the form of regular dues and special levies and imposed them uniformly on all members. In addition, the central executive sometimes taxed particular branches, as when Aba, Umuahia, Port Harcourt, and Calabar were asked to pay the fine and court costs incurred when Abiriba lost a case against a neighboring community in 1956.[24] All branches submitted reports of their activities and membership roles yearly. If branches did not submit these reports or the correct dues, they became subject to a fine. Similarly, all branches could be fined for failing to attend any meeting summoned by the central executive. By 1960, however, the tendency toward poor attendance at meetings and the general difficulty of all branches in collecting dues made the central executive wary of applying these sanctions. Instead, it merely issued complaints at every meeting about the failure of most branches to submit the requisite reports, membership roles, and dues. The central executive sometimes instructed branches to undertake special activities on its behalf. It sent delegations of active branches to delinquent ones to report on their problems and to help reform them. It sometimes instructed urban branches to make purchases on behalf of the union, as when the Port Harcourt branch bought science equipment for Enuda College in 1959.[25]

The control exercised by the central executive over the agenda for the meetings further consolidated their influence over the affairs of the ACIU. Branches could submit proposals for the agenda. In fact, the administrative secretary reminded them to do so before each conference. However, the central officers composed the final agenda. If they disapproved of a proposal, such as the suggestion made before the September 1960 meeting to grant children of Abiriban residents a special discount on school fees in Abiriban schools, they could reject it at the meeting without opening the matter to discussion. Another ploy used by the central executive to retain the initiative was to claim that the measure was under consideration by the union. Branches rarely followed up this claim to make sure that the officers acted on it. The frequent proposals of the Enugu branch to have the union undertake an active campaign for the recognition of the eze as a first-class chief by the Eastern government was an exception. Proposals for improvements that the officers did not want to undertake could be placed on a priority list of projects presented to the age grades, which indefinitely postponed without openly rejecting them.[26] The only clear instance of a proposal by one of the branches being immediately acted on was the appointment of a committee in September 1961 to write a history of Abiriba.[27]

The central executive formulated policy and then referred it to the general meeting for ratification. If the central executive stayed united, it was extremely unlikely that their suggestions would not be approved. Disagreement among the officers occurred infrequently, since most of the members of the central executive had worked together for years.

When a man was elected who would not cooperate with the other members, such as I. O. Onyeije, the first principal of Enuda College, his tenure of office would be brief.

Two recent instances in which the decision of the executive was reversed occurred as a result of a division among the officers. After several years of management and financial problems, the officers of the union and the board of governors of Enuda College at a joint meeting in September 1964 decided to turn the operation of Enuda over to another voluntary agency.[28] N. A. Otisi, the incumbent president of the ACIU, who was not present at the meeting, disagreed with the decision. In order to reverse the decision, he made an emotional appeal at the December general meeting, volunteering to resign his position as educational secretary to the Church of Scotland Mission and to devote his life to Enunda College. Delegates awarded him a two-year trial period as principal to remedy the chronic difficulties encountered by the school.[29]

The second change of policy related to the financing of the rubber plantation. In order for the union to be able to negotiate a loan from the Eastern government for £10,000 to finance the plantation, the officers petitioned two wealthy merchants, Nnana Kalu and M. C. Ugboaja, to stand surety for the union in December 1964. At that time Nnana Kalu, a representative from Aba in the Eastern House of Assembly, the elected legislative body, was also vice president of the union. He apparently agreed to ensure the entire loan, but asked that Enuda College be given to him as security.[30] The specter of Enuda College becoming the private property of one man enraged many of the branch unions and some of the officers, who sent letters of protest to the secretariat. Moreover, the election of Nnana Kalu as president of the ACIU in 1965 meant that he would have been in charge of disbursing the very funds for which Enuda College would be the final collateral. At the April 1966 conference, delegates finally agreed to negotiate a loan directly with the Fund for Agricultural and Industrial Development of the Eastern government, offering the 162 acres of land owned by Enuda College as surety.[31]

Like most other improvement unions, the ACIU followed parliamentary procedure in conducting its meetings. Meetings opened with a hymn or prayer. An agenda, prepared in advance by the central executive, determined the order of business. Officers were elected, usually yearly. Meetings were conducted in Ibo, while the minutes were kept in English. Members cited the conciseness of expression possible in English, in contrast to Ibo, as the reason for taking minutes in English. An additional factor that members sometimes mentioned was the desire to appear modern or educated.

The ACIU raised money through dues, fees, levies, and contributions. Initially, in January 1942, the union assessed one shilling as the regular yearly dues. In an attempt to increase its educational fund, the union reintroduced in 1944 customs that could be performed by the payment of fees: the ekpe fee was six shillings; the egwamang, thirty-six shillings; and the uche £5. These fees were to be shared between the educational fund and the townspeople. In 1945 officers first collected a compulsory levy of £1 to be paid yearly in addition to dues. The rate of dues and of levies usually reflected the nature and volume of projects undertaken by the union. Most commonly the officers set dues at £1.4.4. From 1951 through 1954, and again in 1955 and 1959, they imposed a rate of £2.10. In 1957 members were taxed £2.4.[32]

The central executive issued appeals for additional voluntary contributions on several occasions. In May 1957, when £1,000 was owed to a contractor for a building at Enuda College and the union lacked the funds, branches were asked to provide the money. In February 1959 Echerue Emole, the minister of finance in the Eastern Region government and the legal adviser to the ACIU, convened an emergency meeting to raise £3,125, one-eighth of the cost of installing water pipes, which Abiriba had to provide before the Ministry of Works would contribute the remainder.[33]

At first members regularly paid the dues imposed by the union. In 1950 the executive committee initiated a resolution, which was passed by the general meeting, invoking the right of the union to seize property and take other measures to secure payment of the levies by recalcitrant members. As the willingness of the members to pay their dues decreased, the repayment of scholarship loans by students educated by the union offset this loss for several years. Then the union did not have a reliable source of income. Several members conceived of the rubber plantation as the means of providing such an income for the future. In order to meet financial obligations, the union was eventually forced to borrow money. In 1959 it negotiated a £1,000 loan from the Eastern Region government to construct teachers' housing at Enuda. In 1960 it borrowed the sum of £3,000 from the Church of Scotland Missionary Educational Authority to pay for the First Century Gospel School, now the Enuda Primary School. The 1963 financial report revealed that the ACIU had to borrow large sums of money from Enuda College and Enuda Primary School to defray its operating expenses.[34] In 1966 the union was negotiating a £10,000 loan to finance expansion of the rubber plantation.

The union may be able to lift itself out of this financial morass. According to its revenue estimates, the union balanced its budget by reducing operating expenditures in 1965–1966.[35] Enuda College and Enuda Primary School supported themselves through fees and grants-in-aid from the government. In 1966 the Egwuena Girls' Secondary School was inspected, as a preliminary to receiving aid from the government. The rubber plantation was initially profitable, because the union received a subsidy from the government. The success of all these alternatives, of course, depends on economic rehabilitation.

ALTERNATIVE STRUCTURES

In order to assess the influence of improvement unions on political development, one must first understand their role in the political system, that is, the functions they perform. To operate effectively, a government must be able to receive and apply information, make and implement authoritative decisions, ensure compliance with its policies, and extract resources. The functions undertaken by the government in conjunction with other institutions to ensure survival of the system include the establishment and preservation of legitimacy, the production and allocation of goods and services, the recruitment of new personnel, the provision for participation by members of the society, and the resolution of disputes. An analysis of the organizations that perform these activities in Abiriba indicates that the ACIU was the effective government there, in the sense that it executed most of the requisite functions.

In addition to the Abiriba Communal Improvement Union, two other structures formerly existed in Abiriba that could have possibly performed the functions of government: a local council established by the colonial administration in the early 1950's, and the Owuwa Anyanwu County Council, whose jurisdiction included Abiriba. Both of them were dissolved by the Ironsi regime. From its inception, the local council, however, lacked the requisite capabilities to operate and performed few functions, while the county council tended to disregard purely Abiriban affairs.

The local government council consisted of thirty men who lived in Abiriba. The chairman, elected by the members of the council according to local convention, had to have resided in Abiriba for his entire life. Consequently, the backgrounds of the council members differed from the majority of Abiribans, who as traders spent most of their time away from home. Furthermore, the council lacked channels of communication with the citizens abroad. Many of the traders whom I interviewed in Port Harcourt in 1966 were not even aware of the continued existence of the council, assuming that it had disbanded several years ago.

Theoretically, councillors could have made policy decisions at their monthly meetings, but poor attendance led to the postponement of many meetings. Councillors lacked incentives to attend, since they received no remuneration. Their parochial views—since the majority of those willing to serve on the council were old and illiterate farmers—and their lack of administrative experience inhibited them from initiating community development projects. Consequently, the local government council rarely undertook responsibility for significant activities. It also lacked the apparatus to implement decisions or enforce compliance with them. The council had only one employee, a part-time messenger, who circulated notices of meetings.

One of the most significant indications of the limited capabilities of the local council was its inability to raise resources. The government never conferred the power to levy taxes directly on it, nor did it receive a regular subsidy from the Owuwa Anyanwu County Council. With no resources, it could not have undertaken community development projects even if it had been so inclined, unless members of the community had voluntarily contributed funds. Crippled by a low level of assets, the local council performed few services. As an artificial creation arising neither out of tradition nor to serve any particular and useful purpose, except to advance the policy of a colonial government, the local council did not inspire convictions of legitimacy. Being a pragmatically oriented people, the Abiribans merely ignored this rather useless institution.

Moreover, the local council in no way contributed to the integration of the community. In a tradition-conscious town imbued by the need for community development, the only service provided by the local council that a former chairman could list was the maintenance of law and order. Even this activity must be somewhat discounted, since the chairman could not describe how the council actually contributed to the preservation of order. Had a disturbance occurred, it seems that there was no way the council could have independently ended it. The council did not contribute even symbolically to the provision of goods and services through membership on the boards of schools, the hospital, or the post office, despite the councillors' requests to the ACIU for representation.[36]

The difficulty of the local council in recruiting able members originated in part from the absence of any benefits accruing from participation, since councillors were not paid, and membership did not confer prestige. It also derived from the small number of educated men available in Abiriba. In 1958 the ACIU passed a resolution making the only educated group remaining in Abiriba, the teachers, ineligible for membership on the council, apparently to ensure its continued ineffectiveness.[37] An effective local government council might have challenged the position of the ACIU. Although the election of the thirty councillors provided for a measure of participation, the elections lacked meaning, since the candidates would not be performing a useful role. Consequently, apathy characterized these elections, in sharp contrast with the interest generated during the elections for office in the ACIU.

The council was prodded into action only at the bidding of another agency, usually the ACIU. As a registered cultural organization, the ACIU sometimes found it embarrassing to negotiate with government officials. Hence, on several occasions the ACIU sent council members to interview government officials on particular matters or included them in delegations led by union officers. When the Owuwa Anyanwu County Council decided to erect new market stalls in Abiriba, it vested the local council with the responsibility and necessary resources to clear some land. With its usual domineering attitude, the ACIU held that the local council was accountable to it and demanded detailed figures on how the council spent the money.[38]

Unlike the local council, the Owuwa Anyanwu County Council was a viable, operating unit of government. It consisted of thirty-seven elected members, six of whom represented Abiriba, and four traditional members, one of whom was the eze of Abiriba. In addition to Abiriba, the jurisdiction of the council extended to an area embracing three other clans and including one small provincial city, Ohafia. Abiriba, which according to the 1963 census constituted about twenty-one percent of the population of the county council area, elected only sixteen

percent of its members. Since the census figures for Abiriba underestimated the population, Abiriba probably constituted one-fourth the
total population of the country council area. The largest number of
representatives, sixteen, came from Ohafia; Abam had nine; and Npkoru
elected six.

With almost half of its members from Ohafia, the county council
directed most of its resources and energy there, performing few functions in Abiriba. The primary service it provided for Abiriba was the
maintenance of four government-sponsored junior elementary schools.
Since the Ministry of Education in Enugu formulated educational policy
for government-sponsored schools, the county council merely contributed the funds. Its also allocated a yearly subsidy of £500 for the
hospital in Abiriba, in lieu of maintaining a medical dispensary, which
it maintained in the other three towns. The only independent project
it undertook in Abiriba was the erection of new open market stalls.

THE FUNCTIONS OF THE ACIU

With branches in every major center in which Abiribans lived and a
permanent administrative secretariat in Abiriba, the ACIU maintained
contact with the citizens of Abiriba, whether at home or abroad. The
branches submitted membership lists and sent reports of their major
activities to the secretariat. They sometimes forwarded proposals for
the agenda of the annual conference to the secretariat. In return, the
secretariat supplied them with yearly reports on the state of the entire
union, copies of important speeches, memoranda, letters, and minutes
of the annual conferences. Annual conferences, to which each branch
was entitled to send four delegates, brought representatives of the dispersed groups together to communicate with one another.

The central executive made most major decisions and then submitted
them to the conference for ratification. There was widespread acceptance of the central executive as the preeminent decision-making center
in Abiriba. The executive did not consult with either the traditional
authorities or the local council prior to formulating policy. The branch
organizations, coordinated by the secretariat, furnished the central
executive with a mechanism through which to implement its policies,
as well as to collect information.

Like governmental bodies in other subsystems, the ACIU lacked the
ability to apply physical coercion. It did, however, have other means

with which to evoke compliance. In 1950 a general meeting passed a resolution invoking the right of the union to seize property and take other measures necessary to secure payment of levies from recalcitrant members.[39] According to interviews with members, though almost everyone paid up, the union did seize property of members from time to time. When residents of Amaeke Division refused to pay their eg-wamang and uche fees, the union sued them in court, eventually securing a favorable judgment. The union had one effective sanction, the ability to humiliate individuals through publicly criticizing them. Just as the capturing of an enemy's head in battle was once the sign of manhood in Abiriba, more recently Abiribans have identified their coming of age with the responsibilities imposed by membership in the ACIU. Of course, this potential sanction of implying one had shirked the obligations of manhood would have no effect on someone who had ceased to identify with his community of origin, but such a development, sometimes called detribalization, has yet to occur among citizens of Abiriba. The loyalty of educated young men and the traders residing abroad equaled that of the farmers, who rarely left Abiriba for a prolonged period of time.

Insofar as operational capability is related to the ability to extract resources commensurate with needs, the ACIU declined in this aspect of its performance in the middle sixties. The resources of the ACIU, however, should be compared with those available to the Owuwa Anyanwu County Council. The county council had an estimated revenue of £62,990 in 1964.[40] For the same year the revenue of the ACIU, minus the school fees for Enuda Primary School and the contribution of the age grades, equaled £12,745.[41] During that year the Egwuena Girls' Secondary School opened, built at a total cost of £40,000. Two representatives of the American Friends Service Committee living in Abiriba organized international work camps to help construct an x-ray unit for the hospital built by and named after the Akahaba age grade organization. Also, the Erinma age grade finished collecting money for its town hall. Because there were so many different sources of income, it is difficult to estimate the precise resources of the union and its subsidiaries for 1964, but a conservative estimate of the total amount raised on behalf of the union would be £15,000.

In comparing the capability of the two organizations to extract resources, one should remember that according to the official estimate, Abiriba constituted only 21 percent of the population of the county council area and hence contributed only that proportion of the total amount of levies. Another factor affecting the comparison is the substantial contribution made by the government to the county council: by 1962 the Eastern government had donated half of the revenues of the county councils through recurring grants. In addition, the county council derived part of its revenues from a rebate on taxes levied by the regional government.[42] Hence, Abiriba's total direct contribution to the Owuwa Anyanwu County Council in 1964 was probably less than £6,000.

Legitimacy derives from conviction of the validity of a form of government. There was widespread acceptance of the role of the ACIU in Abiriba, and when asked, most Abiribans described the union as the government of Abiriba. A few emphasized that the ACIU should be considered only as a cultural organization, but even after January 1966 in Nigeria, with the new sensitivity about the political role of the ethnic unions in the discredited parliamentary system, this interpretation had few adherents.

The ACIU created and preserved a sense of legitimacy by linking itself with Abiriban tradition and by providing most of the improvements in the town. For example, the union sought and routinely received the approval of the chiefs for almost every important decision. When the chiefs refused to ratify ACIU decisions on a few occasions, the officers ignored their criticism and went ahead with the projects. Given the importance of education and community improvement to the residents of Abiriba, the accomplishments of the ACIU conferred tremendous prestige on the organization.

Not only had the ACIU linked itself to Abiriban tradition, but it also actively fostered that tradition. For example, it revived the three festivals that Christianization had suspended in 1944. It undertook several projects to increase the prestige of the chiefs, as in 1947 when the central officers commissioned three branch unions to make gowns for them. Intermittently, the union petitioned the government to recognize the eze as a first-class chief entitled to membership in the Eastern House of Chiefs. On two occasions, in 1947 and 1960, the union sought to have a history of Abiriba written: in 1947 it sponsored a contest and in 1960 the central executive appointed a committee to write a history.[43] By helping to define a new role for the age grades, the ACIU helped to preserve them.

The most important way in which the ACIU fostered the integration of the community was by providing the mechanism by which the citizens abroad were linked to those at home. Residents from Abiriba in each city and town throughout Nigeria came together several times a month. These meetings renewed the identity of the city dweller and reminded him of his obligations to his home community. At these meetings the officers at both the branch and central levels inculcated civic consciousness. The ACIU promoted a set of values emphasizing communal obligations, which were accepted by the community. To gain prestige, members of an age group presented a project to the community, as they once had sought recognition through heroic conduct in battle.

Aside from the few primary schools, the tarred road, and the new open market stalls, the ACIU provided all the existing facilities or services for the community. There were seven primary and two secondary schools in Abiriba. The first school to open, the Church of Scotland Mission elementary school, had an enrollment of about five hundred students in 1966. In 1948 the ACIU had financed the extension of the school, and although the school was owned and operated by the mission, the ACIU held the headmaster accountable to the union. In 1956, at the general meeting the officers called on the headmaster to answer complaints, specifically that no pupils had taken entrance exams for secondary schools for two years. The central executive suggested that the headmaster submit a yearly report to the union. Since the headmaster was also the second vice president of the ACIU, he admitted the deficiencies in the administration of the school and indicated how they would be remedied.[44]

The largest primary school, with an enrollment of eight hundred students, was Enuda Primary School. Established by the First Century Gospel Society in 1934, The ACIU bought the school in December 1960 and continued to run it. In addition to the schools operated by the ACIU, four local authority schools, with a combined enrollment of one thousand students, opened during the late 1950's. Financed by the Owuwa Anayanwu County Council and managed by the government, these four schools were the only significant ones in Abiriba with which the ACIU was not intimately connected. In an attempt to gain converts in Abiriba, the Roman Catholic Missionary Society opened a junior primary school in 1961, offering the first three grades. But few Abiribans considered themselves Catholic, so that the school was able to attract less than two hundred children.

As indicated previously the ACIU conceived, financed, built and staffed Enuda College. The second secondary school, Egwuena Girls' Secondary School, bore the name of an age grade, but a study of the details surrounding its construction confirms that the union, not the Egwuena age grade, was primarily responsible for the school. After 1954 any age grade wishing to carry out a development project had first to submit its proposals to the ACIU for prior approval. In December 1956 the Egwuena age grade offered to build a dormitory for Enuda College. At that time Enuda College, although coeducational, could admit few girls owing to a lack of dormitory facilities. The following year the Egwuena age grade canceled its proposal to construct the dormitory in favor of building a maternity center instead.[45] This time the union refused to approve the project. The third project selected by the age grade was a series of closed market stalls. Most of the necessary money had been collected when several influential officers of the union decided that, rather than building more dormitories for Enuda, a separate girls school should be constructed. A few of the officers attended the general meeting of the Egwuena age grade and prevailed on the members to accept the construction of the school as their project. Since the age grade lacked sufficient resources, other groups in Abiriba donated several buildings. Originally estimated at £30,000, the school eventually cost £40,000. One of the strongest advocates of opening a second school, Echerue Emole, finance minister in the Eastern government and legal adviser to the ACIU, donated a dormitory. A group of traders financed a classroom building, and the Abiriba Women's Cultural Organization, the women's wing of the ACIU, funded the staff quarters.[46]

The union also brought about the construction of the Akahaba Hospital. In 1955 the Akahaba age grade decided to build a post office. After receiving a plan from the government, the officers of the age grade called a general meeting for May. The officers of the ACIU favored the construction of a hospital, believing that it answered a greater need. The previous year they had made preliminary inquiries and found that the Ministry of Health would provide some of the equipment for a cottage hospital. I. U. Eke, the general president, met with a contractor, who was a member of the Akahaba age grade. Without consulting the age grade, the two went to the government and acquired a plan for a cottage hospital.

Eke appeared at the May meeting with the plan and a detailed estimate of the costs made by the contractor. Addressing the meeting, he stressed the need for a hospital in Abiriba and asked the age grade to finance its construction. He informed the age grade that the ACIU would acquire the land on their behalf. Also, the government would finance half the total cost of the hospital, to the extent of paying £10,-000 for equipment.

The age grade members agreed to finance a sixteen-bed cottage hospital. After the project was begun, the union discovered that for a larger hospital with more facilities, the government would assume most of the recurring costs of operation. Since the Akahaba age grade had just taxed its members to raise £3,000 more in order to have the £10,000 required to construct the cottage hospital, it was reluctant to finance a more expensive project. When the ACIU undertook, along with the people of Abiriba, to contribute most of the difference in cost between the two hospitals, the Akahaba age grade agreed to the change. The total cost of the seventy-eight bed hospital, excluding the equipment donated by the Eastern government and the x-ray unit built by the American Friends Service Committee in conjunction with the Red Cross, was approximately £20,000.[47] Before it opened, the union negotiated an agreement with the American Mennonite Board of Missions to staff and operate the hospital.

The ACIU maintained a list, which the age groups consulted, of priority projects. In August 1955 the union sent out a circular requesting all branches to inform the age grades that Abiriba needed a postal agency. The Nekina age grade decided to undertake the project in 1956, and three years later it was constructed at a cost of £5,000. The postal agency formally opened on January 1, 1960. In September 1960 the ACIU agreed to operate the Abiriba postal agency in order to raise it to the standard of a subpost branch office.[48]

Akahaba Hospital trained nurses, as well as providing medical services. When the medical officer, realizing the need for a separate nursing and midwifery school, consulted the ACIU, the officers told him that only an age grade would have the resources to finance one. At the request of the Okezie age grade, the ACIU gave them a list of several priority projects, stressing the need for a nursing and midwifery school. After the ACIU had presented the list, Dr. Ibe, the medical officer, at the suggestion of the central officers, spoke with two influential members of the Okezie age grade, the president and the legal adviser. Ultimately the Okezie age grade agreed to undertake the nursing school, whose cost has been estimated at £12,000.[49]

The prestige and influence conferred by an office in the ACIU enabled the union to recruit competent officials. Annual elections were the formal mechanism through which recruitment to office occurred. Appointment to committees, which were formed to perform specific tasks, was a second means through which recruitment took place. Initially the central executive attracted the most educated and distinguished men in occupations other than trade. Later, the tendency of this first group of men to perpetuate themselves in office blocked the rise of younger, more educated men.

The ACIU also recruited Abiribans for political offices. In 1948 the union decided to elect its president, O. A. Otisi, to represent Abiriba in the Bende Native Authority.[50] In 1951 the union directed him to submit his name as a candidate in the Bende Division election.[51] Since it had sponsored him, the union subsidized the £159.12 he spent on canvassing. At the August 1953 general meeting the union endorsed Echerue Emole, then a young barrister who had just completed his education, as their candidate for the seat in the Eastern House of Assembly district encompassing Abiriba.[52] In subsequent elections the union discouraged rivals from contesting the nomination and campaigned for him.

Through attendance at weekly or fortnightly meetings, at which every person had the right to speak, the union granted to each member some means of participation. Each branch also held annual elections for officers at which all contributing members could vote. Branches participated in the formulation of over-all policy by submitting proposals for the agenda of the general meetings and by ratifying or rejecting the programs of the central executive presented at the general conference.

Disputes arose in Abiriba from various sources during the life of the ACIU. Competition between the three component divisions of Abiriba sometimes engendered disagreement. In 1948 the union adjudicated a dispute between Agbaji, Amaogudu, and Amaeke over ownership of farmland. Although the union decided to allocate scholarships for higher education equally among the divisions to minimize complaints, Amaeke refused to continue paying its assessments for the festivals after its students had returned. After prolonged litigation, in 1956 the High Court ruled in favor of the union.[53] Since virtually all of the union's projects were designed for the entire community and were sited according to the availability of land, the potential sources of conflict between Amaeke, Amaogudu, and Agbaji were minimized.

Although each trading house was supposed to be autonomous in regulating its affairs, occasionally the union was called upon to help resolve disputes. In 1949 the union settled a case involving the division of property between two trading houses.[54] When a conflict arose between two groups of trading communities at Aba—the original land-based houses and those formerly based in the Rivers territory—which undermined the functioning of the Aba branch of the ACIU, the ACIU arranged for arbitration.[55]

The predominance of the Church of Scotland Mission and the exclusion of a Roman Catholic Mission until recently prevented a religious division of the community, such as characterized many parts of Eastern Nigeria. A close association existed between the union and the Church of Scotland Mission, resulting from their mutual concern with education and the employment of two past union presidents, O. A. Otisi and N. A. Otisi, in high positions in the mission's educational department. The most significant religious minority, the Assemblies of God Missionary Society, frequently requested permission for absence from compulsory Sunday meetings of the ACIU. The refusal of the union to grant such permission probably prevented the formation of a cleavage between religious groups.

Disputes sometimes arose between the more parochial farmers, who remained at home, and the traders. Since the leaders of the ACIU spent a significant portion of their own lives abroad, the farmers and chiefs sometimes transferred their resentment directly to the union. In 1950 the farmers accused President O. A. Otisi of being responsible for their high income tax assessment. After investigating the claim, the union absolved him. Subsequently Chief Ikpe Mba tried to block the endorsement of O. A. Otisi by the union to enter the 1951 election to the Bende Native Authority, because Otisi had failed to give him proper respect.[56] The ACIU dealt with this demand, as it commonly has with similar demands from the chiefs and farmers, by ignoring it. The overwhelming predominance of the more cosmopolitan members who had lived abroad rendered the farmers and chiefs impotent to block most decisions of the ACIU.

II | Patterns of Influence and Leadership in Abiriba

Influence, the "ability to get others to act, think or feel as one intends," is a concept that has been used in several studies of community power structure in American cities.[1] In Abiriba, the most significant issue areas in which patterns of influence and leadership emerged were the formulation of educational policy, the evolution of community development, and nominations for office, particularly in the political system of the Eastern Region. The union was intimately connected with the history of community development in Abiriba and with the evolution of education, for which interviews and minute books furnish abundant evidence. The data relevant to political nominations, however, is more limited, since one man, Echerue Emole, represented the Eastern House of Assembly constituency encompassing Abiriba from the first direct election in 1953 until the dissolution of the parliamentary system in 1966. A member of the faculty of the University of Nigeria, Kalu Ezera (from Ohafia), represented the Federal House of Representatives constituency, which included Abiriba. The central role played by the ACIU in the political system of Abiriba determined that the leadership of the ACIU was to a significant extent also the leadership of Abiriba. A high correlation between office and influence in the ACIU resulted from the centralization of power in the executive committee. Hence, any study of leadership in Abiriba must begin with an analysis of the incumbents of offices in the union.

SOCIOECONOMIC CHARACTERISTICS OF LEADERSHIP

The relatively short period of time that the ACIU has existed precludes a search for major historical changes in the socioeconomic characteristics of its office holders and members of committees. For only twenty of the years since its founding in 1941 could complete lists of ACIU officers be obtained for this analysis.[2] Informants furnished specific information on the officers' level of education, occupation, and length of residence in urban areas. In the absence of evidence to the contrary, all officers, with the exception of the presidency, were considered of equal importance. During the twenty years for which data was available, members filled 165 offices, or an average of about eight officers were elected each year. During this period, electors chose twelve men five or more times for a total of 110 terms, representing two-thirds of the total number of offices. Hence, the analysis of the socioeconomic characteristics of leadership of the ACIU concentrates on these long-tenure officers. Had lists of officers for the six omitted years been available, these twelve officers would probably have shown even longer tenures. Table 1 presents the data on the three variables of education, occupation, and residence for the twelve key officers. Table 2 compares the profiles for the five presidents elected during the first twenty-five years of the ACIU. Two of the five, P. O. Iboko and Nnana Kalu, did not serve long enough to be considered long-tenure officers.

Every officer considered spent a substantial portion of his life living away from Abiriba, including most of his tenure of office. This situation reflected the fact that the vast majority of delegates to the annual conference that elected officers came from the towns and cities, rather than from Abiriba. Only the administrative secretary, a paid, appointed position, had to reside in Abiriba. The more cosmopolitan, outward orientation of the officers sometimes caused friction between them and the farmers and chiefs, the permanent residents of Abiriba. The 1950 dispute between the Abiriba Communal Farmers' Association and O. A. Otisi, the incumbent general president of the ACIU, was a case in point. Although the union absolved Otisi of all responsibility for the high income tax assessment, at the same time it reminded him that, in view of the "underdeveloped condition" of the people, he should deal with them gently and patiently and not "forcefully command them" until they had learned "the modern way" to do things. Apparently the decision did not satisfy the farmers, for shortly afterward someone set fire to Otisi's house, and the chiefs unsuccessfully attempted to block his 1951 electoral bid.[3]

In 1955 when the central officers of the ACIU forced I. O. Onyeije, the first principal of Enuda College, to resign, the farmers in Amaeke,

Table 1. Socioeconomic characteristics of key officers of the ACIU for twenty years[a]

Officer	Terms	Schooling	Occupation	Principal residence
O. M. Agbagha	5	None	Trader	Calabar
O. Agwu	10	Three years elementary	Trader	Calabar
E. Akuma	13	Standard six (six years primary school)	Trader	Calabar
I. U. Eke	14	Standard six (six years primary school)	Trader, dispenser	Abroad[b]
U. Eme	14	Higher elementary teacher's certificate (primary school; four years teacher training)	Teacher, principal	Abroad
K. Ifekwu	5	Professional teacher's certificate (secondary school; one year teacher training)	Teacher	Abroad
K. Kalu	5	Standard six (six years primary school)	Trader	Aba
O. Onuoha	8	Professional teacher's certificate (secondary school; one year teacher training)	Teacher	Abroad
U. Onwuka	8	Professional teacher's certificate (secondary school; one year teacher training)	Teacher	Ohafia
N. A. Otisi[c]	12	Professional teacher's certificate (secondary school; one year teacher training)	Educational administrator, principal	Abroad
O. A. Otisi[c]	11	Higher elementary teacher's certificate (primary school; four years teacher training)	Educational administrator	Abroad
A. M. Ume	5	Higher elementary teacher's certificate (primary school; four years teacher training)	Teacher	Abroad

Source: Minute books and interviews.

a. The following years were used: 1941–1945, 1947–1948, 1952–1960, 1962–1965.

b. "Abroad" refers to any area of residence in Nigeria outside Abiriba or another African country.

c. Otisi is a common name in Abiriba. O. A. and N. A. Otisi were not directly related.

his division, began to boycott the activities of the union. The union had to take them through the courts in order to have them pay their educational levies at the uche and egwamang festivals.[4] The generally negative reaction of the people in Amaeke to Onyeije's forced resignation ultimately caused the union to hold a special meeting in 1956 to re-

Table 2. Socioeconomic characteristics of presidents of the ACIU for its first twenty-five years[a]

President	Terms	Schooling	Occupation	Principal residence
P. O. Iboko	2	None	Teacher	Calabar
O. A. Otisi	13	Higher elementary teacher's certificate	Educational administrator for Church of Scotland Mission	Abroad-Abiriba
I. U. Eke	4	Standard six	Trader, dispenser	Abroad-Abiriba
N. A. Otisi	5	Professional teacher's certificate	Educational administrator for Church of Scotland Mission, Principal Enuda College	Abroad-Abiriba
N. Kalu	2	Standard six	Trader, politician	Aba

Source: Minute books and interviews.

a. The data in this table for O. A. Otisi, I. U. Eke, and N. A. Otisi differs from that in Table 1 because it is based on all twenty-five years and concerns only their terms as president.

view and explain his case. Although the home community readily conceded Onyeije's faults, they asked that he be restored as principal. The refusal of the union to do so engendered more animosity between the farmers and the officers. The hostility climaxed in 1958 when the union accused certain cliques in Amaeke of trying to assassinate the general president.[5] In May 1960 the chiefs reported the unwillingness of the home community to contribute anything toward the acquisition of the First Century Gospel elementary school by the union. Finally in September 1960 the officers called on the chiefs to attempt to restore peace in the home community.[6]

Sometimes officers returned to Abiriba subsequent to their election. After becoming president, O. A. Otisi was transferred to Abiriba by the manager of the Ohafia District Schools of the Church of Scotland Mission, in order to improve its primary school there. U. Eme and I.U. Eke worked in Abiriba for almost their entire tenure in office, the former as a teacher and then headmaster of Enuda Primary School and the latter as a dispenser. N. A. Otisi briefly became both president of the ACIU and principal of Enuda College. The officers' subsequent residence in Abiriba did not change their identification with the modernist trade and professional group.

In conclusion, the ACIU was established through the efforts of Abiribans living in other areas of Nigeria. These same groups continued to control it, since the preponderant number of representatives at each general meeting was from branches abroad. The outlook of the officers, elected by these delegates, reinforced the bias in the union. Considering that at any one time more Abiribans reside abroad than remain at home, this bias proved functional.

The officers of the union represented two occupational groups, educators and traders. Five of the twelve long-tenure officers, or about 42 percent, were traders, and seven of them were educators, or approximately 58 percent. Three of the five presidents were traders, and two were educational administrators. Inasmuch as the two educators served a total of eighteen terms as president, while the three traders served only eight, the educators predominated. In view of the fact that as many as three-fourths of all Abiriban males were traders, the educators were represented far out of proportion to their numbers. This preponderance of educators in the central executive was not duplicated either in the branches or in the offices of the age grades. The overwhelming majority of officers of the Port Harcourt branch, the most important and active branch, were traders. For example, in 1965 nineteen of the twenty officers whose occupations are known were traders, and one was a lawyer. The one lawyer, the legal adviser of the branch, attended few meetings of either the executive or the residents of Port Harcourt and could be discounted as anything more than an intermittent influence. It is likely that the three officers whose occupations could not be ascertained were also traders.

A similar preponderance of traders existed in the central executive of the Okezie age grade. In 1966 the Okezie age grade was constructing a nursing school in preparation for their celebration of the uche festival. Previously Okezie had inaugurated the competition between age grades in presenting community development projects by building a town hall for their egwamang celebration. In 1965 eleven of the twelve members of the central executive of the Okezie age grade were traders, and one, their legal adviser, was a lawyer.

The Abiriba Youth Movement (AYM) was the only organization embracing Abiribans abroad that had a higher proportion of nontraders among its officers than did the central executive of the ACIU. The AYM originated in 1962, specifically to try to improve the management of Enuda College. It remained in existence as a kind of pressure group generally representing the views of the more educated elements. A tabulation of the occupations of the central executive, the Eastern executive, and the executive of the Port Harcourt branch of the AYM, which counted each man only once even if he held several offices, showed that three were professionals, two civil servants, one a university lecturer, and two traders.[7]

Although the ACIU was sometimes dependent on the support of the wealthy merchants for its financing, the election of officers did not reflect this situation. On two occasions the ACIU composed lists of wealthy traders assisting the union—in 1948, naming the guarantors to the chief inspector of education in Enugu should the union fail to complete the secondary school, and in 1964, listing those who provided the surety for a loan to finance the rubber plantation.[8] None of the five traders on the 1948 list was either appointed a trustee of the union, despite the selection of the first group of trustees a year after their guarantee, or elected to central office. The officers nevertheless placed three of the wealthy merchants on committees at various times.

M. C. Ugboaja and Nnana Kalu, who were asked to provide the surety for the £10,000 loan from the Eastern government for the rubber plantation, were more influential than the first group of guarantors. Both became trustees of the ACIU in 1964, along with Emole, N. A. Otisi, and E. Oko. At the same meeting in December 1964 where the union composed the draft loan agreement with the two traders, delegates elected Nnana Kalu general president of the ACIU. However, these two incidents do not seem to be directly related. Correspondence in the files of the Port Harcourt branch indicate that the delegates elected Nnana Kalu "to use his much accumulated experience and influence both as director of many companies and as an Honorable member of the Eastern House of Assembly."[9] Shortly after his election, the union reconsidered its loan policy, because many people were adverse to having one of the guarantors administering the borrowed money.

The preponderance of educators over traders in the central executive probably reflected the emphasis on education that has characterized the union from its inception, as well as indicating the union's broad financial base. The traders, most of whom were illiterate, lacked the qualifications for formulating educational policy and administering it. When he was elected president in 1943, O. A. Otisi represented the most qualified Abiriban to direct the development of the educational program and the most prominent citizen among the nontraders. During most of his tenure as president, he lived near or in Abiriba and could devote his time to the union's affairs. In the ten years prior to 1966, however, the teachers elected to office were neither the most prominent professionally nor the best qualified educationally.

Just as the occupational structure of the ACIU officers was atypical of the general membership, the educational levels attained by them were somewhat higher. It is unlikely that more than one-fifth of all Abiribans born before 1945 attended school. Only one of the twelve long-tenure officers did not receive any education, and another failed to complete primary school. Three of the twelve attained a standard six certificate, indicating that they had completed the full primary school course. Another four held higher elementary teacher's certificates, the approximate equivalent in length to a secondary school education.

The highest standard achieved was the professional teacher's certificate, held by three officers. A professional teacher's certificate required at least one year of study after the completion of secondary school. Table 3 gives the educational profile of the twelve long-tenure officers.

Table 3.   Schooling of long-tenure officers of the ACIU

Schooling	No. of officers	Combined no. of terms
None	1	5
Some primary	1	10
Standard six	3	32
Higher elementary teacher's certificate	4	35
Professional teacher's certificate	3	28

Source: Minute books and interviews.

Of the five ACIU presidents, only the first one was not educated. Two completed primary school, and two received higher elementary or professional teacher's certificates. As with the occupational structure, the two presidents with the highest level of attainment, O. A. Otisi and N. A. Otisi, held office for most of the time, eighteen out of twenty-six terms.

That the central executive attained a more advanced level of education than did the branches is shown by an analysis of the education of the officers of the Port Harcourt branch in 1965. Six of the twenty-three members lacked any education; five had received some elementary education; and six had studied through standard six. One had received some secondary schooling; one had completed secondary school; and one had attained a university degree. Information regarding the education received by three of the officers was not available. Thus, at least eleven members, or almost 48 percent of the Port Harcourt executive, had not even completed primary school, as compared with 17 percent of the central officers. While 58 percent of the central officers studied had gone beyond primary school, possibly only 13 percent of the Port Harcourt executive had done so.

The record of the Okezie age grade executive more closely resembled that of the Port Harcourt officers than it did the central executive. Three members of the twelve man executive had some elementary schooling; eight had studied through standard six; and one, their legal adviser, had attained a university degree. While no member of their executive was illiterate, only one officer had studied beyond primary school.

Although the central executive was better educated than the general membership, it did not constitute the most advanced group in Abiriba. Three-fourths of the officers of the AYM had studied beyond primary school. Not one of the ACIU's long-tenure officers had attended a university, which indicates that it failed to utilize the talents of the university graduates who emerged in increasing numbers after 1951, the year that I. O. Onyeije, the first scholarship student sponsored for higher education by the union, returned. At least twenty Abiribans had received university degrees by 1966, five of whom were educated by the union: I. O. Onyeije, A. O. Uche, O. O. Otisi, C. O. Odu, and O. A. Okorie.[10] These five are listed with their university degrees in Table 4.

Table 4. ACIU scholarship students

Student	University	Degrees	Year of return
I. O. Onyeije	Edinburgh	B.A., M.A. in education	1951
A. O. Uche	Edinburgh	G.S., M.A. in education	1952
O. O. Otisi	Ibadan	B.A.	1953
C. O. Odu	Howard, South Hampton	B.A., M.A. in education	1956
O. A. Okorie	Howard, Harvard	B.A., M.A., Ph.D. in science	—[a]

Source: Minute books and interviews.

a. Okorie had not yet returned in 1966 but was expected shortly, according to members of his age grade who claimed to have corresponded with him.

The union sponsored the education of the five so that they could staff Enuda College and assume leadership roles in Abiriba in at least educational policy-making. Shortly after the return of Onyeije, the union appointed him principal of Enuda College. In 1954 delegates elected him secretary of the ACIU, with O. O. Otisi as his assistant. Almost immediately friction developed between Onyeije and the older, less educated officers. The charges preferred against him by the president, O. A. Otisi, in May 1956, at the last of a series of emergency meetings called over Onyeije's resignation as principal, included several charges relating to his tenure of office as secretary: that he had refused to enter important records into the minute books, especially those pertaining to himself, and that he had written discouraging letters to scholarship students in the United States (presumably about finances) without any authorization.[11] Apparently Onyeije failed to disguise his feelings of contempt for the other officers. In any case, delegates refused to reelect either Onyeije or O. O. Otisi. Until 1965, when C. O. Odu became one of the two joint treasurers, delegates did not elect any scholarship student or university graduate.[12] O. O. Otisi's term as publicity secretary for a few years provoked criticism about his lack of effectiveness. However, since this particular office did not entitle its incumbent to meet with the central executive and participate in the formulation of policy, it has not been included in the group of offices on which this analysis of leadership is based.

Some officers attempted to justify the systematic exclusion of university graduates by claiming that the five scholarship students failed to fulfill their obligations, despite the sacrifices made on their behalf by the community. This claim cannot be substantiated. Only one student, O. A. Okerezie, did not return by 1966. Onyeije served the community for four years, Uche for six, Odu for eight, and Otisi was in his thirteenth year of service in 1966. Otisi, Odu, and Uche completely repaid the union for the cost of their education, and Onyeije partially repaid it, in accordance with a High Court judgment in 1958, after his dismissal as principal. Furthermore, Onyeije and Uche probably would have served longer had the board of governors not forced them to resign. According to two observers, Uche was incompetent and did a poor job. Emole, on behalf of the union, used his influence to get Uche an appointment at the Advanced Science Secondary School at Lagos. Demoted as principal in 1961 after serving for several years, Odu resigned in 1964 along with Uche. In terms of qualifications, interest, and service to the community, O. O. Otisi was more deserving of election to office in the union than any other Abiriban. Not only did he fill many key educational appointments, including headmaster of Enuda College and principal of Egwuena Girls' Secondary School, a position for which he was recruited in 1963, but he also served as chairman of both the Abiriba Local Council and the Owuwa Anyanwu County Council several times.

The frustration of many of the better educated young men over their inability to influence the formulation of educational policy inspired the formation of the AYM. None of the members of their executive gained election to the ACIU. In 1965 Ezima Otisi, the assistant secretary of the central executive of the AYM and the secretary of the Eastern zonal board, was finally appointed to the education committee and the board of governors of Egwuena.

Hence, at one time the officers of the ACIU numbered some of the best educated Abiribans. As a result of the stability of leadership, these men remained in office, despite the superior educational qualifications of many younger men. It seems that after their initial unhappy experience of having their competency to lead challenged by Onyeije, and hence their legitimacy, the long-tenure officers used their influence to exclude other university graduates from office in the central union.

CONSTRAINTS ON THE ACIU EXECUTIVE

While there was a significant correlation between office in the ACIU and leadership in Abiriba, other positions also provided an access to influence. These other sources of power acted to limit the scope of influence exercised by the central executive of the union. Two groups could wield direct influence: the politicians and the professionals who were called upon by the union to manage the schools and community development projects. In addition, annual elections conferred indirect influence on the delegates to the conference, who selected the executive.

The member of the community most prominent in the larger regional political system was Echerue Emole, a frequent minister in the Eastern government. When he returned from England in 1952, as the first Abiriban to win a law degree, he acquired a great deal of prestige. Almost immediately he became involved in politics. In 1952 he sent a circular letter to all ACIU branches, reminding them that they would soon be called upon to nominate a candidate to represent Abiriba in the Bende Native Authority and stating his willingness to serve if elected.[13] Various branches then arranged receptions for him. Following constitutional reforms, the candidate nominated for a constituency encompassing Abiriba was to serve also in a newly formed House of Assembly legislating for the Eastern Region.[14] One other candidate from Abiriba seriously challenged Emole, Ikwam Onyeije, who also tried to mobilize support through correspondence with the branches. The union played a decisive role in the nomination of Emole, first by endorsing his candidacy at the general meeting and second by persuading Onyeije to withdraw.[15]

After his election Emole became a minister in the government of the Eastern Region. Although the union was decisive in securing his first election, his high position in the NCNC, the ruling party in the one-party regional political system, conferred on him an independent base of influence. Emole frequently enacted a ritual of accountability to the ACIU by reporting the services he had performed for Abiriba at union conferences, but it was almost unthinkable that a community would renounce the benefits of patronage by not reelecting an important minister.

Frequently one of the branches would petition Emole to remind him of his obligations. For example, a welcome address presented to Emole during his visit to Port Harcourt in 1965 listed the following deficiencies for him to remedy: absence of any Abiribans on the boards of established industries in the Eastern Region or in executive positions in the civil service, and failure of any Abiriban youths to be awarded scholarships for higher learning by the Eastern scholarship board. In addition, the Port Harcourt branch asked Emole to use his influence to site an industry in Abiriba, to tar the Amogudu-Abiriba road, and to exchange the plot of land in Port Harcourt assigned to the branch for a town hall for a more favorable location.[16]

From time to time the central executive depended on Emole to complete certain projects. In 1959 Emole arranged for the installation of water pipes by the Ministry of Works: the Abiribans had to pay only one-eighth of the total cost of £3,125, although the government policy was to require a contribution of one-half from the community.[17] In 1961 the Eastern government paved two miles of roads. It is likely that the projected electrification of Abiriba was facilitated by arrangements executed by Emole prior to the formation of the military regime. To justify the inclusion of Abiriba on the priority list for electrification, the government claimed Abiriba to be particularly suitable for the development of small industries—something it was not.[18]

Although Emole never accepted elective office in the ACIU, serving rather as their legal adviser, he definitely must be considered one of the most important men in Abiriba. Appointed by the union to many important committees, he also became chairman of the board of governors

of Enuda College in 1966. Emole played a decisive role in the controversy over whether to build a separate college for girls. Enuda College
opened on a coeducational basis, limiting the number of girls only to
the availability of dormitory space. In December 1956, when the Egwuena age grade offered to build a girls' dormitory for Enuda College,
the union approved the proposal and sent for plans.[19] Emole and many
of the union officers, who apparently were quite conservative on the
subject of coeducation, favored building a separate girls' school, rather
than making Enuda the comprehensive school advocated by many of
the more progressive, educated members of the community. In addition,
Emole seems to have advocated the opening of another secondary school
for the prestige it would confer on Abiriba. Many union officers began
pressuring the Egwuena age grade to build a girls' secondary school.
Emole became the adviser to the age grade, a newly created position,
in 1961 and as such attended the meeting at which they finally consented
to build the new school.[20] Emole's commitment to erect a dormitory for
the new school made the project financially feasible.

One other Abiriban, Nnana Kalu, was elected to the Eastern House
of Assembly from an outside constituency, becoming a member from
Aba in 1961. Since he did not represent Abiriba, Kalu did not need the
political support of the ACIU. Moreover, evidence suggests that the
union did not offer its support to secure his political position. The delegates elected him president apparently as a result of his political position, hoping that he would use his influence on their behalf.[21] In
addition to being president of the union, Kalu became chairman of the
board of governors of Egwuena Girls' Secondary School in 1966.

Since the union was the proprietor of Enuda College, Enuda Primary
School, and Egwuena Girls' Secondary School, the general president
managed the three schools. The administration of the two secondary
schools was vested in a board of governors selected by the ACIU and
responsible to the general assembly of the ACIU and the minister of
education of the Eastern Region or his representative. Five officers of
the ACIU automatically became members: the president, vice-president,
secretary, treasurer, and financial secretary. Each board selected a
chairman from among its members to serve for one year. The boards
dealt with all matters concerning general policy, finance, buildings,
appointments and their termination, salaries, allowances, tuition, and
fees.[22]

Normally the two boards met only twice yearly and vested day-to-day
management of the secondary schools with the principals. According to

the constitution of Enuda College, the principal, who was subject to confirmation by the board, had the following powers and responsibilities:

(a) Power to suspend any member of the teaching staff and report immediately to the Chairman of the Board.

(b) The engagement of such administrative, domestic, and outdoor staff as may be provided for in the Annual Estimates.

(c) The academic efficiency, social welfare, and discipline of the staff and students.

(d) Religious Instruction and Observances.

(e) The maintenance of discipline, with power to expel any student, such expulsion to be reported to the Board at its next meeting.

(f) The collection of all funds of the College in accordance with the instruction of the Board, and the immediate payment of these funds to the Treasury of the ACIU. The treasurer disburses all the funds of the College.

(g) The submission to the Board of an Annual Report, Annual Statements of Account and Auditor's Report thereon and an Annual Estimate of Income and Expenditures.

As a result of the need for making daily decisions, the principal often predominated in the formulation of educational policy. The specific role of the respective boards and the union resembled that of the American Congress in the evolution of foreign policy: they could obstruct the systematic formulation and implementation of policy by the executive but could not substitute their own constructive measures.

This division of responsibility between the board and the principal, with its inherent potentialities for friction, all but destroyed the schools. Enuda College had five principals in its first twelve years, while the third principal in less than four years was appointed at Egwuena in June 1966. Disagreements between the officers of the union and the principal inevitably led to his dismissal. Listed below are the tenures of the principals of Enuda College:

Principal	Tenure
I. O. Onyeije	1953–1956
C. O. Odu	1956–1961
Rev. R. H. Paulson	1962–1963
O. O. Okerezie	1963–1964 (interim)
N. A. Otisi	1965——

Following are the tenures of the principals of the Egwuena Girls' Secondary School:

Principal	Tenure
Mrs. Paulson	1962
O. O. Otisi	1963–1966
Miss Gladice Strongface	1966

I. O. Onyeije's forced resignation primarily resulted from his attempt to formulate school policies without consulting the executive of the ACIU and the board of governors of Enuda College, both of whom he considered incompetent. Rather than requesting prior authority for his decisions, he deliberately attempted to conceal the affairs of the school from the scrutiny of the union or the board. The union charged him with surreptitiously raising his salary £100 a year and, when discovered, refusing to refund the money; knowingly disregarding the manager of Enuda by failing to give him the log book to sign; refusing to show the accounts of the college to members of the board of governors; continuously leaving the college without permission; refusing to form a food committee as directed by the union; and retaining and paying a cook fired by the union.[23]

Apparently friction developed initially between his successor, C. O. Odu, and the executive over Odu's more progressive educational attitudes, a common problem encountered by returning scholarship students. Odu's primary fault, however, was his inability to maintain discipline. The inherent pressures experienced by anyone directing a school in his home community under the continuous surveillance of a somewhat hostile board of governors were complicated by Odu's lack of experience with secondary schools: he had attended a teachers college rather than a secondary school. The rapid turnover in his teaching staff, itself a reflection of the insecurity and frustration engendered by the policy controversies, further handicapped Odu.

The extent to which the resulting friction undermined the educational standards of the college was indicated by the 1961 examination results, when only two students from Enuda passed the school certification exam taken at the completion of secondary school, and then only with the lowest mark possible, a grade three pass. An Enuda College Reform Committee, launched by many of the younger, educated men and women and later transformed into the Abiriba Youth Movement, protested the "deplorable state of affairs." Suggested reforms included greater autonomy for Enuda College, the reconstitution of the board of governors, and a review of the competency of the staff by the reconstituted board.[24]

An expatriate principal from the United States, the Reverend R. H. Paulson, arrived in 1962 to attempt to improve educational standards. The appointment of an expatriate, despite the education of five students by the union specifically to direct Enuda College, constituted an admission of at least partial failure by the ACIU executive. Paulson reorganized school administration to place it on a more democratic operating basis, such as by establishing a student council. His innovations, particularly the elimination of physical punishment, infuriated several union officers and Emole. He further decreased his popularity by opposing the encroachment of the rubber farm on school property and the recruitment of his students as unpaid laborers. By 1963 his position had become untenable and Paulson submitted his resignation.

While the union searched for a new principal, O. O. Okerezie served in an interim capacity. Overwhelmed by the bankruptcy of their management policies, the board and the officers of the union decided at their joint meeting in September 1964 to transfer the operation of Enuda College to another voluntary agency. Only an emotional appeal by the incumbent president of the ACIU, N. A. Otisi, at the December general meeting reversed that decision.

As a member of the governing elite of the union, N. A. Otisi, the last principal, was able to maintain good relations between himself and the board, which was the fundamental prerequisite for a successful administration denied to his predecessors. Three-fourths of the students taking the school certification exam in 1965 passed, almost half of them with either a first or second class grade.

The Eastern government refused to certify the first principal of the Egwuena Girls' Secondary School, Mrs. Paulson, claiming that she lacked the necessary qualifications. Since they could not recruit another woman, the central executive drafted O. O. Otisi, then headmaster of Enuda College. In his three years as principal he established the school on an operating basis. Unfortunately the officers of the union believed that it was only proper for a girls school to be directed by a woman. Ignoring the competency of their principal and his advice, the union in 1966 appointed a recent and inexperienced graduate of the University of Nigeria from Opobo, Miss Gladice Strongface.[25]

Professionals also managed the Akahaba Joint Hospital. The Mennonite Mission rather than the union supervised the recruiting of the hospital staff, including the medical and administrative superintendents. Ultimate responsibility for the management of the hospital was vested in a board of governors, to which the union appointed only three of the eight members, two representing the Akahaba age grade and one the general community. The Mennonite Mission and the Eastern government appointed the other five members. The government also assumed the annual deficit up to two-thirds of the operating cost. Hence, the union theoretically had very little to do with the operation of the hospital. It did, however, intervene from time to time, as in 1965 when complaints were made at the general meeting pertaining to the failure of the hospital to give preference to Abiribans in the hiring of nonprofessional staff.[26]

Since the ability to make the decisions distinguishes the leadership of any organization, the general membership was by definition not likely to be influential in the formulation of policy. It would be wrong, however, to discount completely the role of the membership of the ACIU. Annual elections ensured that any officer repugnant to the delegates of the general meeting would not retain his office. On sensitive issues the executive sometimes made an effort to secure prior or subsequent approval for its policy from the conference. For instance, it convened a special meeting to present the point of view of the union on Onyeije's resignation after the town had complained about the lack of information. The officers requested and received a motion of confidence in December 1956 in connection with the legal suit brought against Onyeije to recover their money and books.[27]

The general membership never determined policy-making. Even its potential instrument of influence, annual elections, was dissipated in several ways. Not only did candidates rarely contest elections openly, but on several occasions delegates at the conference gave all the officers a second term by a general vote of confidence. The limited role played by the general conference resulted in part from the nature of the delegates. With the exception of the few coopted officers of the youth and women's wings, the delegates were officers of the branches, who tended to be traders with little or no education. As a group, the delegates probably did not exhibit an active concern with the details of policy-making, particularly in the educational sphere.

CONTINUITY IN OFFICE

Being neither the most competent nor the most educated group, the single most important resource possessed by the leadership was experience. Social scientists have noted the tendency for a small proportion of the total membership of an association to exercise considerable influence over the affairs of that association, even in a democracy.[28] In Abiriba this oligarchical tendency emanated from the perpetuation of the same men in leadership positions. In the twenty-five years from 1941, when the union was founded, to 1966, when the data for this study was collected, twenty-six presidents were elected. Five men filled the office during this period. If the first two and last two years are excluded, only three men served as president. Delegates elected one man, O. A. Otisi, thirteen times. Had Otisi wished to remain in office, he probably could have stayed almost indefinitely. In both 1952 and 1958 he asked the union to relieve him of his post. Table 5 shows the five presidents and the years during which they held office.

Table 5.   Tenure of presidents of the ACIU

President	No. of terms	Years
P. O. Iboko	2	1941, 1942
O. A. Otisi	13	1943–1952, 1955–1957
I. U. Eke	4	1953, 1954, 1958, 1959
N. A. Otisi	5	1960–1964
Nnana Kalu	2	1965, 1966

Source: Minute books and interviews.

The three presidents following O. A. Otisi all had considerable experience as officers of the ACIU. I. U. Eke was vice-president of the ACIU for ten years before he first succeeded O. A. Otisi, and another four years before the second time he succeeded Otisi as president. N. A. Otisi served as an officer of the union for eight years prior to his election. Nnana Kalu's somewhat shorter tenure as an officer—he was vice-president twice and might also have been elected as an officer in 1961 and 1962, years for which no records were available—was supplemented by service on many important committees.

As indicated previously, during this twenty-year period, twelve men were elected five or more times: O. M. Agbagha, O. Agwu, E. Akuma, I. U. Eke, Kalu Ifegwu, K. Kalu, Obasi Onuoha, U. Onwuka, U. Eme, N. A. Otisi, O. A. Otisi, and A. M. Ume. The total number of terms served by these twelve men represented two-thirds of the 165 offices filled during the twenty years. Moreover, eight of these men—Agwu, Akuma, Eke, Eme, Onuoha, Onwuka, N. A. Otisi, and O. A. Otisi—accounted for eighty terms or almost half of the total. The executive officers also had themselves appointed to most of the important committees selected by the union during this period. The union appointed two sets of trustees, one in 1949 and the second in 1964; eleven of the thirteen men chosen had held office at one time. Delegations to conferences in 1948, 1952, and 1957 included four officers out of the five men sent. Eleven of the fourteen men chosen to fill vacancies on various boards of governors were either central officers or the legal advisor of the ACIU. Twelve separate committees formed by the union had a total of sixty-seven members; of those members, fifty had been officers. Of the seventeen general members appointed to the committees, thirteen served on two large committees. Out of a total of ninety-nine appointments, seventy-six, or more than three-fourths, were incumbent, former, or future central officers.

The group of twelve officers filling two-thirds of the terms during these twenty years also served on a dispropotionate number of committees. Of the seventy-six appointments filled by officers of the central union, these twelve men accounted for fifty-seven appointments. This represented three-fourths of all the positions filled by officers.[30]

Aside from E. Emole and Nnana Kalu, no Abiriban devoted his time primarily to politics. The most important resource possessed by the long-tenure officers was experience. The twelve longest tenured officers averaged nine terms each, and during these nine years a substantial portion of their time went to affairs of the union. Furthermore, during this time the general membership did not effectively participate in the formulation of decisions. Given their experience and motivation, the leadership developed considerable administrative skill.

In Abiriba, moreover, resources did not tend to be cumulative; groups possessing one influence base rarely had access to others at the same time. There was a definite structural limitation to pyramiding resources in Abiriba, since the wealthiest group, the traders, usually lacked education. Most of those with university and advanced degrees became educators and thus did not receive high salaries. Advanced degrees often acted as a hindrance rather than an asset, because the long-tenure officers were wary of the university graduates. Wealth did not have the inhibiting effect of education, but neither did it necessarily confer any advantage. Status, aside from the symbolic role of the chiefs, followed from achievement.

The conclusions reached here regarding patterns of leadership are somewhat speculative, owing to the relative absence of data on the role of individual members in the formulation of decisions. By 1966 the president was probably more of a *primus inter pares* than a predominant executive. As a group, the officers had worked together for a long period of time, and several of them had more direct experience in managing the affairs of the union than did the incumbent president. As the only full-time officer, the administrative secretary rather than the president, directly controlled the communications network. He also managed the rubber plantation. While the president managed the three schools, actual responsibility for directing them remained with the principal and the board of governors. Nnana Kalu, the incumbent at the time of this research, as an elected politician and businessman could not possibly have devoted a substantial portion of his time to the union, at least before the installation of the military government. His predecessor, N. A. Otisi, lived at Itu while serving as educational secretary to the Church of Scotland Mission, so that important meetings of the excutive committee took place when he could not attend them, such as the one convened in September 1964 on the status of Enuda College.

It is likely that more power was centralized in the president during O. A. Otisi's tenure. When he was first elected, the union was new and the other officers were inexperienced. Initially he served for ten straight terms. However, his position as educational general manager of the Church of Scotland Mission probably occupied much of his time. During most of his initial ten-year tenure, his general secretary, Ejim Akuma, handled the correspondence, audits, and administrative reviews. Akuma, along with I. U. Eke, the vice-president also held office during these ten years.

One would be justified in calling the ACIU a limited oligarchy in terms of the concentration of power in the executive and the predominance of a small group of men in office. This centralization of power and stabilization of personnel is not uncommon in governments widely acknowledged to be democracies, and the ACIU was the government of Abiriba. Members of the central executive did not use their influence for their advantage, as far as could be ascertained, but to bring about development in Abiriba. Prestige alone, as well as the satisfaction of seeing their plans spring directly to life, accrued to them as a result of their continuation in office.

III | The Development of Mbaise

Mbaise in the Ibo language means five village groups. As the name implies, the county of Mbaise, located in Owerri Division, Owerri Province, consists of several groups or clans joined together to form a single unit. British administrative policy, rather than a tradition of cooperation, called the unit into being. For this reason, it is necessary to examine the evolution of the colonial administration in the area.

Reflecting the ethnic diversity of the area was the plurality of improvement unions in Mbaise, based on villages, on clans, and on the county itself. This diversity, along with the tendency for the jurisdiction of the unions to overlap, created conditions conducive to conflict and competition among the unions—a situation that was precluded in Abiriba by the unitary Abiriba Communal Improvement Union. Since the strengths and weaknesses of various levels of unions tend to reflect characteristics of the units they represent, the nature of the clans in Mbaise must also be explored. In some respects the federation of clans forming Mbaise offered a microcosmic view of the processes uniting the Ibo people. Hence, an analysis of the bonds amalgamating the diverse ethnic groups in Mbaise should illuminate the factors promoting their expanding horizons of identification. An assessment of the extent to which Mbaise superseded the more primary and primordial units, the villages and clans, should also furnish insight into the possibility of maintaining multiple levels of identity.

BRITISH ADMINISTRATION IN THE EASTERN REGION

A military expedition to suppress the oracle at Aro Chukwu passed through Owerri in 1902. Two years later a district commissioner went

69

into the area to establish a primitive system of administration, appointing headmen to be responsible for serious breaches of the peace. During the early years of British administration, the government divided the East first into provinces headed by a provincial commissioner, then into subdivisions administered by a district or divisional commissioner. Shortly afterward the government partitioned the districts into smaller units called native court areas. Mbaise, situated immediately to the east of the Imo River, the western boundary of the Owerri Division, became part of that division. In 1909 two native courts were established at Nguru and Okpala, under whose jurisdiction the present Mbaise area was placed. The jurisdiction of both court areas encompassed large numbers of people, some of whom, particularly those attending the court at Okpala, did not become part of Mbaise. Most of the 100,000 inhabitants of the Nguru court area later became regrouped as the unit of Mbaise.[1]

In order for the courts to function, the British had to establish panels of judges. At first the British assumed that there would be chiefs or strong traditional rulers, as in the northern part of the territory, whom they could appoint to the courts. The dispersed power structure of the Ibo village government, however, had precluded the emergence of permanent, stable leadership. Rather than merely confirming a traditional status through recognition, therefore, the administration had to create chiefs. These men, who were appointed as judges by government warrant, were called warrant chiefs.

Under this system of administration the government met the expenses of operating the courts and the salaries of the judges through compulsory labor and from revenue collected by the native courts rather than by direct taxation. In 1927 the government decided to introduce taxation as part of a program for the transforming of the entire system of local government into a more efficient structure. Although the tax was supposed to be calculated on an assessment of the average farmer's income, it in fact was merely a poll tax based on a census of the adult male population taken by the warrant chiefs the previous year. Partially in protest against the introduction of taxes, partially as a reaction to the reduction of palm oil prices because of a trade recession, and partially as a consequence of the excesses of the warrant chiefs, women's riots erupted. One of the casualties of the riots, the court at Nguru, closed in 1929 because of extensive damage inflicted on the building by the rioters.

One of the major defects of administration through the warrant chiefs was that while the traditional Ibo form of government was democratic, the British system was not. In the Ibo system, when one leader lost support, he was displaced, a not infrequent occurrence, but the warrant chief could not be replaced except by orders of the central administration acting through the district commissioner, despite the chief's lack of popularity with his people.[2] This stabilization of rulership with the accompanying withdrawal of the mechanism of "dethronement," the means by which power had previously been limited, permitted excesses to occur.

Following the women's riots, the British government undertook a fundamental revision of the local government system, not very different from the one contemplated but never completed in 1927. After preliminary anthropological investigations by the administrative officers, new native authority areas were established, supposedly based upon pre-existing clan units. On the advice of an assistant district officer who, after conducting two months of surveys, concluded that there were three distinct subtribes in the Nguru court area—the Ekwerazus, the Ezinihittes, and the Agbajas—the colonial administration set up three separate native authority areas, each with its own court.[3] Two other native court areas, based on the Ahiara and Oke clans, were also created from previously existing courts. These five supposed clans now constitute Mbaise.

The new native authorities never became effective or efficient units of local government, according to the annual administrative reports.[4] The British attributed their ineffectiveness to the small size of the units, and thus, four years after the reorganization of Owerri Division had finally been completed, the administrators began strongly "encouraging" the formation of federations. After three years of sponsored meetings, one group of five clans agreed in 1941 to federate under a single native administration with a common treasury and took the name Mbaise meaning five village groups or by extension five clans.[5] In 1956 after a plebiscite, two small villages seceded from Mbaise and joined neighboring Ngor-Okpala. Otherwise the Mbaise area has remained as a unit since federation took place. A treasury opened in 1942 at Enyiogugu and shifted in 1948 to Aboh, a new administrative center for Mbaise. Eventually the British reconstituted Owerri Division into six federations.

In a major transformation in 1952 the government replaced the native administrations, both the clan and the federal units, by a system of local government councils patterned after those existing in Britain. A

Mbaise County Council was inaugurated in 1956, and local councils were established at Ahiara, Ekwerazu, Enyiogugu, Ezinihitte East, Ezinihitte West, Ezinihitte Central, Nguru, Oke-ovoro, and Okwuato. (Enyiogugu, Nguru, and Okwuato are parts of Agbaja.) Prior to the installation of the first military regime in 1966, various citizens had undertaken a campaign to have Mbaise recognized as a separate division.

THE FIVE CLANS

Ideal models of varying kinship groups are always more easily defined than are the existing units of social organization. The Ibo use the same terms for units of varying size and nature, which complicates the application of kinship terminology. In this study a clan will be considered a maximal lineage, the largest kinship group whose members claim common descent and are linked by shared activities.

Not only did all but one of the supposed five clans in Mbaise fail to fulfill these criteria, but those four differed considerably from each other. In view of the administrative officer's lack of anthropological training and the brevity of his investigation when first defining the clans, it is not surprising that his conclusions were incorrect. Despite these incorrect conclusions, the five former native court areas in Mbaise have since become clans, at least in the sense that the members of Ezinhitte, Ekwerazu, Oke,[6] and Ahiara commonly refer to themselves as clans, largely because the British administration designated them as such. The common identities of the Ezinihittes, Ekwerazus, and Okes have been partially infused as a result of colonial policy.

Edwin Ardener, an anthropologist who studied Mbaise, considered one clan, the Ahiara, to be a maximal lineage. Members of this group claimed descent from a common ancestor. While genealogically unified, as expressed in a number of common activities and rituals, Ahiara was divided into ten village groups organized into an eastern and western segment. Until recently each of the ten village groups had its own central market and some of its own deities.[7]

The four groups constituting the Oke clan also claimed common ancestry. However, Ardener seemed to consider them as approaching the model of a maximal lineage less perfectly than Ahiara, probably because they engaged in very little common activity.[8] Without much shared activity, the four component village groups had been virtually autonomous and hence represented the largest significant units for their members. These four village groups belonged to the larger Tche-Okpala cultural unit and thus were members of the Okpala rather than the Nguru court. They apparently chose to join Mbaise at its formation, rather than remaining with Okpala, in order to increase their independence.

The most disparate of the five so-called clans was the Agbaja. Meaning "land without water," Abgaja referred to an administrative area rather than an ethnic group. Three separate kinship groups lacking cultural or traditional ties—Nguru, Enyiogugu, and Okwuato—were joined together to form this unit under the misconception that they constituted a traditional entity. In a report concerning the formation of new courts in the Nguru court area in 1929, the assistant district officer concluded that the Agbajas were a distinct subtribe because all of them worshipped the same Ndichie juju.[9] As a consequence of that report, the government established one court for the area. At the time of this research residents of Agbaja continued to reject the existence of a single overall clan and persisted in identifying with one of the three kinship groups. They resented the very name of Agbaja as a symbol of the subordination of each separate ethnic group.

The three towns constituting Okwuato—Umuhu, Ibeku, and Lagwa—were traditionally affiliated with Ezinihitte. For several years the Ezinihitte Clan Union engaged in a campaign to reunify Okwuato with the remainder of Ezinihitte, inviting them to participate in the *iwoji* ceremony or passing of kola nuts, which symbolized the unity of Ezinihitte. The three towns did not accept the invitation nor confirm any desire to become recognized as part of Ezinihitte.[10]

Enyiogugu was a self-contained village group based on a maximal lineage. Whereas Ahiara consisted of ten village groups with a combined population of 24,000, according to the 1952 census, Enyiogugu's population was concentrated in one village group of about 8,000 and was thus more unified.

Nguru was also a maximal lineage descended from a common ancestor. Although the inhabitants regarded Nguru as a single entity, some functional differentiation emerged, such as five separate markets. In size and population Nguru came between Enyiogugu and Ahiara, having some 18,000 residents. Historical factors may have fostered the unity and patriotism of the Nguru group. The force conscripted by the administration in 1906 to avenge the murder of a British citizen, Doctor

Stewart, who had been bicycling through Ahiara, consisted primarily of men from Nguru. The most influential warrant chief from the Mbaise area, Nwathoracha, came from Nguru. As the center of the large court area, Nguru gained prestige and recognition.

Ezinihitte, the largest of the designated clans, had a cultural but not a genealogical unity. Common cultural charatceristics mentioned in the anthropological surveys and affirmed by elders of Ezinihitte included the presence of the Okonkwo society, a title society of wealthy and influential men; the worship of the same god, Chileke; and the use of manilla coins at the same rate of exchange for shillings. The inhabitants of Ezinihitte used the term *ohuhu,* meaning "roasting," to refer to themselves. According to legend, in the course of a migration they became separated from the remainder of the Ngwa group when they stopped to roast yams on the right bank of the Imo River, where they presently reside. Other groups have also referred to Ezinihittes as ohuhu, but in a derogatory sense to describe the nasality of their dialect.

It was difficult to draw precise boundaries for the Ezinihitte group. Five villages incorporated into Ezinihitte were originally under the jurisdiction of the Okpala court. After the women's riots in 1929, these villages successfully petitioned to be transferred to the new court established at Itu for the Ezinihitte group. Three towns in the Okwuato group in Agbaja had traditional ties to the Ezinihittes. One village group in Ezinihitte, Onicha, was ethnically related to Nguru as two segments of a lineage agnatically descended from a common ancestor. Lacking geographical contiguity, the two segments ceased to participate in any common activities. E. M. Dickenson in his intelligence report on the Ezinihittes did not include four towns with the twelve he acknowledged as Ezinihitte, despite the claims of their inhabitants to have always been part of Ezinihitte, and the concurrence with this assertion of the remainder of the group.[11]

Ekwerazu was not a genealogical unit, and was even less culturally unified than Ezinihitte. But since the various intelligence reports described Ekwerazu as a clan, the administration constituted it as a separate native court area.

According to the 1953 population census, the clans varied in population, with Ezinihitte, the largest, more than twice the size of Ahiara, the smallest.[12] The census estimated the total population of Mbaise as 186,274 persons, which after the secession of Isuobiangwu and Umuohiagu would have been reduced to 175,794. The individual clan estimates were: Ezinihitte, 57,600; Agbaja, 49,418, or 38,938 after the secession; Ekwerazu, 29,501; Oke, 25,611; and Ahiara, 24,144. Table 6 lists the complete population breakdown according to the 1953 census.

THE MBAISE COMMUNITY

Mbaise, an artificial creation called forth by the exigencies of colonial administration, was neither a genealogical nor a cultural unit. In its 185 square miles a number of disparate kinship groups lived. Three Ibo cultural-linguistic areas—the Oratta, the Ngwa, and the Isu—met in Mbaise, blending into one another at their boundaries. The dominating culture was the Ngwa, which extended over Ezinihitte, the major part of Oke, and the Okwuanto section of Agbaja and influenced eastern Ahiara. The Isu area, generally called Isoma in Mbaise, included Ekwerazu and parts of Ahiara. Portions of Enyiogugu and Nguru were Oratta, and the remaining parts of Enyiogugu and Nguru were a blend of Oratta and Isoma.[13]

It would be a mistake, however, to discount Mbaise as a unit. The history of Mbaise demonstrates the contingent nature of ethnic identification. Ethnic units among the Ibo traditionally were associated with a geographical area. Hence, when contiguous areas were united to undertake common activities, they often developed a new communal identity based on the larger unit. This occurred not only at the federal level in Mbaise, but also when established units were divided to form separate local councils or constituencies.

The groups constituting Mbaise had a relatively long history of co-operation under the British administration. Much of Mbaise belonged to the Nguru court area. During the more than twenty-five years that Mbaise existed as a unit, the people were subjected to uniform administrative policies, offered the same opportunities, and faced many similar problems. Throughout Mbaise, the scarcity of water was a constant limitation on economic development and the economy of the area depended entirely on the sale of palm oil. As one of the most densely populated areas in Eastern Nigeria, all parts of Mbaise suffered from constant population pressure.

Christianization, economic development, and political activities rendered many of the cultural differences less important. Predominantly Roman Catholic in religion and NCNC in political orientation, the Catholic-Protestant, NCNC-independent rivalries supplanted or supple-

Table 6.   Population of Mbaise, 1953

Clan	Town	Population	
Agbaja			49,418
	Ibeku	2,818	
	Inyeogugu	9,886	
	Isuobiangwu[a]	6,583	
	Lagua	3,656	
	Nguru	18,394	
	Umuhu	4,184	
	Umuohiagu[b]	3,897	
Ahiara			24,144
	Aguneze	1,785	
	Akabo	1,130	
	Amuzi	3,004	
	Lude	1,593	
	Nnarambia	2,376	
	Obobo	2,022	
	Obodo Ujieji	1,122	
	Ogbe	5,410	
	Ogwuana	763	
	Orlu	1,761	
	Otulu	3,178	
Ekwerazu			29,501
	Ekwerazu town	859	
	Initteafouku	5,191	
	Mpam	5,569	
	Obohia	5,261	
	Oparandam	5,154	
	Omuokrika	7,467	
Ezinihitte[c]			57,600
	Akporku	696	
	Amaumara	6,154	
	Ezegborgu	2,799	
	Ezuido	5,966	
	Ife	4,431	
	Ihitte	5,079	
	Itu	3,350	
	Obeama	2,772	
	Obizi	4,153	
	Okpoffe	3,283	
	Oniche	10,785	
	Udo	1,590	
	Umuchoko	1,526	
	Umudim	1,573	
	Umueze	1,553	

Table 6 (continued)

Clan	Town	Population	
	Umunama	1,530	
Oke			25,611
	Amuzu	5,796	
	Lorji	2,991	
	Mbutu	7,327	
	Ovoro	9,577	

Source: Population Census in the Eastern Region of Nigeria, 1953.
a. Seceded from Mbaise in 1956.
b. Seceded from Mbaise in 1956.
c. Ezinihitte was probably underestimated relative to the other clans.

mented older cleavages. Increased mobility within Mbaise and occasional intermarriage between groups helped to unify the area. As young men emigrated to cities throughout Nigeria in search of employment, their Mbaise identity, the one recognized by outsiders, became more important. Before the mass exodus of Ibos from the North and West after the Northern army mutiny, at least one-sixth of the Mbaise community resided in urban areas, while of those remaining at home, more than one-fourth took short business or pleasure trips into an urban center each week.[14]

The unity of Mbaise was a theme constantly reaffirmed to outsiders by members of the community. Apparently few perceived an incompatibility between professing this unity and engaging in activities that tended to weaken it. For example, almost everyone either directly engaged in or supported attempts to maximize the resources received by his primary ethnic group. Individuals and groups, while criticizing others or even condemning arrangements as being unfair because they themselves did not receive a sufficiently large portion of the available resources, rarely threatened dismemberment of Mbaise, and even more infrequently seriously considered it. The maintenance of unity for the advantages it conferred was the function of several organizations, including two improvement unions, the Mbaise Federal Union and the Mbaise Youth Movement. In addition, traditions evolved, such as the celebration of Mbaise Day, to symbolize the Mbaise community.

In gauging the advantages that unity conferred on the Mbaise community, one might theoretically assume that the larger the unit, the more effective would be the corresponding improvement union, since it would have an expanding resource base. In fact, there seemed to be an inverse ratio between the size of an improvement union and its effectiveness, particularly in Mbaise, at least regarding the initiation and execution of development projects. The primary advantage reaped by Mbaise as a consequence of its position as the most numerous and cohesive Ibo community was political influence. Four members of the Eastern House of Assembly and two delegates to the Federal House of Representatives represented constituencies either completely or predominantly located in Mbaise. In urban areas in the Eastern Region the Mbaise immigrants could often wield influence equal to entire divisions. One Mbaise man, D. D. U. Okay, represented Port Harcourt, the industrial center of the Eastern Region, in the Federal House from 1957 to its dissolution in 1966. Two members of the House of Assembly from Mbaise became ministers: Chief Pius Nwoga, who held a continuous series of offices from the time ministers were first appointed in the Eastern Region, and Dr. A. N. Ogbonna, who joined the Eastern Council of Ministers after the 1961 regional election. He also served as provincial commissioner of Owerri for a time.

In the one-party political system of the Eastern Region political influence was often directly translatable into economic gains. With ethnic nepotism an accepted principle of government, Mbaise received generous grants for its county hospital and secondary school; a new tarred road linked Mbaise with Owerri Province, and the government located some of the first water pipe installations in Mbaise, initially in Ogbonna's and Nwoga's home villages.

Cognizant of the ties that bound the formerly disparate groups into one unit, the Mbaise community sometimes repelled attempts to loosen those bonds. Whenever the grievances of one group against the community approached the threshold of explosion, such as those of Ahiara in 1964, some means was found to accommodate them. A ten-year campaign to have Mbaise recognized as a separate division in order to increase its share of amenities from the region made people more aware of the size and potential influence of the community as a unit. Originally proponents linked the proposal to constitute Mbaise into a division with a plan to dismember the present county council area into three separate counties within the new Mbaise division, because all of the divisions then existing in the Eastern Region had been divided into more than one county area. But the realization that the formation of three separate county council areas might lead to the fragmentation of Mbaise as an effective unit caused the leadership to reformulate their proposal. Prior to the suspension of local government by the military, the Mbaise County Council and the Mbaise Federal Union sought the elevation of Mbaise into a separate division with only one county council area, the present one, constituting the division.

POLITICS AND DIVISION IN MBAISE

While the interest in politics and economic development rendered many cultural divisions archaic, the dynamics of political activity reinforced others. At first glance the monopoly of the NCNC in the area would seem to have reinforced its unity. The NCNC first appeared in Mbaise in 1946 through the sponsorship of Joseph Iwunna of Nguru, one of the first agitators for independence in the area; in the same year Nnamdi Azikiwe and his delegation toured some of the native court areas in Mbaise. In 1966 each of the nine local council areas had its own branch of the NCNC, and representatives of these nine branches constituted the Mbaise District Executive of the NCNC.

Until 1961 constituencies located primarily in Mbaise elected two members of the Eastern House of Assembly and two representatives to the Federal House of Representatives. In 1961 the twenty-seven multi-member constituencies for the Eastern House of Assembly were divided into single-member seats, and new constituency boundaries were drawn. As a consequence of this reapportionment, Mbaise received two more seats, precipitating a marked increase in ethnic politics. In most areas of the Eastern Region problems emerged during the 1961 election from matching candidates with the new, smaller constituencies or eliminating representatives because of an inadequate number of seats in their home areas. Difficulties arose in Mbaise from the new grouping of local government areas into constituencies that joined Ezinihitte East with Ezinihitte Central, Ezinihitte West with Oke, Nguru with Enyiogugu and Okwuato, and Ahiara with Ekwerazu. The new constituencies either split a recognized group, giving rise to a kind of irredentism, or included two groups who considered themselves incompatable, which engendered conflicts between them for control over the seat. Dissatisfied groups—a category that soon included almost everyone—searched for scapegoats on whom they could blame the unfavorable reapportionment.[15]

In constituencies with two somewhat hostile ethnic blocs the NCNC was unable to contain the conflict between them. Party organization was weakly articulated in the rural areas of the Eastern Region, and even in its urban strongholds the NCNC was never a monolithic centralizing party. There was no weapon other than expulsion from the party with which the NCNC could threaten those who refused to support the official party candidate. Furthermore, expulsion constituted a rather mild threat, since the NCNC always reincorporated former members who had run as independents against the official nominee. Not only did political blocs tend to form around ethnic groups, but the clan unions directly assumed an active role. When a group was disappointed by the NCNC, it turned to its clan organization to rectify the situation. Hence, independent candidates proliferated at each election.

THE MBAISE COUNTY COUNCIL

One of the major forces unifying Mbaise was the existence of a single effective unit of government, the Mbaise County Council. The nine local councils at Ahiara, Ekwerazu, Ezinihitte East, Ezinihitte Central, Ezinihitte West, Oke, Nguru, Enyiogugu, and Okwuato lacked both the resources and the power of the Mbaise County Council. Most projects undertaken by these local councils were financed by and thus required the approval of the county council. As a consequence, most groups looked to the Mbaise County Council for amenities and improvements, ensuring continual interest in its activities.

The Mbaise County Council consisted of forty-six elected councillors and five appointed traditional members. Each year the councillors elected a chairman and a vice-chairman from their midst. Councillors were elected by and theoretically represented the villages, but groups usually formed around the larger ethnic divisions, with each one jealously guarding the size of its delegation to ensure that it received at least a share of amenities equal to its proportion of the total population of Mbaise. Hence, councillors usually considered themselves representatives of their clan and not their village. The number of councillors from each area was as follows: Ezinihitte, sixteen; Agbaja, nine; Ekwerazu, eight; Oke, seven; and Ahiara, six.

Subsequent to the transformation of the native authorities into the Mbaise County Council, elections took place in 1955, 1958, 1961, and 1965. Three men served as chairman: N. D. Ukah of Ekwerazu from 1955 to 1958, D. N. Abii of Ezinihitte from 1958 to 1964, and Donatus Onu of Ezinihitte from 1965 until the council was suspended. All three men were leaders of the NCNC: Ukah and Abii had served terms as members of the Federal House of Representatives from Mbaise, and Onu had organized the Okpara Youth Brigade in Owerri Province and become its national financial officer and a member of the national executive council of the NCNC. Politicians, while representing Mbaise in other capacities, frequently sought election to the Mbaise County Council in order to pyramid their bases of influence and remain in public view.

The Mbaise County Council delegated much of its business to standing committees assembled monthly in conjunction with the meeting of the county council. Three of the most important were the finance and staff committee, the education committee, and the development committee. Aspiring politicians pursued election to the chairmanships of these committees along with the chairmanship of the county council.

The Mbaise County Council was reputed to be one of the most effective councils in the Eastern Region by the district commissioner in his 1957 annual report.[16] In 1965 Mbaise still had the lowest tax rate in Owerri Division, while providing more services than any comparable unit. To a great extent the success of the Mbaise County Council derived from its ability to extract resources. Its estimated revenue for 1964–1965 was £108,748, and for 1965–1966, £110,972.[17] The Mbaise County Council formulated a five-year development program in 1965 at a cost of £100,000, of which the council expected to raise £85,000 out of current revenues during the period and borrow the balance.[18]

As one of the most influential communities, with two representatives in the Federal House of Representatives and four in the Eastern House of Assembly, including two ministers in recent years, as well as having a member of the community elected from Port Harcourt to the Federal House since 1957, Mbaise received several grants from the government. For example, the Mbaise County Hospital was predominantly financed by the government, rather than by the local community as in Abiriba. In order to finance the development program, the county council commissioned the two ministers from Mbaise to negotiate a loan with the Ministry of Local Government.

The resources of the county council should also be considered relative to those existing in Mbaise from other sources. With one of the highest population densities and smallest water supplies in the area, Mbaise, unlike Abiriba, remained a relatively poor community. The water scarcity was so critical that young boys used to sleep on the banks of ponds to prevent neighboring villages from raiding their supply. Unlike Abiriba, Mbaise did not have a trading tradition to divert the surplus population. The exodus of Mbaise citizens to the towns and cities of Nigeria resulted more from economic necessity than from enhanced opportunity. While a multiplicity of ethnic improvement unions existed, few of them actually completed projects. Rather than concentrating on self-improvement, they focused their efforts on petitioning the county council for desired amenities.

Most of the improvement projects completed in Mbaise and the amenities provided were sponsored and partially financed by the county council. All of the bridges in the area were built with substantial assistance from the county council. With the exception of one tarred road through Mbaise that the government constructed, the council maintained all roads. It also sponsored the health centers at Ezuido and Onicha (Ezinihitte), and Ekwerazu, and a central post office for the community at Aboh, the center of Mbaise. The council assumed responsibility for the maintenance of all the water supply installations after their completion. Two of the most important projects in the Mbaise area, the Mbaise County Secondary School and the Mbaise County Joint Hospital, were sponsored by the county council. At the time of its dissolution the council had spent £3,120 on secondary school scholarships and £2,100 on grants to the secondary schools in Mbaise. Formerly the council also extended loan scholarships to university students, but discontinued the practice owing to the refusal of recipients to repay them. In January 1966, just prior to the coup, the council assumed management of the thirty-five primary schools constructed under the universal primary education scheme, which had been managed by various voluntary agencies since 1957.

The 1965 development plan projected three more bridges at Obohia and Oparandim, Ekwerazu and Itu, Ezinihitte, as well as health centers for Ezinihitte West, Agbaja, Ahiara, and Oke. Proposed recreational facilities included a stadium, a central library, and thirteen separately located reading rooms. Another project mentioned was a Mbaise national hall at Aboh with facilities and offices for the county council at a cost of £25,000. In order to take advantage of the economic effects of the new road linking Mbaise with Ahoada, Etche, and Ngor, the council would construct a new modern market in Nguru.

Financial limitations, however, reduced the role of the Mbaise County Council in providing goods and services. Two of the most important projects sponsored by the council, the Mbaise County Secondary School and the Mbaise County Joint Hospital, were completed only after the council had received substantial assistance from the government. At no time did the county council manage either of the institutions. It placed both under the auspices of the Bishop of Owerri, who recruited their staff and supervised them. This arrangement proved somewhat unsatisfactory, since it evoked charges of religious discrimination from the Protestant minority. After complaints of maltreatment, mismanagement, and arbitrariness had gone unheeded, the chairman of the county council threatened that the people of Mbaise would be provoked into a showdown unless the bishop removed the head of the hospital and transferred the order of sisters who operated it.

The great majority of primary and secondary schools in Mbaise were managed by mission societies, most of them by the Roman Catholic Mission and a small number by the Christian Missionary Society. Although the Mbaise County Council contributed a small sum toward their operating expenses, it could not influence their educational policies. Dr. A. N. Ogbonna built the first hospital in Mbaise and operated it until he became involved in politics. He also provided most of the financing for a secondary school, the Obizi Community Grammar School. The Nguru Development Union built the only full post office in Mbaise, one of the few examples of an improvement union completing a project there.

The provision of a reliable water supply, along with the installation of pipes to carry the water throughout Mbaise, was one of the most crucial projects for the development of this extremely dry area. With the exception of Obizi in Ezinihitte, Ogbonna's village, the government refused to undertake a water project until the community had provided a portion of the necessary funds. The need to raise money to finance the installation finally galvanized some of the unions into development activities. At the end of 1965 the Enyiogugu and Ekwerazu schemes had been completed, along with parts of Ezinihitte.

Rather than resolving conflicts that existed within the community, the Mbaise County Council tended either to reflect or to generate disputes. Mbaise was predominantly Catholic as a result of the early arrival of the Roman Catholic Mission in the area. Significant minorities existed only in Ezinihitte and Oke. Although Protestant councillors often alleged religious discrimination, the district commissioner claimed in his report on Mbaise in 1957 that decisions of the county council did not reflect a religious bias.[19] Although systematic and intentional religious discrimination may have been rare, several council resolutions concerning the management of the Mbaise County Secondary School and the Mbaise County Joint Hospital indicated that it was difficult to ensure that Protestants received equal treatment at facilities managed by the Roman Catholic Church. [20]

Even more disruptive than Catholic-Protestant friction was the never-ending competition between ethnic blocs for concrete amenities or prestige. It was popularly assumed that with the chairmanship of the council went the vast majority of amenities. Groups denied the chairmanship therefore delivered a constant barrage of criticism claiming that the chairman's home area had received all of the resources. Though the chairman's group did have an advantage, an analysis of the minutes of the council describing its allocation of projects over a ten-year period shows that all groups eventually shared the development funds.

Mounting dissatisfaction with Chairman Abii of Ezinihitte had virtually disrupted the council by 1964. The Ahiara union in particular claimed that an organized conspiracy existed to relegate the Ahiara area to "last in the scheme." The union issued three specific demands: that amenities be distributed according to local councils rather than court areas (so that Ahiara would be third among nine rather than last among five), that an Ahiara man be made chairman of one of the committees, and that Ahiara school children not be made to march last in the Mbaise Day celebrations. Although at the time the third demand was the most inflammatory, as a matter of prestige, the underlying source of discontent was the sense of impotence resulting from the absence of a parliamentary representative from Ahiara in the Mbaise delegation. When the county council refused to change the order of marching to give the Ahiara children a more advantageous position, the Ahiara community boycotted the Mbaise Day celebrations. From time to time the leaders of Ahiara ominously warned that the community might seek ways to withdraw from Mbaise.[21] The selection of A. T. Mbegbu, a barrister from Ahiara, as the NCNC candidate for one of the two seats of Mbaise in the Federal House of Representatives ended the dispute.

Generally the Mbaise County Council refused to hear disputes between groups in the same clan, preferring instead to refer them to the relevant union for resolution. Since profound disputes sometimes shattered unions for a period of years, this policy often meant that conflicts festered and remained unresolved. The perpetuation of dissension within clans did not, however, affect the operation of the Mbaise County Council.

IV | The Role of Ethnic Unions in Mbaise

The multiplicity of ethnic unions, formed to further the interests of villages, clans, and the whole of Mbaise, reflected the complex patterns out of which the fabric of Mbaise society was woven. Individuals commonly belonged to three of these organizations: a village association, a clan union, and the Mbaise Federal Union. The role of the last two—the clan and the federal unions in Mbaise—is assessed here.

Contrary to the pattern prevailing in Abiriba, an effective unit of government existed in Mbaise, for unlike the Abiriba local government council and the Owuwa Anyanwu County Council, the Mbaise County Council fulfilled the requisite functions of the political system. It received information about needs through the demands made by its clan representatives, and the record indicates that it could make authoritative decisions and implement them with a fairly high measure of compliance. Furthermore, the council had the greatest resource base per capita of any organization in Mbaise. Although the county council was a new form of government and Mbaise was an artificial unit created in 1941, the success of the Mbaise County Council in providing amenities bred a conviction of legitimacy. Leading members of the Mbaise community, realizing the advantages conferred by the size of their community, resisted attempts to dismember the county. Prestige and possible influence activated aspiring politicians to seek seats on the council, which led to meaningful elections and the recruitment of fairly competent candidates.

Nevertheless the ethnic unions still performed some significant functions in the Mbaise political system. One important set of activities of the associations involved only their immediate members and related to the internal role of the clan unions and the Mbaise Federal Union. Another significant contribution of the unions in the Mbaise system was in terms of their demand and support inputs. These categories of demands and supports derive from a list suggested by Gabriel Almond. His four types of demands included the need for goods and services, the regulation of behavior, participation in the political system, and symbolic outputs, such as displaying the majesty and power of the political system and affirming the norms. Almond also classified support inputs under four headings: material supports, obedience to laws and regulations, participation, and deference to public authority, symbols, and ceremonies.[1]

INTERNAL ROLE OF ETHNIC UNIONS

In order to understand the internal role of the unions, one must first be aware of the context in which they originated and the nature of their organization. Educated men from Mbaise participated in the Owerri divisional union before the existence of clan unions in the Mbaise area. In 1937 after two of these men, Joseph Iwunna of Nguru and D. N. Abii of Ezinihitte, had become officers of the Owerri divisional union, this young group of educated men decided to sponsor the formation of clan unions. The first two such unions in the area, the Nguru Patriotic Union and the Ezinihitte Clan Union, originated in that year. Shortly afterward unions formed in Ekwerazu and Ahiara. The Oke-ovoro Union, founded as a branch of the Okpala Union, remained as such until 1944, despite the secession of Oke from the Okpala court area to join Mbaise when it was established.

At the time that the clan unions originated, Mbaise did not yet exist. In 1944, several years after the establishment of the clan unions and three years after the federation of the clans to form Mbaise, the same group of educated men originated the Mbaise Central Union. Joseph Iwunna, who first brought the NCNC to Mbaise, served as the president of both the Mbaise Central Union and the Nguru Patriotic Union during their initial periods, establishing the precedent for a nexus of clan union leadership and political activism that was perpetuated.

Most village unions originated later than either the clan unions or the Mbaise union. As intimate and immediate units, the towns and villages could command an intense loyalty from their members. The general ineffectiveness of the village unions as vehicles for political and improvement activities derived from the small size that they represented. The clans in Mbaise consisted of up to seventeen villages, as compared with the three divisions of Abiriba. And only one clan in Mbaise, Ezinihitte, equaled Abiriba in size. Hence, it is more fruitful to focus on the groupings of villages into ethnic blocs through their clan unions than on the village associations.

The clan and Mbaise unions adhered to the same basic organizational pattern as did the Abiriba Communal Improvement Union, having a home branch coordinated with branches abroad through conferences to which both sent representatives. They differed in the number of branches abroad, their location, and the frequency of general conferences. Most organizations had only one general meeting at home during the Christmas holidays. At times various clan unions and the Mbaise union employed intermediate levels of organization between the branches and the general conference. A reorganization of the Ezinihitte Clan Union in 1948 added regional groupings, which in turn sent representatives to the general conference. For a similar period of about five years the Mbaise Federal Union had three regional groupings of unions, the eastern, the western, and the northern, but only one of them, the northern, actually operated.

The size of some urban branches became unwieldy when the members attempted to meet together. To remedy this situation, several urban branches introduced indirect membership. Usually each village sent two or more representatives to a clan union, and each clan sent a delegation proportionate to its members in the area to the Mbaise Federal Union.

None of the unions had compulsory membership or dues. Attendance at meetings tended to be low and the amount of dues collected inadequate to finance ambitious improvement projects, the main exception being the Nguru Patriotic Union, which raised £5,000 to construct a post office. Several of the unions were temporarily immobilized by internal disputes between subgroups of the clan.

The Mbaise union also had a somewhat tenuous existence. Following its inauguration in 1944, it underwent two drastic transformations. In 1951 the Mbaise Central Union (abroad) was transformed into and renamed the Mbaise Federal Union, Nigeria. The minutes from that and subsequent meetings imply that the Mbaise Central Union had become defunct. In fact, delegates to the first meeting called it an inaugural meeting rather than a reorganization. Again in 1955 a "reorganization" in actuality resembled a revival, since according to the administrative report of C. O. Onuoha, then assistant general secretary and formerly president, the branches of the Mbaise Federal Union in the East and the West were by then either moribund or nonexistent.[2]

The Mbaise Federal Union, as well as the clan unions, lacked the ability to extract resources. An educational levy of £100 for each regional union was never paid by the eastern and western unions and only partially by the northern. The eastern regional union never even refunded the money advanced to it by the Mbaise Federal Union for the fare of its officers to the federal meeting. In 1955 the conference resolved that every Mbaise citizen abroad should pay ten shillings a year to his branch union.[3] But the local branches of the Mbaise Federal Union never collected this money.

The Mbaise Federal Union held yearly conferences on a fairly regular basis. However, the number of branches sending delegates—despite the coincidence of the annual meeting with the Christmas holidays over which many people return to Mbaise—was rather dismal. In 1956, one year after the revitalization, only eleven branches attended the meeting or contributed even part of the ten-shilling levy.[4]

As in Abiriba, the leadership of the unions was usually assumed by members living outside the home area, or residing "abroad" according to the colloquial term. Initially several of the unions specifically included the word "abroad" in their title. The membership in the cities and towns outside Mbaise always greatly exceeded that of the local branches. When unions imposed financial obligations, they always taxed members abroad more heavily, as a consequence of the poverty of Mbaise. Frequently unions only asked residents of areas outside Mbaise to pay dues, and substituted a communal cutting of the oil palm trees for the farmers at home.[5]

To distinguish between leaders according to their residence, however, would obscure the modernist orientation of all of the officers. Most of the Mbaisans with the equivalent of a secondary or university education became educators, many of whom taught in both Mbaise and other areas of the Eastern Region. The great majority of the central officers of the unions came from this group.

When questioned on the functions of their unions, members usually replied that they promoted improvements for the clan. Few unions, however, completed any improvement projects, because they lacked the requisite resources. The primary role of the clan unions vis-à-vis their members was to symbolize and thus foster the unity of the group, a prerequisite for development in the Mbaise system. At the time that the clan unions originated, only one of the court areas, Ahiara, really fulfilled the criteria for a clan. The four villages of Oke-ovoro undertook little common activity. Ezinihitte and Ekwerazu had some common cultural characteristics, but the units constituting them lacked genealogical connections. The formation of Agbaja as a single unit had followed either from a grave error in the analysis of the nature of the area or from a deliberate attempt to punish the people for razing the court at Nguru.[6] Agbaja included two units which in themselves could be considered clans, Nguru and Enyiogugu, and a third group related to Ezinihitte, Okwuato.

By 1966 members considered four of the former court areas to be clans: Ahiara, Ezinihitte, Ekwerazu, and Oke. Clan unions consciously promoted the integration of the court areas by inaugurating festivals and ceremonies in which all the villages participated and by declaring the unity of the group through ceaseless propaganda. The operation of the union itself constituted one important common activity for members of the court area. Emigrants to the urban areas joined branches of the clan unions, since no branches existed at first for the village associations. Thus, their links with the home community came through the more general clan rather than the village identity. Later the inauguration of the Mbaise County Council transformed the clan into the relevant unit for participation in the Mbaise political system. Thus, utility reinforced the conscious attempts of the educated leaders of the unions to foster integration.

Significantly Agbaja was the only court area for which no clan union was ever formed. At one time a union calling itself the Agbaja Clan Union did exist, but the Enyiogugu Union had merely usurped the name without widening its base of membership.

Ironically, while modernization diminished both the objective differences between the clans and their relevance, the activities of the clan unions, combined with the exigencies of political participation, reinforced the clans as units of identification. Prior to the dissolution of the Mbaise County Council by the military regime, the clan unions played an important role in the political system of Mbaise. In order to present a united front to the rest of Mbaise, when two or more members competed for one position, the union held a primary to eliminate all but one of them. Thus the unions presented an official nominee behind whom the entire clan could unite. When conflicts arose between members of subunits, the clan unions attempted to mediate them in order to maintain the effectiveness of the clan as a cohesive political unit.

THE DEMANDS OF CLAN UNIONS
IN THE MBAISE SYSTEM

The extension of suffrage and the increasing interest in politics as independence neared made the clan unions the most important formulator of demands within the Mbaise system. As a pre-existing cohesive unit with an organizational arm to protect and promote its welfare, the clan was the most likely group through which participants in the Mbaise system could act. The small size of the villages, despite their cohesiveness, undermined their potential effectiveness. Since almost everyone belonged to the same political party, political affiliation could not be an organizational base on which to formulate demands.

The two most insistent kinds of demands made by the clan unions—for goods and services and for political participation—were interrelated. Because few of the clan unions actually initiated improvement projects, they attempted to increase their group's share of amenities by competing against the other clans for allocations from the Mbaise County Council, the guardian or the largest pool of resources in the immediate Mbaise system. This campaign to secure as large a slice of the development pie as possible devolved upon the clan union as the most important organized subunit in the Mbaise system. In turn, the campaign strengthened clan bonds and forestalled possible permanent ruptures. People in Mbaise commonly assumed that political representation constituted the one guarantee of access to economic resources. Consequently unions strove to have one of their members elected to an influential position as a delegate to either the Federal House of Representatives or the regional House of Assembly, or alternately as chairman of the Mbaise County Council or one of its important committees. Such active political participation often precluded undertaking community development. When confronted with a political crisis, unions diverted funds collected for other purposes, such as scholarships, into financing electoral activity. For example, the Nguru Patriotic Union was about to launch a scholarship program when the NCNC constituency committee failed to nominate the Nguru candidate in 1961. The union thereupon used the money to finance his campaign as an independent.

So intense was the competition for goods and services that when one subunit of a clan decided that it was being discriminated against in favor of another subunit, the discovery often induced the subunit to act in such a way that it undermined both the unity of the clan and the effectiveness of the relevant ethnic union. Ezinihitte West, one of the three local council areas in Ezinihitte, boycotted the Ezinihitte Clan Union for several years because members felt that the two Ezinihitte politicians, Dr. A. N. Ogbonna and D. N. Abii, both of whom were from the Eastern subunit, had systematically denied them an equal share of favors. They became particularly incensed when the government sited the first water project for Ezinihitte in Obizi, the home village of the minister of commerce, Dr. Ogbonna, rather than in their area, although they alone had collected the requisite £2,500 demanded by the government. The leaders of Ezinihitte West also charged that D. N. Abii, a whip for the NCNC in the Federal House of Representatives, had conspired with the constituency delimitation committee to separate Ezinihitte West from the remainder of the clan in order to render it politically impotent.[7] As if to confirm their suspicions, in the 1961 election the official candidate of the NCNC for the constituency embracing Ezinihitte West and Oke, a man from Ezinihitte West, lost to an independent put forth by Oke, the more populous group. The Ezinihitte Clan Union finally resolved the dispute in 1966, after it had proved politically disastrous, by an agreement among the officers to send a petition to Lieutenant-Colonel Ojukwu protesting the merger of Ezinihitte West in a constituency with Oke, and another petition to the Water Planning Committee asking it to initiate a project in Ezinihitte West.[8]

A similar dispute between subunits rendered the Ekwerazu Assembly impotent for several years. All five villages in Ekwerazu belonged to the same local council area, but two of them, Umuokrika and Obohia, were more advanced than the others. Reflecting and contributing to this unequal development, all the prominent politicians from Ekwerazu came from Umuokrika: Chief Pius Nwoga, the minister for local government in the Eastern Region; N. D. Ukah, at one time a member of the Federal House of Representatives from Mbaise; D. D. U. Okay, the representative from Port Harcourt in the Federal House; and

Donatus Onu, the chairman of the NCNC in Mbaise and chairman of the Mbaise County Council from 1964 to 1966. The county council located the health center and the dispensary built for Ezwerazu in Umuokrika and Obohia respectively. Chief Nwoga used his influence to have the first water pipes in Mbaise installed in Umuokrika. The installation of the entire water scheme for Ekwerazu, the first clan area to complete their project, alleviated most of the friction between the two groups, especially since the main reservoir was located in Mpam rather than in Umuokrika or Obohia.

The demand for participation in the political system was directly associated with the overwhelming desire for goods and services, as a result of the link observed between political influence and economic gains. A second factor precipitating the demand for participation was the prestige associated with political office.

The initial target of the clan in its drive for political recognition was the NCNC nominating committee for the relevant constituency. Frequently the clan union held a primary of its own before approaching the NCNC nominating committee with its choice. An announcement would be made that all those seeking the nomination should apply to the clan union. At a designated meeting the members would then select the clan's candidate from this group. Thus, in 1961 the Nguru Patriotic Union presented its president, E. O. Osuagwu, to the Agbaja constituency nominating committee, and the Oke-ovoro Union drafted its most prominent member, S. M. Ahamba, author of several books on the Ibo language, for their joint constituency with Ezinihitte West. Similarly before the 1964 federal election the Ahiara Clan Union chose A. T. Mbegbu, a barrister, from a field of four candidates.

Neither Osuagwu nor Ahamba received the NCNC nomination. Although Nguru included more people than Enyiogugu and Okwuato combined, each of the three units had an equal number of representatives on the nominating committee. The two smaller units, having decided to cooperate in order to prevent Nguru from dominating them, selected E. M. Mbator from Enyiogugu. Oke-ovoro was also the larger unit within its constituency. The nomination of Francis Uwalaka from Ezinihitte West by the NCNC reflected the political predominance of the Ezinihitte clan.

When the NCNC nominating committees rejected their candidates, the Nguru Patriotic Union and the Oke-ovoro Clan Union decided to sponsor campaigns for their candidates as independents. The Ahiara

Clan Union, which was successful in having its candidate officially nominated, also campaigned actively. All three unions donated money and
had the officers canvass for their candidate.[9] A failure to support the
campaign of one's fellow-clansman was looked upon as a violation of
ethnic obligations.

Participation in politics, like the competition for goods and services,
could be a two-edged sword precipitating cleavages within clans. Prior
to the 1964 federal election Ekwerazu had two political representatives, Chief Pius Nwoga, a minister in the Eastern government, and
N. D. Ukah, a member of the Federal House of Representatives. Of the
two, Chief Nwoga had more influence, since he was a minister. Also,
the people tended to associate benefits from government with the Eastern regional government rather than the federal government. The crisis
in Mbaise resulting from Ahiara's boycott of the Mbaise Day celebrations took place a few months before the nomination of the candidates
in 1964. In retrospect, Ahiara seems to have generated a great deal of
sympathy for its demand for political recognition, since at that time it
was the only one of the original five court areas not to have a representative. Ahiara and Ekwerazu constituted one regional constituency
and with Agbaja elected a member of the Federal House. Consequently,
Ahiara could only gain representation at Ekwerazu's expense. In order
to protect his own position, Pius Nwoga decided to join forces with the
Ahiara group attempting to replace N. D. Ukah with A. T. Mbegbu. His
success in eliminating Ukah contributed to the conflicts that rendered
the Ekwerazu Assembly ineffective.[10]

Ezinihitte West's complaints about the new constituency arrangements became vociferous only after a member had lost the 1961 election. The ensuing dispute between Ezinihitte West and Ezinihitte East
cost D. N. Abii both his federal seat and the chairmanship of the Mbaise
County Council. Despite his position in the NCNC and his presidency
of the Ezinihitte Clan Union, Abii lost the NCNC nomination for his
federal seat in 1964 because representatives from Ezinihitte West joined
with those from Oke on the nominating committee to block him.
Along with Ezinihitte West and Oke-ovoro, the federal consituency included a small section of Ngor Okpuala, an area outside Mbaise. Not
only did Abii lose the nomination, but the NCNC committee selected
an outsider from Ngor Okpuala, Nnana Ukaegbu, in his place. Hence,
Ezinihitte West's hostility toward Abii and the other two sections of
Ezinihitte was so great that it preferred to forfeit the prize of a seat in

the Federal House to an outsider rather than allow Abii or the other candidate from Ezinihitte East to gain the nomination.[11] In the same year Donatus Onu of Ekwerazu replaced Abii as chairman of the Mbaise County Council. Again disunity in the Ezinihitte delegation prevented the victory of its candidate. One of the primary factors motivating the reconciliation between sections of Ezinihitte in 1966 seems to have been a recognition of these disastrous political consequences of disunion.

A third type of demand made by the unions, in addition to the ones for distribution and participation, was that for symbolic recognition. The most volatile issue leading to the Ahiara boycott was the placing of the Ahiara school children last in order of marching for the Mbaise Day celebrations. The leaders of Ezinihitte West complained not only about the discrimination in drawing of the constituency boundaries and in allocating amenities, but they also objected to the division of the clan into two customary court areas designated Eze and Ihitte, symbolically separating Ezinihitte West at Ihitte from the remainder of the clan. Although most of the competition over the location of development projects resulted from economic factors, some followed from the desire for prestige. For example, construction of the post office at Nguru by the Nguru Patriotic Union climaxed a long campaign by other clans to have the post office located in their communities. Although having a post office situated nearby involves an element of convenience, it does not confer any economic advantage.

Nguru and Enyiogugu expended a great deal of energy in an attempt to undermine the Agbaja identification and gain distinct recognition as clans in their own right similar to the other four court areas. The colonial administration had located the first court, which most of Mbaise attended, at Nguru. The early preeminence of Nguru was reversed by the women's riots of 1929, during which the original court was razed. In 1966 members of the Nguru clan still claimed that the renaming of the area as Agbaja, along with the transfer of their court to Enyiogugu, came as a form of punishment for the riots. They therefore resented this name and refused to use it.[12]

Enyiogugu also had a set of grievances. When the federation of the five native court areas took place, the government placed the first treasury at Enyiogugu. Enyiogugu continued to be the headquarters of the Mbaise Group Council until 1948, when the administration federalized Aboh, a small part of Ezinihitte, to become a neutral center not associated with any clan. Just as the people of Nguru resented their subordination, those of Enyiogugu felt bitter about the removal of the headquarters from their area. On several occasions members of other clans asserted that the residents of Enyiogugu did not participate fully in the Mbaise Federal Union and the Mbaise Youth Movement because of their resentment over this transfer.[13]

The Nguru Patriotic Union sent petitions to both the Mbaise County Council and the Mbaise Federal Union demanding recognition as a distinct entity. In one of its more recent petitions to the county council it also requested that all committee appointments be on a local council basis. Unlike the other local councils, Nguru was not represented by a traditional ruler; nor did it have a representative on the hospital board or the road safety committee. Enyiogugu complained to the same two organizations about its relationship to Nguru and its lack of representation.[14]

The fourth type of demand, for the regulation of behavior, was rarely made by clan unions within the context of the Mbaise political system. Each ethnic union attempted to regulate the conduct of its members in order to preserve its good reputation. On the infrequent occasions when members of one clan requested action by the Mbaise County Council against another group, the councillors usually refused to become involved. The Mbaise County Council avoided even more strenuously mediating intraclan disputes. This particularization of the function of regulating behavior testified to the incomplete integration of the Mbaise system.

THE ROLE OF THE MBAISE FEDERAL UNION

According to the constitution of the Mbaise Federal Union, the objects for which it was established "are and shall be the social, educational, economic, political, religious and cultural advancement of Mbaise in general and its members in particular." In order to further the social, educational, and economic advancement of Mbaise, the union embarked on a number of projects, none of which it completed successfully. It never collected a ten-shilling levy instituted to finance a secondary school and a small hospital. After the Mbaise County Council took over these two major projects, the Mbaise Federal Union decided to award a number of scholarships instead, but the decision was never implemented. In August 1956 the union established a special committee to suggest future plans for Mbaise. The projects recommended by the committee included construction of a post office, transformation of Aboh into a model township, establishment of a new daily market, and a campaign for the recognition of Mbaise as a separate division.[15] With the exception of the post office, which the Nguru clan completed, none of these projects ever materialized. A campaign for the establishment of a separate division for Mbaise by the Mbaise Federal Union preceded the committee's formal endorsement but was never brought to fruition. Despite its failure to implement any of its projects, the Mbaise Federal Union remained undaunted. As its contribution to the new Mbaise development plan, it set up an Industrial and Commercial Company in 1964 to launch an unspecified industry for which capital of £150,000 was to be raised through the sale of shares.[16] This grandiose scheme predictably miscarried just like the others; the Industrial and Commercial Company never sold enough shares to establish any industry.

The Mbaise Federal Union, like the other improvement unions in Mbaise, dabbled in politics from time to time. In 1951 it selected four candidates and campaigned for them in the indirect elections to the Eastern legislative council. When the three successful candidates stood for reelection in 1953, it again endorsed them. Part of its political role was to reinforce the NCNC monopoly in Mbaise. In 1952, in response to reports linking the president of the Mbaise Federal Union, J. A. Iwunna, with the Action Group, the dominant political party in Western Nigeria, the union called on him to explain his heresy.[17] On two occasions when Premier Azikiwe's position was threatened—in 1956 during the African Continental Bank controversy, and in 1958 when one of his principal ministers was attempting to wrest control of the party—the Mbaise Federal Union passed resolutions expressing confidence in him.[18] The Mbaise Federal Union, like the clan associations, sent letters to political representatives reminding them of their obligations to the community. The tendency of the union to ratify a successful politician's position by electing him to office in the Mbaise Federal Union strengthened the bonds between the two groups.

The failure of the Mbaise Federal Union to complete any of its proposed projects or to become more directly involved in the nomination of candidates resulted to a great extent from the emergence of the clans as the focal group in the Mbaise political system. Most Mbaise citizens could potentially belong to at least three improvement unions— those of their village, clan, and the Mbaise Federal Union. Most people,

however, lacked the resources, time, or interest to support and participate in all three levels of unions. In the competition for members,
dues, and commitments the Mbaise Federal Union was the most disad-
vantaged of the three types of union, in terms of both emotional and
utilitarian appeal. The village and the clan had existed for a longer
period of time and, as more immediate and less inclusive units, could
command a more direct identification. As an inclusive body representing Mbaise as a whole, the Mbaise Federal Union could not be
used as an instrument to gain economic advantage for only one part.
After the initial elections in 1951 and 1953, no constituency embraced
all of Mbaise.

The inverse ratio between the comprehensiveness of an improvement union and its effectiveness in sponsoring community improvement
also derived from the difficulty of the larger union in deciding upon and
locating projects. Few projects could be equally advantageous to all
groups, except perhaps new roads through Mbaise, which only the
government had the requisite resources to build. If scholarships had
been awarded, it is likely that there would have been controversies
over the method of their allocation. Had projects been proposed primarily benefiting one clan, even if only in terms of the prestige gained
from the location, other clans would have refused to contribute toward
it.

One should not discount the role of the Mbaise Union completely
however. Just as the clan unions became integrators and arbitrators for
their respective groups, the Mbaise Union assumed these functions to
an extent for Mbaise. The mere existence of an improvement union for
all of Mbaise symbolized the unity of the area—a unity that was very
fragile when the first Mbaise Central Union was founded in 1944. After
its revival in 1955 the Mbaise Federal Union attempted to strengthen
the sense of unity by resolving conflicts between the clans. At an emergency meeting called in August 1964 by Secretary General C. O.
Onuoha, the union appointed a committee to probe into the grievances
of certain groups in Mbaise against the county council, in order "to
enhance the economic progress and stability of Mbaise in general." After hearing preliminary testimony, the committee disbanded for the
impending federal election, so as not to prejudice the chances of the
chairman, D. N. Abii, for reelection to parliament.[19]

Perhaps the single most important activity of the Mbaise Federal
Union was its sponsorship of the campaign to create a separate division

for Mbaise. The union spearheaded the drive as early as 1955, before it became a generally accepted goal of the community. In 1956 it sent a petition to the premier of the Eastern Region requesting an administrative reorganization. In the petition it stated that since the government allocated all amenities on a divisional basis, Mbaise was not receiving its fair share, because Mbaise compared favorably in size with at least eight existing divisions. Another reason cited in favor of the reorganization was the poor condition of the roads, which made it difficult to travel from Mbaise to other parts of the Owerri Division.[20]

Although the road system improved considerably, other unions and the Mbaise County Council took up the demand for a separate division. Many members of the Mbaise community believed that the Eastern government had accepted their request just before the military regime suspended parliamentary institutions. The opposition of the politicians had delayed this acceptance by undermining the campaign for a separate division until 1965, when they acceded to the strong feeling for the proposal and agreed to support it. Their opposition had resulted from their belief that they would no longer be recognized in the NCNC as representatives of all of Owerri Division, as well as Mbaise, which would weaken their resource base in the party councils.[21]

ETHNIC UNIONS AS SUPPORTS
IN THE MBAISE SYSTEM

Along with the local and county councils and the missions, the various improvement unions constituted a major structure of authority in the Mbaise system. As such, they contributed toward the regulation of behavior. Deviations from accepted norms of conduct would be a source of embarrassment to the clan. A potential offender, aware that his action would probably provoke a reprimand and possible ostracism by all his relations, might be deterred. Reciprocally, a manifestation of civic responsibility would reflect on the clan as well as the actor; the recognition involved would thus reinforce the desirability of undertaking such an action.

Since the clan identity was more salient than the Mbaise identity, individuals responded more strongly to clan symbols and ceremonies than to those involving Mbaise as a unit. Despite the relatively modern nature of the clans, many of the ceremonies celebrating their unity were vested with the sanctity of tradition because they were adaptations of pagan religious rituals. Mbaise ceremonies, like the observance of Mbaise Day, seemed more obviously new and contrived. Nevertheless, clan unions enthusiastically participated in Mbaise ceremonies.

As indicated previously, in Mbaise the clan unions did not contribute to the material improvement of the community, as they had in Abiriba, by promoting and financing major community development projects. The collection of funds for the installation of water pipes was the first such constructive activity for several of them, and not all the unions were able to raise the requisite sum despite an intensive effort. By lobbying for a larger slice of the development pie for their group, the unions probably increased the level of aspiration in Mbaise. Coupled with this elevation of aspiration, the unions reinforced the tendency to look to a unit of government, whether it be on the county or regional level, rather than attempt to undertake a project oneself. While Mbaise lacked the resource base of Abiriba, the union should have been able to finance some middle-range projects. Certainly Ezinihitte, the largest and most advanced clan area, had the resources for self-improvement. Clan members justified the noninvolvement of the Ezinihitte Clan Union in community development by citing the relative advancement of Ezinihitte, instead of attempting to utilize their greater resource base to further develop the area. In the context of a reorganized political system with a regional government having fewer resources or being less responsive to the demands of Mbaise, the predominantly political orientation of the unions would bring frustration.

One of the primary reasons that the clan unions did not promote development projects was their overwhelming preoccupation with political participation. Through such participation, the clan unions helped legitimize the system. While groups complained about their particular allocation of economic or political resources, they never made a serious challenge to the system. According to one officer of the Ahiara Clan Union, its threat to investigate ways of contracting out of Mbaise in 1964 did not reflect an actual consideration of such a course of action; the union made the threat merely to demonstrate the depth of Ahiara's grievances to the other clans.

The continuous involvement of the clan unions in politics can be considered pernicious only if one is committed to the principle that so-called ethnic improvement unions should confine their activities to the developmental and cultural spheres. After the 1959 federal election the unions rather than the NCNC primarily performed the function of political recruitment. While fostering the spontaneous creation of several protopolitical ethnic parties, the unions' involvement did not undermine the NCNC. Unions strove to achieve their goals within the NCNC, circumventing the party only when blocked. By running as independents rather than accepting an opposition party label, the union-sponsored candidates were able to rejoin the NCNC after their election. The same unions which sponsored and organized an electoral campaign in opposition to the NCNC would promote the return to the fold, complete with ceremonies and celebrations.

Just as the Mbaise Federal Union played a secondary role in the formulation of demands within the Mbaise political system, it performed a limited role in eliciting supports. The Mbaise Federal Union could only assume a greater role in the context of a more comprehensive political system, where the Mbaise identity, rather than the more particular one, would be significant. Its primary contribution to the maintenance of the Mbaise community at home was on the symbolic level.

Over-all the unions had a beneficial impact on the Mbaise system. Although they fostered clan consciousness, the disappearance of the clan unions would not have ensured the evolution of a more perfectly integrated Mbaise. The primary raison d'être for the role of the unions was the competition for scarce resources and not pre-existing cultural or ethnic rivalries. This competition would have promoted the formation of some type of subgroup, probably based on local government councils, had Mbaise been a more integrated, traditional entity. Given the nature of Mbaise as a federation of previously existing units, even without the unions to structure and direct them, subgroups probably would have emerged with an ethnic basis, because few alternate bases of organization existed. In fact, if the urban migrations had not called the clan union into being, the competition over development resources probably would have done so.

The only other probable form the competition might have assumed was blocked by the strength of the NCNC in the area. Had the NCNC been either less firmly established or less capable of absorbing the ethnic maneuvering, it might have fragmented into two or more parties. These parties probably would have had an ethnic or religious base.

The specter of ethnic parties in Mbaise highlights the advantages of the system in existence before the suspension of parliamentary government. While struggles over the allocation of resources were unceasing, they were rarely ever very bitter. Disappointed groups changed their strategy but did not call for the destruction of the institutional frame-work. Had formal opposition political parties emerged, the struggle would certainly have been more intense and less contained. With all groups at least nominally under the aegis of one party, the same party in power on the regional level, the motivation for and the possibility of compromise continued to be present. One of the great sources of strength in the existing system was that groups did not consider them-selves to be engaging in a zero sum game. That is, their failure to gain one nomination or one type of development resource could always have been compensated with the substitution of another at some later date. A plurality of political and economic assets existed, and the competition for any one of them remained fairly independent of the struggle for the others.

In a two- or three-party political system, competition would have been more acrimonious, because access to resources tended to be cumulative. If groups lost a single election, such as the chairmanship of the Mbaise County Council, they could have been refused not only a particular health center or aid for the construction of a certain bridge, but access to development funds for a period of years. This situation would probably have been intolerable for the loser and might have led to the breakdown of the system.

In places where several parties competed for control over local gov-ernment councils, as in the Western Region of Nigeria, the results were often disastrous. Action Group ministers in the regional government frequently charged NCNC-controlled local authorities with irregularity as an excuse to suspend them. When the Nigerian National Democratic party (NNDP) came to power, it used the same kind of methods against Action Group-dominated local councils. If these councils re-fused to change their party affiliation, they were replaced by caretaker committees. Under both Action Group and NNDP administrations in the West, local councils often harassed supporters of the minority party in the council area. The Mbaise system had marked advantages to the situation in the West.

V | Patterns of Influence and Leadership in Mbaise

In order to assess the patterns of leadership and influence in any community, one should examine the process by which decisions on significant subjects are made. The earlier analysis of Abiriba focused on three issue areas central to the community: educational policy, community development, and political recruitment. The dispersion of authority in Mbaise complicates the application of this methodology. The ethnic complexity of Mbaise with the resulting multiplicity of improvement unions, the existence of local and county councils that functioned according to statutory instruments, and the management of key educational and medical facilities by individuals and religious missions contrast with the centralization of most activities in Abiriba in the Abiriba Communal Improvement Union. An investigation of the same three issue areas in Mbaise yields less clearly delineated spheres of authority; more persons participated in the decision-making process, which rendered it more difficult for a single group to prevail continuously.

When correlating the socioeconomic characteristics of the leaders in Abiriba, it sufficed merely to consider the past and incumbent officers of the ACIU. Since the officers of the improvement unions in Mbaise constituted only one among several potential elites, their qualifications should be compared with those of another core group, the holders of political office. It should also be determined whether the patterns of influence and leadership reflected the fragmentation of authority among the several clans and the local government council. To what extent and in what manner could potential leaders overcome the dispersion of authority?

THE SOURCES OF INFLUENCE

As in Abiriba, this analysis focuses on the three core issues affecting the community: educational policy, community development, and political recruitment. No one agency formulated educational policy for the whole of Mbaise, as did the ACIU for Abiriba. The two groups that assumed the greatest role in determining educational policy in Mbaise, the Roman Catholic Mission and the Ministry of Education in the Eastern government, were external agencies over which the community had virtually no control. Consequently, an analysis of educational policymaking does not yield information about patterns of influence in Mbaise but merely reveals the dependence of the community on outside assistance in this sphere.

In terms of the number of schools managed, the Roman Catholic Mission predominated, with the Christian Missionary Society also well represented. Even the Mbaise County Secondary School, supposedly a public, nondenominational institution which had been constructed with large-scale governmental assistance, was managed by the Bishop of Owerri. Various voluntary agencies—usually one of the missions—also operated a group of primary schools established by the government during the movement for universal primary education in the Eastern Region. The Mbaise County Council had planned to assume control of the schools in 1966, but the transfer was prevented when the military government dissolved the local government councils in the Eastern Region.

In terms of control over the formulation of fundamental educational policy, the Ministry of Education predominated in Mbaise, as elsewhere in the Eastern Region. The Ministry of Education made the important decisions and issued guidelines to assist in their implementation for private as well as public schools.

The desire for education in Mbaise prompted interest in educational policy, despite the relative impotence of the community to influence it. When the Eastern government reintroduced school fees for all but the first two years of primary education in 1958, after an experiment in free primary education had proved too costly, more than a thousand men and women in Mbaise demonstrated in protest. Venting their anger on the Mbaise County Council in a manner reminiscent of the women's riots of 1929, they damaged several buildings in Aboh, including the one in which the council met.[1] Protestants issued several protests to the county council concerning the treatment of non-Catholics in the Mbaise County Secondary School. However, the county council could no more influence the educational policies of the Roman Catholic Mission than it could reverse the reintroduction of school fees by the Eastern government. Its ultimate sanction against the mission, withdrawal of the right to manage the secondary school, would have been rather meaningless, because the council apparently lacked the ability to manage the school itself, and the predominantly Catholic population would not have accepted any other voluntary agency.

The predominance of the Roman Catholic Church in the area both religiously and educationally ensured that the personnel attached to the mission, particularly the priests, filled a vital role in the life of the community. Since the great majority of the priests were Irish rather than Nigerian, and practically none came from the Eastern Region, they remained an external elite grafted onto the community. Their external position limited the spheres in which they could exercise influence. In general, the priests refused to become involved in internal disputes in Mbaise. Consequently, aside from purely religious matters and some prerogatives in the management of the schools, the priests tended to have prestige rather than influence. Even at nontraditional celebrations, such as the one sponsored in 1966 by prominent clan members following the ordination of the first priests from Ekwerazu, the priests attended as representatives of the church and as observers, not as participants.

The limited change effected in the convert by Christianization also tended to inhibit the role of the clergy. Articles of the Christian dogma frequently did not replace the convert's former network of religious loyalties, but were superimposed on them. In part this reflected the peaceful entrance of the Catholic Church and its general acceptance. Probably some converts embraced Christianity only nominally, accepting the label for the sake of the educational opportunities and prestige it conferred. Many others may have sincerely subscribed to elements of the Christian faith, while clinging to pagan beliefs as well. In fact, membership in the church did not preclude participation in other rites, since former pagan festivals were transformed to celebrate the secular unity of the community, rather than the beneficence of a deity.

In Abiriba levels of influence could be observed through a second policy area, community development. Because intense aspirations for economic development existed in Mbaise as well, the ability to determine the location of projects both reflected and increased a participant's influence. Unlike Abiriba, the primary focus in Mbaise was on the allocation of resources rather than the formulation of development policy.

The individuals best placed to influence the distribution of development funds were members of the Eastern House of Assembly, particuuarly the ministers, members of the Federal House of Representatives, and officers of the Mbaise County Council. The competition for these offices precipitated the entrance of clan unions into the political arena. Considering the universality of the interest in political office, nominations and elections demonstrated the relative influence of various groups and individuals.

Listed below is the location of some important projects completed by the Mbaise County Council during the period 1958 through 1964 when D. N. Abii of Ezinihitte was chairman:

Project	Location
Health center	Ezinihitte
Health center	Ezinihitte
Health center	Ekwerazu
Bridge	Ezinihitte
Bridge	Ekwerazu
Sub post office	Ahiara

The location of projected facilities or those already begun by the Mbaise County Council in 1965–1966, during the chairmanship of Donatus Onu of Ekwerazu, were as follows:

Project	Location
Health center	Ezinihitte
Health center	Agbaja
Health center	Ahiara
Health center	Oke-ovoro
Bridge	Ekwerazu
Bridge	Ekwerazu
Bridge	Ezinihitte
Postal agency	Ekwerazu
Postal agency	Ezinihitte
Market	Nguru

The council did not have unlimited discretion in assigning project locations. Only a certain number of health centers, bridges, or post offices could be built in any one community, and the completion of one of them engendered demands for similar projects by other communities, which would have been difficult to deny permanently. Within these bounds the clan controlling the chairmanship had some advantage, as demonstrated by the preceding lists. It should be remembered that Ezinihitte, being the most populous of the former native court areas, had the largest delegation to the Mbaise County Council. Relative to its size, Ekwerazu gained more projects than Ezinihitte, despite the longer tenure of Abii from Ezinihitte as chairman.

During the ten years preceding the military takeover the Eastern government extended grants for the construction and operation of the Mbaise County Secondary School and the Mbaise County Joint Hospital and completed a tarred road linking Mbaise with Owerri and Umuahia. The government also financed the water supply schemes initiated in parts of Ezinihitte and completed in Ekwerazu and Enyiogugu. Most of the assistance granted by the government subsidized projects benefiting the Mbaise community as a whole. The one exception to this non-discriminatory policy was the location of the first two water supply schemes in Nwoga's and Ogbonna's home villages.

Membership in the Eastern House of Assembly placed a representative in a better position to obtain governmental assistance than did a seat in the Federal House of Representatives, because most development programs were undertaken on a regional level. Conflicts between legislators in the federal and regional houses erupted from time to time, with the Mbaise Federal Union providing the forum for their mutual recriminations.[2] When questioned, most inhabitants correctly attributed the increased assistance from the government to the activities of the regional legislators.

Contrary to popular expectation, mere membership in the Eastern House of Assembly opened few channels of influence for a representative. Once the member had been elevated to the cabinet the situation changed: ministers could tap numerous sources of patronage to assist their communities. Even some of the most important ministers, however, were circumscribed in this respect by the competition for limited resources and the over-all development plans. Many communities demanded that ministers site industries there, while very few new factories were actually built, with the result that no minister would squander his personal resources attempting to locate a steel mill, a textile facility, of a bottling plant in the rural hinterland.

Another major issue vital to the community was in the area of nominations and elections. The intrusion of the clan unions into the recruitment process, formerly reserved either for the community or for the NCNC party apparatus, elevated office in one of the unions as a potential source of influence. One candidate, E. O. Osuagwu, definitely benefited from his position as president of the Nguru Patriotic Union in the competition for endorsement by the union for the Agbaja constituency. Pius Nwoga had been president of the Ekwerazu Assembly for about fifteen years prior to his election to the Eastern House of Assembly in 1953. D. N. Abii, one of the founders of the Ezinihitte Clan Union and its president since 1945, gained election to the Federal House of Representatives in 1954.

Office in one's clan union did not become a prerequisite for a community-sponsored nomination. Frequently this high office was conferred on a member after he had been elected, so that his victory would bring prestige to the union, rather than the reverse. Almost simultaneously with their electoral victories Dr. A. N. Ogbonna, S. M. Ahamba, and N. D. Ukah became high-ranking officers in their respective unions. The Ahiara Clan Union endorsed A. T. Mbegbu, although he had never been an officer.

Even the chairmanship of the clan union did not guarantee continued influence over the members. Both N. D. Ukah and D. N. Abii were the presidents of their respective unions when they lost their bids for renomination to the Federal House of Representatives in 1964. In fact, Abii's position as the official leader of the Ezinihitte Clan Union seems to have directly contributed to his defeat, since the dissidents held him, rather than Dr. Ogbonna, responsible both for. the division of the clan into two court areas and for the discriminatory allocation of amenities. These allegations, coupled with a repudiation of his reputed arrogance in claiming to be the eze of Mbaise, motivated the defection of one section of the clan, Ezinihitte West. Despite Ukah's position as president of the Ekwerazu Assembly, a majority of the members accepted Pius Nwoga's political maneuvers that denied Ukah his renomination, although they may not have supported or approved of those maneuvers.

Office in the Mbaise Federal Union seems to have conferred prestige rather than influence, since the Mbaise Federal Union did not have direct access either to economic resources or political nominations, which were the two commodities in most demand in Mbaise. Almost all prominent politicians held office in the Mbaise Federal Union at one time. Dr. Ogbonna became president of the union in 1954, shortly after his initial election. Pius Nwoga, the secretary since 1954, resigned in 1957 when he became a full minister. According to Nwoga, the duty of an officer to protest to the government in order to protect the interests of his union would conflict with membership in the government.[3] Ukah and Oswagwu were both officers of the Mbaise Federal Union prior to their election to federal and regional political offices: the former was treasurer for a total of four years, and the latter was vice-president for ten.

Office in the NCNC apparatus in Mbaise did not confer as much influence over the nomination procedure as did election to the Eastern House of Assembly or the Federal House of Representatives. The ministers and representatives from Mbaise normally did not hold party offices in the Mbaise NCNC organization. Donatus Onu, who became chairman of the Mbaise County Council in 1965, had been chairman of the NCNC branch in Mbaise for several years. His election probably owed far more to Nwoga's support than to any other single factor.

RELATIVE INFLUENCE OF THE CLANS

Ezinihitte, the most numerous in population and reputed to be the most advanced, was the most successful of the clans in securing political representation and economic amenities. One need only glance back at the lists indicating the location of projects by the Mbaise County Council to perceive the advantages reaped by Ezinihitte's large delegation. After the delimitations commission redrew the constituency boundaries, only Ezinihitte independently elected a member of the Federal House of Assembly. From 1953 to 1959 two of the three Mbaise political representatives came from Ezinihitte. Even after 1961 only Ekwerazu matched Ezinihitte's two representatives. Equality in political representation among the clans after 1964 resulted from a split in Ezinihitte. Had Abii retained his seat, Ezinihitte would have been the only clan with more than one representative, since Ekwerazu transferred its federal seat to Ahiara. With its sixteen delegates, at least twice the number of any other clan, Ezinihitte controlled the chairmanship of the Mbaise County Council from 1958 through 1964. Internal divisions alone precipitated the decline of Ezinihitte, so that if the reconciliation effected in January 1966 remains permanent, Ezinihitte should resume its paramount position when representative government is restored.

Ekwerazu, third in population of the three court areas and second to Ezinihitte in size of the clans, was also eminently successful in gaining political representation and having development projects located in its area. For the five years from 1959 to 1964 Ekwerazu had representatives in both the regional and the federal houses. Two inhabitants of Ekwerazu, N. D. Ukah and Donatus Onu, held the chairmanship of the Mbaise County Council. Much of Ekwerazu's political success probably derived from Nwoga's position as the first full minister from Mbaise.

In addition to the support he received as Nwoga's candidate for the Mbaise County Council chairmanship, Onu owed his election in part to the defection of Ezinihitte West. In order to repay his electoral debt after he had become chairman, the council sited several projects in Ezinihitte West. Projects for Ezinihitte proposed in the five-year development program included a bridge, a postal agency, and a health center. Postal agencies were usually located in the center of the clan, which for Ezinihitte was Ife. The plan located both the bridge and the health center in the local council area of Ezinihitte West.

Ahiara and Nguru, smaller than Ezinihitte or Ekwerazu and less prone to internal division than were the two larger groups, attempted to compensate for their numerical disadvantage by greater unity. This unity might have derived from their greater preunion integration. The dynamics of the system of participation through ethnic blocs tended to lend legitimacy to the demands of dissatisfied groups for equal treatment. Although Ahiara constituted less than one-third of the population, to fulfill Ahiara's demands for ethnic equality, the federal constituency seat was awarded to A. T. Mbebgu. The larger clans did not attempt to deprive the smaller groups from having health centers or postal agencies, but employed their superior numbers to ensure that the first such projects were constructed in their own areas. Consequently, there were no dominant and subordinate clans in Mbaise, and influence was always relative, depending on the particular circumstances.

SOCIOECONOMIC CHARACTERISTICS OF THE LEADERSHIP

The men considered as leaders for the purpose of this analysis are those having institutional bases: executive positions in clan unions, membership in one of the legislative assemblies or other political office. This group does not necessarily include all of those who actually wielded influence over the formulation of policy, for the size of Mbaise circumscribed the comprehensiveness of the analysis, but it does include the most influential persons. The multiplicity of unions in Mbaise and the almost universal nonexistence of full records precluded the collection of complete data on the socioeconomic characteristics of the officers since the inception of the unions. Most of the clan unions, however, exhibited a remarkable stability by re-electing the same officers year after year. Hence, although data was confined to those officers serving in 1965–1966, it was fairly representative of the trends in recent years.

Table 7. Educational qualifications of Mbaisan politicians and union officers

Schooling	No. of politicians	No. of central union officers	No. of Port Harcourt branch officers
None	—	2	5
Some primary	—	—	2
Primary	—	5	13
Some secondary	—	1	1
Secondary	—	4	4
Grade two elementary teacher's certificate[a]	—	3	—
Higher elementary teacher's certificate[b]	5	7	—
Diploma in education	1	2	—
University	—	1	1
Bachelor of law	1	—	—
Medical degree	1	1	—

Source: Minute books and interviews.

a. A grade two elementary teacher's certificate requires three years of normal school after primary school.

b. A higher elementary teacher's certificate, sometimes known as a grade one, is received after four years of normal school.

Table 7 gives the educational qualifications of the politicians, central union, and Port Harcourt branch union officers. The unions furnishing data for this analysis included the Ezinihitte Clan Union, the Ekwerazu Assembly, the Nguru Patriotic Union, the Ahiara Clan Union, the Oke-ovoro Clan Union, the Mbaise Federal Union, and the Mbaise Youth Movement. Since the characteristics of the officers of the Mbaise Youth Movement's Port Harcourt branch were atypical, this union was omitted from the tabulations on the branch officers. When a person held more than one union office on the same level, he was counted only once.

As a body, the politicians constituted the most educated group of the three considered. The contrast between the politicians and the central union officials, charged with the responsibility for coordinating the branches, would be even greater if the qualifications of the politicians also serving as officers of the unions were withdrawn from the tabulations. Politicians possessed five of the seven higher elementary teacher's certificates, a diploma in education and a medical degree. All of the politicians had at least the equivalent of a secondary school education, because the higher elementary teacher's certificate required four years of study after the completion of primary school. In contrast to the politicians, only 58 percent of the central union officials and 19 percent of those on the branch level were as well educated.

These figures verify the empirical observation that education commanded respect in Mbaise. Until very recently an elementary teacher's certificate represented the highest level of education attained by members of several of the clans. For example, the first college graduates from the Nguru clan did not return until 1960, after the campaign for Osuagwu had already begun. When O. U. Duruh, one of the first members of the Ahiara clan to receive a bachelor's degree, returned to Nigeria from Belfast, he immediately became an officer of the union. The immense prestige received by A. N. Ogbonna, the first doctor from Mbaise, was vastly increased when he decided to establish a hospital in Mbaise rather than to practice in a more lucrative urban area. Two years after his return he had been elected to the Eastern House of Assembly. The Oke-ovoro Clan Union drafted S. M. Ahamba to be their candidate for the Assembly because of his prestige as an author and as a recognized authority on the Ibo language.

Many unions made it a practice to invite all university graduates and professional men to their annual meetings. More of the recent graduates would probably have been made officers if they had exhibited an interest. Several who became civil servants believed that office in a union was incompatible with their position, since the unions frequently became involved in politics. Others either did not want to sacrifice their time or found the low standards of debate repellent. Several of the unions were also meeting irregularly by the time the university graduates returned. The almost universal respect accorded to education did not have to compete with other sources of prestige to the same extent in Mbaise as it did in Abiriba. Lacking a mercantile tradition, the Mbaisans were impressed by wealth but did not seem to elevate it as a value over education.

The occupational profiles of the politicians and officers reflected their educational qualifications. Educators predominated, as the number of teaching certificates would suggest. Table 8 correlates the occupational data for the politicians, central union, and Port Harcourt branch officers.

Table 8. Occupations of Mbaisan politicians, central union officers, and Port Harcourt branch union officers when first elected

Occupation	No. of politicians	No. of central union officers	No. of Port Harcourt branch officers
Laborer	—	1	3
Trader	—	8	7
Clerk	—	1	13
Administrator	—	3	2
Educator	5	12	1
Doctor	1	1	—
Barrister	1	—	—

Source: Minute books and interviews.

The percentages of politicians and officials who were educators, administrators, or professional men is similar to the educational profiles. Again the politicians ranked highest, with all of them either educators or professionals. The central union officers, including the coopted politicians, were intermediate, with 62 percent of them either educators, administrators, or professionals. By excluding the coopted politicians from the calculations, only 48 percent of the central union officers fulfilled the criteria for inclusion in this grouping. An even smaller number of Port Harcourt branch officers had the necessary qualifications. Only 12 percent of them were educators, administrators, or professional men, as compared with 19 percent of them who had a secondary school education or its equivalent.

Most of the men grouped in this category of educators, administrators, or professionals resided away from Mbaise for at least part of their adult lives, both while attaining an education and later while practicing their occupation. Many of the educators taught for at least a short period of time in Mbaise or in nearby Owerri, making it more convenient for them to exercise positions of leadership in the unions. The predominance of educators is explained by the earlier accessibility of teacher's training as a form of higher education. As was the case in Abiriba, the difference between those groups who lived outside of the home community was not marked. Even the farmers remaining in Mbaise frequently traveled to urban areas. All groups embraced modern values, particularly those relating to consumption.

PATTERNS OF THE LEADERSHIP

While the sources of influence at the intermediate level of leadership were somewhat dispersed, given the multiplicity of institutional alternatives, the pyramiding of positions and the deference to politicians circumscribed the access of individuals to high positions of leadership. In Mbaise the seeming fragmentation of authority was partially overcome by the tendency for men prominent in one sphere to pyramid their influence by participating simultaneously in others.

Membership in one of the local councils or the Mbaise County Council conferred sufficient recognition within the community to elevate a person to the intermediate range of leadership. Similarly someone with a secondary or university education automatically received a degree of deference, which then increased relative to his professional success. The few men who amassed wealth in the urban areas were also accorded recognition, especially if they used some of their money to assist members of their community.

At least four separate organizational bases offered potential access to positions of leadership in Mbaise: the chairmanship of the Mbaise County Council, office in one of the unions, election as a member of the regional or federal houses, and membership on one of the NCNC executive or nominating committees. The disproportionate amount of prestige and influence conferred by political office ensured that the successful candidate could consolidate his position through cooptation to other organizations. Since office in one of the clan unions did not constitute an independent source of influence, unions beseiged successful candidates to accept office. Criticizing this tendency, the editors of the *Ezinihitte Newsletter* commented:

> There is leadership in nearly every walk of life. We have leaders of religion, education, trade unions, societies and associations—be it an ordinary town union or a village assembly or any other thing you may think about. Political leadership is given more prominence, and it is surprising that in Ezinihitte every organization would like to have a Chief, or a Councillor or a Parliamentarian as its Chair-

man. Leaders of thought in other walks of life are relegated to the background with the resultant mad ambition and rush for everyone to become a politician—and therefore a recognized leader.

Perceiving that this tendency was not entirely beneficial, the editors continued:

> . . . unfortunately these political leaders have little or no time to lead. Where they have the time to lead they have made enemies during their election campaigns and these enemies do not let their leadership bear fruit. Even sometimes when their political opponents have accepted defeat and would let byegones be byegones these successful politicians continue to begrudge their opponents with the result that effective leadership cannot be had from these politicians.[4]

Unless the political system is revised so that fewer political offices are available to inhabitants of Mbaise or the fruits of political office are decreased, it is unlikely that the separation of functions between the ethnic and political leadership can be accomplished. In the past this fusion merely reflected the access to economic resources through political influence, along with the emergence of the ethnic blocs as the only viable basis of organization. Politicians also became councillors as well as officers of the clan and Mbaise unions. Subsidiary membership, such as on the Mbaise County Council, helped to keep them known to their constituents. The extent of the cooptation of politicians to other positions is indicated in Tables 9 and 10, delineating the offices held by successful candidates prior to their election and offices assumed simultaneously or subsequently.

Table 9. Offices held by candidates for election to the legislature from Mbaise

Candidate	Office in clan union	Office in Mbaise federal union	Office in Mbaise county council
Pius Nwoga	president	—	—
Dr. A. N. Ogbonna	—	—	—
S. M. Ahamba	—	—	—
E. O. Osuagwu	president	vice-president	vice-chairman
D. N. Abii	president	—	—
N. D. Ukah	officer	treasurer	chairman
A. T. Mbegbu	—	—	—

Source: Minute books and interviews.

Table 10. Offices held by legislators from Mbaise

Candidate	Office in clan union	Office in Mbaise federal union	Office in Mbaise county council
P. Nwoga	patron, president	secretary	—
Dr. A. N. Ogbonna	treasurer	president	vice-chairman
S. M. Ahamba	vice-president	—	vice-chairman
E. Osuagwu	president	vice-president	—
D. N. Abii	president	—	chairman
N. D. Ukah	president	treasurer	member
A. T. Mbegbu	—	—	—

Source: Interviews.

Only one representative, A. T. Mbegbu, either did not seek an alternate source of influence after his election or did not accept one when petitioned to do so by his clansmen. Politicians tended to hold more offices subsequent to their election to the regional or federal legislature than they did previously. Not only did election to one of the legislatures confer a great deal of prestige on the representative, but it was a primary access channel to other important positions within the system.

The close association between politics and ethnic groups impeded the emergence of a leader or group of leaders accepted as representing all the Mbaise, just as the political parties in Nigeria were associated with regions. It was commonly believed that representatives at all levels of the political system would first and primarily be concerned with the interests of their immediate group. Each set of elections and monthly meetings of the Mbaise County Council served to reinforce the ethnic divisions, which precluded further integration of the community.

Part Two | Ethnic Unions
in an Urban
Environment

VI | The Urban Context, Port Harcourt

Ethnic unions operated in two environments: the home village in the countryside and "abroad" in the urban centers. As earlier shown, immigrants to the cities founded the vast majority of unions that formed in Eastern Nigeria and provided the financial resources and leadership to sustain them. The Abiriba Communal Improvement Union, for example, was dominated by its urban branch representatives at general conferences and was controlled by men with considerable urban experience. A complete analysis of the unions must therefore include their operations in urban areas as well as at home. Since Port Harcourt, the largest city and the industrial center of the Eastern Region, offered the greatest economic opportunities and since it was within easy driving distance of Abiriba and Mbaise, large numbers of people from those two communities resided there.

In order to comprehend the role assumed by the improvement unions in Port Harcourt, one must first become familiar with the urban context, the environment in which the unions operated. Within this framework, the role of the unions should be considered vis-à-vis their members and the Port Harcourt system in general.

SOCIAL BASIS OF THE NEW TOWNS

Urban centers did exist in Nigeria prior to the colonial period, notably in the Yoruba kingdoms and in some of the emirates, but all of those in the Eastern Region evolved after the establishment of the British administration. Like most cities in Africa, the new towns arose near the centers of colonial administration and commerce. For example, in 1909

119

there was only one house in the area that was to become Port Harcourt. The discovery of coal in the Enugu area in that year prompted the construction of a port from which to ship the ore. Surveyors selected a natural harbor on a peninsula in the Bonny River about forty-one miles from the sea as the site for the railroad terminus. In 1915 the first shipment of coal from Enugu, the present administrative center of the East, arrived by rail at the harbor, now called Port Harcourt. Economic opportunities lured villagers to Port Harcourt—first the chance of employment on the railroad, then the hope of profits from trading in the town, and most recently the lure of jobs from oil explorations and the industries that have arisen to service the oil companies. After the establishment of the headquarters of Shell British Petroleum in Port Harcourt in 1957, the city became the center of a flourishing oil industry.

A dichotomy between modernity and tradition, which equates the modern society with the urban center, has influenced some conceptions of modernization. Residence in an urban center appeared as one significant index of social change in the models of Daniel Lerner and Karl Deutsch. Deutsch's other indices for social mobilization, defined as "an over-all process of change which happens to substantial parts of the population of countries which are moving from traditional to modern ways of life," included exposure to significant aspects of modern life, contact with mass media, change in locality of residence, practice of nonagricultural professions, urbanization, literacy, and level of income.[1]

The contrast between the traditional and modern society does not illuminate the distinction between the rural village and the urban center in Eastern Nigeria. Traditional Ibo society, that is, the social structure existing prior to the establishment of the colonial administration, incorporated many elements of the cluster of values usually associated with modernity. Conversely, for several reasons the new cities lacked characteristics normally connected with the image of an urban center. Or to employ Emile Durkheim's two models, the organic solidarity resulting from the division of labor inherent in industrial enterprise had not yet superseded patterns of allegiance based on the network of mechanical solidarity; the two types of solidarity, the two patterns of allegiance, coexisted.[2]

In many respects the immigrant to Port Harcourt had already been socially mobilized, according to Deutsch's criteria. He had changed the locality of his residence, experienced many aspects of modern life, including at least one form of the mass media, learned to practice a nonagricultural profession, gained a better income than in the rural area, and obviously lived in a town. The only one of the seven indices he might not have fulfilled was the acquisition of literacy.

Most residents fulfilled Deutsch's indices because Port Harcourt was a community of immigrants. The land on which Port Harcourt evolved had formerly belonged to the Ikwerres, a marginally Ibo community. Two purchases, the first in 1913 and the second in 1928, transferred ownership of the land from the Ikwerres to the government. Although the Ikwerres later undertook protracted litigation to regain the land or to raise the £500 annual rent payment, a series of court decisions, culminating with one by the Privy Council in 1956, upheld the acquisition.

The failure of the Ikwerres to reclaim their ancestral land was paralleled by their inability to participate effectively in and benefit from the development of Port Harcourt. Overwhelmed by the succeeding waves of immigrants from the surrounding countryside, they constituted only about 7 percent of the population by 1963.[3] Ikwerre settlements remained almost symbolically at the outer limits of the city. Although the peninsula marks the dividing line between Ibo and Ijaw areas, the population of Port Harcourt consisted predominantly of Ibos, who were approximately 80 percent of the total. Most of them came from Owerri and Bende Divisions, with significant representation from Onitsha and Orlu Divisions.

Unlike some other African and many Asian cities, Port Harcourt was not constituted so that members of the same community lived in homogenous or segregated neighborhoods. Although virtually the entire population came from outside the immediate geographical area, no *sabon garis* or strangers quarters separated the new settlers from the former residents, as in Northern Nigeria. Residential patterns were ethnically dispersed, with very few concentrations of immigrants from the same clan or town living in close proximity.

Yet an examination of the pattern of social relationships immediately reveals the strong bond that united the immigrant with his community of origin. If social mobilization is a "process in which major clusters of old social, economic and psychological commitments are eroded or broken and people become available for new patterns of socialization and behavior,"[4] then the residents of Port Harcourt did not experience it. Urbanization did not necessarily promote radical social change. The extraordinary growth of Port Harcourt prevented the assimilation of the immigrant upon his arrival. Many cities in Africa experienced a sudden spurt of growth during and after the Second World War, as a result of increased economic activity. The rapid rise of Port Harcourt as the commercial and industrial center of the Eastern Region during the ten-year period from 1953 to 1963 was reflected by a meteoric population growth of 240 percent.

The great influx of predominantly illiterate and unskilled immigrants from the surrounding countryside impeded the transition to a new identity. Virtually all adults were born outside the city. No one of those interviewed, not even those who had spent the better portion of their lives in Port Harcourt, failed to consider himself a member of his community of origin. Port Harcourt could be described as a city of strangers, each of whom regarded himself as only a temporary resident accumulating enough wealth to return to his real home. Although fewer and fewer of the immigrants probably returned permanently to their home community, not even the most Anglicized admitted to any other ambition than to retire to his community of origin. As soon as the immigrant earned enough money, he usually built a house in the home community rather than in the city, as a symbol of his success and a manifestation of his commitment. The close geographic proximity between the city and the home community for the vast majority of the inhabitants allowed them to return for a visit at frequent intervals. Some of those interviewed journeyed home as often as every week, others only once a month, but all at least several times a year.

Other factors reinforcing the reliance on the home community were the high rates of unemployment and underemployment, which resulted from the failure of the economy to keep pace with the population boom brought on by immigration. Relatively few industrial enterprises, with the exception of the oil companies, established plants in Port Harcourt. Those that did tended to be capital intensive and to employ small labor forces.

In Port Harcourt most residents experienced frequent exposure to some aspect of the mass media. By itself this contact could create aspirations for a higher standard of living, something the Ibo was generally predisposed toward even without reinforcement, but exposure did not foster social change. In an article on the relationship between communication and modernization, Daniel Lerner argued that the mass media stimulated frustrations and potential instability by raising expectations, which the economic system could not fulfill.[5]

Research on other Nigerian and African cities confirms that urban residence, at least for the first few generations, did not precipitate radical social change. Ibo communities in Enugu, Aba, Onitsha, Lagos, Ibadan, and Jos maintained their ethnic ties, through ethnic unions, just as did those in Port Harcourt.[6] The expectation that urban residence would lead to a basic transformation in the pattern of social relations in Africa followed in large part from the early dichotomous models that oppose tradition and modernity. Ferdinand Tonnies' model of community and society (*gemeinschaft and gesellschaft*), Emile Durkheim's distinction between organic and mechanical solidarity, and Max Weber's ideal types of customary as against rational-legal domination, all posit total acceptance or rejection of two opposing orders. They presume, as C. S. Whitaker pointed out, that social change is cumulative, that within a particular sphere of activity the introduction of significant new elements promotes consistent modification in most of its other aspects, and that transformations in one sphere of activity spillover and foster reinforcing innovations in others. They also presume a standard of consistency in individuals and groups that would make the retention of fundamentally different cognitive orientations in various fields of activity intolerable.[7] Recent studies of social change in Africa, however, demonstrate that neither individuals nor social systems exhibit the consistency that these models of total acceptance assume.[8] Individuals quite comfortably retain the traditional alongside the modern without social or psychological conflict. After all, societies, even those acknowledged to be modern, always retain certain elements of tradition.

THE EVOLUTION OF PORT HARCOURT'S POLITICAL SYSTEM

In his excellent studies of Port Harcourt, Howard Wolpe delineated four distinct historical periods in the evolution of the political system.[9] During the first period, 1913–1920, Port Harcourt was governed by a colonial administrator and a township advisory board consisting of European officials and representatives of European mercantile firms. Unlike most other Nigerian cities, Port Harcourt was never subjected to indirect rule based on native authorities. Instead, its political system evolved from this form of direct rule.

During the next period, 1920–1943, Africans were added to the township's advisory board. The African "patricians" who were appointed to the advisory board came from the groups that had early access to Western education and therefore were not predominantly Ibo. Of the twelve

Africans who served on the advisory board, two were Yorubas, two Sierra Leonians, one Gambian, three Ijaws, and four Ibos. No Ibo member was invited to join the advisory board until 1937, eleven years after the board became multiracial. Ibos began to migrate to Port Harcourt in large numbers during this period and clearly constituted a majority of the population. With this migration came the new organizations, particularly the ethnic unions. Political forces gradually coalesced, and the African population groped toward a confrontation with the colonial elite, who still monopolized political power.

In the third period, 1944–1954, the challenge to colonial rule became explicit with the rise of nationalist militancy following the war. In 1949 the basis of political power in Port Harcourt was democratized by replacing the colonial officer and his advisory board with an elected town council. The town council and the NCNC branch in Port Harcourt assumed the paramount position relinquished by the administrator and his board. As this occurred, the social basis for leadership in the African community also changed. Ibos from Onitsha, the first Ibo area to receive extensive Western education, assumed leadership, along with some Mid Western Ibos, another educationally advantaged section. The Onitsha and Mid Western Ibos compensated for their small numbers, as compared with the Owerri Ibos, by their greater political sophistication and organizational skill.

As independence approached in the fourth period, 1954 to 1966, numbers came to be the major criteria for political power. Consequently the Owerri Ibos gradually displaced the Onitsha and Mid Western Ibos from their political positions. By 1955 the composition of the municipal council reflected this change in the basis of political power, when the Owerri Ibos for the first time comprised a majority. During this period wealth replaced occupational status as another source of political power, which facilitated the Owerri advance because they constituted a significant proportion of the businessmen and traders. It should be noted that Owerri Province incorporated both the Abiriban and Mbaise communities until 1959, when the original five provinces were split into twelve. After 1959 the division between the Owerri and Onitsha communities (still based on the old inclusive provincial lines) became an explicit and salient basis of organization for political activities in the main township.

Port Harcourt consisted of a main township and an adjacent slum area, Diobu Mile Two. Diobu was the original stopping-off point for immigrants when they arrived in Port Harcourt. Since Owerri Ibos constituted a larger proportion of the population of Diobu than of the main township, the social basis of political competition there centered on divisions within the Owerri provincial grouping. In Diobu, Ibos from Owerri Division often united against an alliance of Ibos from Okigwi and Orlu Divisions, once part of the same administrative unit.

THE PORT HARCOURT COUNCIL

From 1949 until 1954 and again from 1955 until 1966 an elected council governed Port Harcourt. The one-year hiatus resulted from the council's suspension by the Eastern government for reasons of corruption and maladministration, two organizational vices that continued to plague the council until its final dissolution by the military government. Originally the council administered only the wards in the main township, but a reorganization in 1960 extended its jurisdiction to Diobu, the slum area. In 1966 the military government replaced the council with a civil servant, a British expatriate, as sole administrator. The size of the city, combined with the presence of some industry and a heterogeneous residential pattern, precluded the emergence of a nongovernmental association as an effective replacement for the functional deficiencies of the local council, similar to the manner in which ethnic unions compensated for the shortcomings of councils in the countryside. Consequently the ethnics unions could not play the same role in the city that they did in rural areas.

Each member of the municipal council usually came from a different community than did the majority of his constituents, which sometimes made communication between them more difficult. The weakness of the NCNC at the ward level accentuated this problem. Since it was impossible for all of the rural communities represented in Port Harcourt to have a delegate on the council, many people considered themselves to be without direct access to communication channels.

Because councillors represented multiethnic constituencies, ethnic factors did not often enter into council deliberations. Most subjects within the competence of the council—finance, schools, roads, sanitation, market maintenance—did not directly concern communal interests. As Wolpe indicated, "'communalism' in Port Harcourt impinged only upon issues of political *recruitment* and *patronage*—issues upon which the prestige and recognition of immigrant groups depended—and did not affect routine Council deliberations." When the council considered subjects that did not have immediate communal implications, councillors and party members "either divided themselves according to their *residential* interests (as when amenities, such as paved roads and electric lighting were to be allocated) or followed the direction of the Council's informal leaders." Leadership in the council in that case depended on soundness of judgment, reputation for integrity, and oratorical skills.[10] Hence, A. D. W. Jumbo, an Ijaw businessman, could become one of the most influential members of the council as a result of his personal qualities, despite his minority communal affiliation.

Councillors ofter seemed to be more concerned with the distribution of jobs and contracts or other patronage issues than with the problem-solving activities of the council. To judge from the incidence of corruption, the possibility of access to this potentially lucrative source of income must frequently have motivated persons to seek election to the local council. Many councillors also apparently lacked the competence to contribute significantly to technical discussions.

As with most municipal governments, lack of autonomy and the inability to control major factors in its environment restricted the scope of decision-making and implementation for the municipal council. For instance, the destiny of Port Harcourt was inextricably linked with the fortunes of the oil industry; as the oil industry prospered, so did Port Harcourt. The rapid rate of population growth brought on by rural immigration was one of the primary determinants of conditions in Port Harcourt, yet this situation depended on subjective factors and objective conditions in the countryside, not on council decisions. Similarly the number of skilled expatriates arriving resulted more from developments in the oil and other industries than it did from conscious policy devised by the council. Large grants to undertake major improvements or develop new industries could only be secured from the Eastern government. Although Port Harcourt was the industrial center and largest city in Eastern Nigeria, Enugu remained the focus of regional political power. Although politics in Port Harcourt had important consequences for the Eastern Region because the city had such a high concentration of Ibo wealth and skills, the NCNC branch in Port Harcourt often could not ensure that favorable decisions were made in Enugu.

In many instances there was a distinct time lag between the formulation of policy by the municipal council for Port Harcourt and its effective implementation, indicating the somewhat limited capabilities of the municipal council. For example, hand carts continued to be pushed along the roads, interrupting the flow of traffic, long after the council had promulgated an ordinance banning them. Several months and sometimes years intervened between the decision to undertake a project, like the tarring of roads, and its completion.

One continual problem was the inability to extract resources commensurate with the vast needs of the city. The rapid population growth, increasing 240 percent in the ten-year period from 1953 to 1963, outstripped the increasing resources available from the economic development of the city, despite the fact that Port Harcourt had the highest revenue base of any council in the Eastern Region. In 1963–1964, for example, the council received £275,000. On occasion the municipal council raised loans of up to £100,000 from commercial banks for which the Eastern government provided the guarantee. The municipality of Port Harcourt, along with the five largest urban county councils, received a six shilling per person grant, the highest rate of assistance awarded by the Eastern government.[11] However, these resources were not sufficient, given the special needs of the city.

The municipal council did not provide even minimal social services for most of the people, many of whom were in dire need of assistance. In addition to denying social services, the lack of funds prevented the municipal council from improving the sewage system and the roads. The open gutter drains were unsanitary, as well as aesthetically unpleasing. With the exception of a few main roads through the center of the city, the roads remained ungraded and untarred. During the rainy season, which lasted for about six months a year, large potholes abounded, and many of the roads became quagmires.

Conditions were especially poor in Diobu. Large numbers of people crowded into flimsy houses with a few small rooms. Most of the people living in Diobu had recently arrived from their home villages with no skills, little education, and no immediate prospects for employment. Moreover, the distance they had traveled from their villages to Diobu, while often relatively short in actual mileage, had exposed them to a whole new pattern of life. Although the needs of the Diobu residents were great, the council spent little time and minimum resources attempting to ameliorate conditions in this densely populated area. As with slums throughout the world, Diobu had fewer roads, poorer sanitation facilities, and less police protection than the rest of the city, with little hope for significant improvement.

Ethnic unions arose in Port Harcourt to fill the social and economic gaps resulting from the residential patterns, the rapid population growth, and the low capabilities of the municipal council. They were never actually counted, but hundreds of branches of various types of ethnic unions operated in Port Harcourt. These branches both catered to the needs of their members in Port Harcourt and sponsored economic and educational development at home. Generally meeting once a month, the unions provided a physical link and a communications network between the immigrants in Port Harcourt and the community at home. Union meetings often were the only means for members of the home community to come together as a group. The immigrant turned to the unions, rather than the municipal government, for assistance, comfort, money, and support. When an immigrant arrived in Port Harcourt, his clan union tried to find him a place to live and often lent him money.

In addition to town or clan unions, division and provincial associations proliferated in Port Harcourt. Throughout the various administrative reorganizations in Eastern Nigeria and Biafra, the divisional boundaries (sometimes called districts) tended to remain stable. Hence, residents from the same division often had elements of a shared heritage or tradition, as well as common interests. Some of the divisional and provincial unions existed for a longer period than many of their constituent clan and town unions. For example, the Port Harcourt branch of the Owerri Progress Union was formed in 1932, twelve years before the Mbaise Federal Union.

Membership in a divisional union was usually indirect, requiring prior participation in a constituent union. The nine clan unions forming the Bende Development Union each sent four to six representatives, depending on their size, to the meetings. As a result, the general membership of the clan unions usually concerned itself with the affairs of the divisional union in a peripheral manner, and the concrete activities of the divisional unions related only to the direct participants—some held send-offs or welcome home parties for people from their area going abroad to study, and one, the Owerri Progress Union, built a meeting hall in Port Harcourt.

In April 1966 the Bende Development Union decided to transform itself into a direct membership organization and sent notices to constituent unions that every member should now register individually. If they ever have an opportunity to implement this policy, it will be the first attempt to integrate divisional members through the activities of a union. Presumably representatives would still represent union branches, not groups of individuals.

The importance of the division union lay in its potential for mobilizing support behind a member, particularly in a direct political confrontation with someone from another division. For this reason their infrequent meetings could be misleading indices of the role of the divisional unions in Port Harcourt. Only one division union in Port Harcourt, the Onitsha Division Union, met with any regularity, once a month. The Bende Development Union theoretically scheduled a meeting every three months but often postponed it. At election time, however, all the divisional unions resumed functioning.

Voluntary associations based on economic and functional divisions could not completely replace the ethnic improvement unions, because when an immigrant arrived in Port Harcourt, only his clan union could find him a place to live and lend him money. But the clan union could no longer either provide the immigrant with a job or secure his advancement once he began working. With the formation of trade unions management became increasingly hesitant about dealing with outsiders. Unofficial estimates placed the industrial labor force in Port Harcourt in 1966 at eighty thousand, of which between one-fourth and one-third had joined unions. Some eighty unions existed in Port Harcourt. A few were branches of larger unions, but most of them were local organizations having only one hundred members or less. Although most of the unions were small and relatively new, during the general strike in 1964 they halted virtually all industrial production in Port Harcourt.

An industrial relations adviser believed that the general strike initiated a new identity for the workers based on class distinctions. It seems unlikely, however, that at this stage of their development the trade unions could replace the clan unions, even in those industries with large, well-organized unions, such as Shell British Petroleum, the United African Company, or the Nigerian Ports Authority, because only the clan union provided assistance in times of personal need. Also several of the trade unions in Port Harcourt were themselves beset by ethnic divisions. There was a three-way division in the Port Harcourt Glass Factory union between men from Onitsha, Umuahia, and Calabar. Alcan Aluminum's union never recovered from the intrigue employed by a Mbaisan in 1962 to displace the inefficient president, an Ibibio from the Rivers area. In several other industries people gained employment through political influence exercised on their behalf by men from their community, which constituted a kind of ethnic nepotism.[12]

While the 1964 general strike lasted, workers in Port Harcourt followed the directives of the trade union leaders and acted on the basis of their working class solidarity. For two weeks the strike effectively halted all industrial production in the city. But once the strike was over, the trade union leaders could not politically capitalize on the militancy expressed by the workers. As Wolpe showed, the leaders of the strike were drawn predominantly from minority ethnic groups and had previously broken with the dominant NCNC organization.[13] Just as most matters concerning the Port Harcourt municipal council did not depend on ethnic factors, the working force apparently divorced most trade union activities from communal considerations. However, once the trade union leaders attempted to infringe on ethnically relevant matters by trying to form a new political party, the workers refused to follow them. Instead they returned to their former network of allegiance, the ethnic unions and the NCNC.

Similarly some residents of Port Harcourt temporarily became involved in political controversies on the basis of their religious affiliations. In 1956 and 1963–1964 Catholic protest movements formed against the Eastern government's policy to limit the expansion of denominational schools. Protestants generally supported the government, because Catholic schools were opening at a much faster rate in the East. As with the trade union leaders, the leaders of the local Catholic executive committee did not hold high positions in the NCNC. And like the trade union leaders, they found that using religious issues did not advance their political ambitions.[14]

ROLE OF THE UNIONS IN
THE PORT HARCOURT SYSTEM

The kinds of demands made by the improvement unions reflected the unintegrated nature of the Port Harcourt system. Demands for symbolic outputs or for the affirmation of norms predicate the acceptance of such symbols or norms. In an unintegrated system demands for the regulation of behavior, to the extent that they even exist, are generally confined to rules that limit the activities of opponents. Most improvement unions primarily issued demands for goods and services and for participation.

Economic opportunity had originally attracted the city's several hundred thousand residents to Port Harcourt. Once in the city, they joined clan unions to finance improvement projects in their community of origin. Ambition and their materialistic orientation fostered a desire for amenities in Port Harcourt as well, such as schools and market facilities. But such desires would more likely be voiced generally, as for schools, or individually, as for market facilities, rather than through the homeward oriented improvement unions. As a result, the only typical economic demand made by the clan unions in Port Harcourt was for a suitable plot of land on which to erect a meeting hall.

The most insistent demands of the ethnic unions were for political recognition through the nomination of a kinsman for political office. Such behavior is typical of immigrants in any political system. Ethnic voting, a still common occurrence in the United States, has two manifestations: affinity for a particular political party because of its identification with one's ethnic group, and the tendency to cross party lines to vote for or against a candidate belonging to a particular ethnic group.[15]

Only one party, the NCNC, existed as an effective political force subsequent to the extension of the franchise in 1949. As a consequence, Port Harcourt had a one-party political system. This party, however, never managed to mobilize its adherents into a disciplined monolithic force infused with a loyalty transcending ethnic divisions. While political influence in Port Harcourt depended on one's position in the NCNC, ethnic factors entered into the determination of that position.

With one major exception for the people from Mbaise, the separate town or clan groupings in Port Harcourt remained too small to participate directly in the political or economic system. The 1963 population of Port Harcourt was estimated officially at 179,563 persons and unofficially at between 300,000 and 500,000.[16] The wards, which determined nominations and elections for regional and federal parliamentary seats, rarely had significant concentrations of residents from one community, which precluded ethnic appeals directed at any one group. In order to win, a candidate had to gain the support of voters of diverse origins. Hence officers in clan unions could not directly translate leadership of their community into a position of influence in the party. Ethnic factors usually entered into political calculations at the divisional level. Division unions, joining together all the clan and town unions in a particular division, furnished the effective organizational media through which ethnicity operated.

In Port Harcourt most groups worked to fulfill their demands through the predominant NCNC. For example, one of the two leading NCNC candidates for election as mayor in 1965 was Chief Akomas from Bende Division, and the other candidate, Francis Ikekinoaba, was from Orlu Division. Each relied on his division for his primary source of support and then made alliances with other divisions. The various candidates vying for the NCNC nomination for the seat to the Federal House of Representatives in 1964 made similar divisional appeals.

When party affiliation and ethnic group loyalty conflicted, the resident had to make a choice between the two. As might be anticipated, the stronger of the two affiliations prevailed. Dissatisfaction with the ethnic division of spoils frequently led to a threat and sometimes actually to withdrawal from the NCNC. The most common expression of this dissatisfaction was support for an independent candidate running against the official nominee.

As the 1964 federal election indicated, the threat of electoral secession was not always an idle one, at least in the federal constituency based on Diobu and the Ahoada rural area; nor was the NCNC an invincible monolith that could rise up and defeat any independent that dared run against it. Once the long dormant Ikwerres awakened to the realization of their subordinate position in Port Harcourt, they attempted to improve their status. They decided that certain prizes in the Port Harcourt system belonged to them, including the parliamentary seat encompassing their home area. The Port Harcourt NCNC nominated candidates for two federal constituencies. When in 1964 the NCNC executive selected candidates from Mbaise for both the first constituency based on wards in the central part of Port Harcourt and the second one including Diobu and Ahoada, the area in which the Ikwerres lived, the Ikwerres recruited a prominent member of their community to run as an independent. The candidate, a barrister practicing in Port Harcourt, defeated the NCNC nominee.[17]

Concerned with preserving a favorable community image in order to enhance their prestige, clan unions also provided supports for the political system. For example, they frequently lectured their members on the necessity of being good citizens. They probably fostered support for the system through encouraging members to pay taxes and obey laws.

Improvement unions also supported the political system more directly through their incorporation into the apparatus of the Social Welfare Department. In 1961 the government demarcated six welfare zones in the Eastern Region, one of which was Port Harcourt and its environs. In each of these zones welfare officers invited town and clan unions to affiliate with a Council of Social Services after satisfying two conditions, proof of continuous existence and financial solvency. The original goals of the Council of Social Services were to assist the Port Harcourt Municipal Council and the local authorities in solving welfare problems in light of community traditions, to increase intercommunal responsiveness and intertribal understanding, and to promote the interchange of ideas between these cultural organizations and international voluntary organs. Some eighty-three town and clan unions had affiliated with the Council of Social Services by 1966. During its first five years the Council of Social Services completed a citizenship center for delinquent youths and began a halfway home for mentally disturbed, senile, and destitute persons.

The most effective organization undertaking social welfare activities in Port Harcourt was the Port Harcourt Christian Council Project, particularly the teams associated with St. Andrew's Anglican Church in Diobu. This group also worked with the Council of Social Services. At St. Andrew's Community Center the teams attempted to work with the clan unions as well in order to gain information about local customs, financial aid, and welfare assistance, such as sending home destitute kinsmen.

EVALUATION OF THE IMPACT OF THE UNIONS

The first and most obvious appraisal of the overall impact of the ethnic unions on the Port Harcourt political system would seem to stress their negative effects, such as their role in maintaining the identity of the immigrants with their community of origin, and thereby focusing their energy and funds on improvements at home rather than in the city. Doubtless their activities and demands fostered separateness rather than integration. They acted to retard the emergence of a Port Harcourt community superseding the rurally based network of commitments.

Within the context of conditions in Port Harcourt, however, such as the heterogeneous residential areas and the absence of welfare facilities, the unions performed vital functions that the state could not yet assume. They provided a kind of welfare insurance and acted as a social watchguard for their members. Without this measure of security and order, the result would more likely have been chaos and anomy than integration. As William Kornhauser observed, the rapid influx of people into newly developing urban areas can engender mass movements by creating discontinuities in the society. Widespread social mobilization that eroded old clusters of commitments would probably have given rise to a mass society, in which large numbers of people were not integrated into any broad social groupings. A mass movement could have evolved out of a mass society if extraconstitutional behavior became organized and acquired a continuity in purpose and effort.[18] A susceptibility to such mass movements would have undermined the political system.

By furnishing an infrastructure through which recent immigrants could organize their experience and comprehend politics, the clan and division unions played an indispensable part in making the political system immediate and relevant. Given the rapid influx of immigrants and the recent origin and lack of comprehensiveness of voluntary associations with an economic base, ethnic unions were probably the only medium through which a majority of the people could organize. Rather than create new animosities, they supplied acceptable outlets through which rival groups could compete.

In the one-party system of Port Harcourt the ethnic unions were the most important independent organizations capable of influencing the NCNC. While divisional unions could not dictate to the party, they played an important part in deciding on nominations for political office. Ethnic groups in at least some constituencies could also ventilate their grievances by fielding independent candidates supported by their union as a kind of safety valve. Thus, the clan unions ensured flexibility within the party by reinforcing the mosaic pattern of the pluralistic Port Harcourt society.

How might the future evolution of the city affect the unions? For the first generation immigrant, his community of origin, in which most of his relatives probably lived and to which he hoped to return, still structured his important sets of commitments. With the passage of time, if Ibos return to Port Harcourt, the strength of these community bonds may weaken, particularly if either the municipal government or the trade unions can provide the social insurance and welfare services presently associated with the urban branches of the ethnic unions. One index of the transformation from Port Harcourt transient to urban dweller will be the decision of the resident to build his home in Port Harcourt rather than in his place of origin. A second will be the redirection of his time and resources from a preoccupation with his community of origin to the improvement of Port Harcourt.

To a very limited extent before the war, both changes were taking place. Several educated professional people had built their first homes in Port Harcourt. In April 1966 the residents of the Diobu slum area formed night patrol groups for mutual protection against robbers, to compensate for the tendency of the police to ignore the area. When the police arrested several of the night patrollers after they had shot a group of alleged robbers, almost all the residents of Diobu joined in a protest the next day. This mass protest, together with several of the organizations formed in Diobu as a consequence of it, pointed to at least a partial concern with the affairs of Port Harcourt.

VII | The Port Harcourt Branch of the Abiriba Communal Improvement Union

How did the improvement unions actually operate within the urban framework? Did the branches of the Abiriban and Mbaise unions differ from one another in Port Harcourt, as the unions did in the home areas? In order to answer these questions, it is necessary to describe the role that the branch unions assumed vis-à-vis their members and within the political system in Port Harcourt. As will be demonstrated, the uniformity of the environment minimized some of the divergences observed in the performance of the unions in the two rural communities.

The role of the Port Harcourt branch of the Abiriba Communal Improvement Union included its activities on behalf of Abiribans in Port Harcourt and at home. One should remember that the Port Harcourt branch probably was the strongest single local unit of the ACIU for the ten years preceding 1966. The Port Harcourt branch also played a role in the political system in terms of its demands and supports. Finally, in contrast to most other branch unions, the ACIU occasionally became involved in regional politics.

THE INTERNAL ROLE

A branch of the Abiriba Youth League was formed in Port Harcourt in 1939, with 198 members.[1] After the inauguration of the ACIU in 1941, the Port Harcourt branch of the Abiriba Youth League was transformed into an ACIU branch. In 1964 there were 212 members on the rolls of the Port Harcourt branch and 250 in the Diobu subbranch formed in 1962. The formal inauguration of the subbranch in 1962, which had been meeting separately for several years, required the ap-

136

proval of the central executive. Poorer members living in Diobu had complained about the cost of transportation to the main town every Sunday for the compulsory meeting. Although the two groups actually functioned as autonomous units, to maintain the unity of the Abiriba community in Port Harcourt vis-à-vis other groups, they described themselves as sections of one branch. When in 1965 the Council of Social Services issued separate invitations to affiliate with it, for instance, they replied that the ACIU was a single entity and sent one member from the Port Harcourt branch to represent both groups. Similarly one delegation composed of four members from the main branch and two from Diobu represented Abiriba in the Bende Development Union before the latter decided to transform itself into a direct membership organization.[2]

In addition to the regular branch and subbranches, whose membership was confined to men, a women's auxiliary operated sporadically. Formed under the guidance of the male branch, it could not maintain itself because a majority of the men preferred that their wives stay at home rather than attend the meetings.

The Port Harcourt branch met once a week on Sundays. Members conducted meetings in Ibo, according to general parliamentary procedure, with minutes taken in English in much the same way as the general conferences. Unlike the central union, the officers did not compose an agenda before the meetings, because the discussion centered on nonpayment of dues, incomplete membership roles, and nonattendance. Officers were elected yearly by all dues-paying members.

Unlike the procedure utilized by the central union, the Port Harcourt branch functioned to a great extent through the age grades. Each age grade maintained lists of all members residing in Port Harcourt, which they periodically submitted to the branch executive. These age grade lists constituted the basis of the membership rolls of the Port Harcourt branch, which it was required to keep by the central executive. Representatives of five of the age grades, appointed each year, collected the dues. In return, the collectors often received a commission of two shillings on each pound as an incentive to undertake the task. For several years the age grades were directly represented in the branch executive, with members electing two persons from each age grade along with the other officers. When the branch encountered financial difficulties, it tried to borrow money from the age grades.

The dependence on age grades by the Port Harcourt branch did not indicate the strength or relevance of the age divisions in the urban environment. In fact, the age grades did not seem to perform any specific function in the general Port Harcourt system. Rather, this dependence resulted from and manifested the weakness of the regular branch organization. It was a lazy way of maintaining the branch in being.

In theory, attendance at all meetings of the Port Harcourt branch was compulsory, and absentees paid a two-shilling fine. Although various incumbent officers claimed nonattendance was not a serious problem, the minute books constantly repeated the complaint of the small proportion of members coming to meetings. Matters such as the election of officers frequently had to be postponed owing to the lack of the requisite number of members. Published figures of the number of persons present rarely exceeded one hundred people, half the total registered membership, and frequently seemed to range around sixty. Even officers sometimes failed to appear regularly.

Unless the member contributed all dues and levies, the union could theoretically seize his property, but this did not happen in practice. Although Port Harcourt along with Aba was generally acknowledged by Abiribans to have the most prosperous group of traders, its fund-raising ability did not reflect this affluence. When the central secretariat kept records comparing the contributions of branches, Port Harcourt rarely came first. In 1948 at the general conference the central officers criticized it for its poor record as the fifth ranking branch after Calabar, the farmers at home, Ifiayong, and Umuahia. Port Harcourt's contribution of £78 at that time nevertheless exceeded the £48 it collected in 1964.[3]

Along with the weekly meetings of the ACIU, Abiribans in Port Harcourt attended fortnightly meetings of their age grades. Both meetings took place on Sunday, the only day on which most people did not work. Generally the age grades scheduled their meetings for the morning and the ACIU for the early afternoon, thus monopolizing a great portion of the leisure time of members.

One of the primary functions of the Port Harcourt branch with regard to its members concerned the reinforcement of the Abiriban identity. The branch did not completely succeed since it could not count all eligible Abiribans as members. Attendance at meetings and the donation of dues declined in the ten years preceding 1966. Relative to other ethnic organizations in Port Harcourt, the ACIU had fairly high capabilities in terms of the frequency of meetings, attendance, and collection of dues. The decline in attendance and in the subscription of dues related to the reaction of members to twenty years of compulsory activities. Attendance figures, while disappointing to officers, compared favorably with other clan unions. The performance of this integrative function was particularly important because of the high proportion of Abiribans living away from the home area.

The small resource base of the Port Harcourt branch—optimally two shillings for each member, or £21 annually if everyone contributed his dues—limited the ability of the branch to provide goods and services for its members. In 1964 a dues subscription of £48.13 left the branch with a revenue of only £5 for the entire year, with the remainder going to the central union. Occasionally members borrowed money from the branch treasury, but they more often sought loans from affluent kinsmen. Frequently the small financial resources of the branch after their mandatory contributions to the central organization were expended on receptions for visiting Abiriban dignitaries, such as central officers, returning scholarship students, and politicians.

The only project that the branch tried to undertake, the construction of a meeting hall in Port Harcourt, never materialized. Members decided to build the hall in 1949. Not until 1959 did the municipal council assign them a parcel of land in Gborokiri, a reclaimed swampland on the outskirts of the city. Seventeen years had thus gone by since the original decision, and the branch had yet to dig a hole for the foundation. By 1966 the central union had disassociated itself from the project. In part the lack of progress derived from a dissatisfaction with the location of the plot assigned to the union.

The trading orientation of the community made it less likely for members to seek industrial employment or join one of the labor unions. In order to receive assistance in establishing themselves as traders, Abiriban immigrants would approach one of their kinsmen or a trading house, not the ACIU.

The Port Harcourt branch was one of the twenty constituent units of the ACIU. Its correspondence files attested to a continuous stream of letters between the central secretariat and the branch, as well as frequent communication with other branches. Hence, the Port Harcourt branch performed one vital function required of all the constituent units by providing the central executive with information. Reciprocally the branch kept its members informed about decisions of the central union by discussing letters from the secretariat and reading minutes of the general meetings.

Occasionally, but only occasionally, the Port Harcourt branch interrupted its preoccupation with attendance, finances, and membership lists in the period from November 1945 to April 1964 to discuss substantive matters concerning Abiriba. These discussions often coincided with visits from officers of the central union or political representatives. But beginning in April 1964 the focus of the meetings changed. Instead of merely discussing the usual organizational deficiencies, the meetings became a forum in which participants reflected on problems in Abiriba and ways to solve them. On several issues the branch even took an initiative. No one obvious factor accounted for this transformation. Few new officers were elected; the president had been in office since 1949. Possibly the school crisis galvanized the branch into action. N. A. Otisi, the general president of the ACIU, unexpectedly visited the branch to discuss this issue. After this visit many of the meetings focused around facets of this problem.

Sometimes the branch actively attempted to influence policy rather than merely to inform the central union about its opinions, particularly after 1964. In May 1964 the branch instructed a four-man committee to contact the sanitary inspector in Abiriba about certain problems. When N. A. Otisi attended another meeting, the branch pressed him for the immediate removal of two members of the Enuda College staff and asked him to persuade Reverend R. H. Paulson, the principal, to withdraw his letter of resignation. On another occasion the branch sent a letter to Enuda College and to the ACIU secretariat urging the removal from the school of a boy alleged to have poisoned a fellow-student. As one of the groups advocating the transfer of Enuda College to another voluntary agency, the branch interviewed several organizations about managing the school. The Port Harcourt branch was also one of the groups that objected to the pledging of Enuda College as security for a loan to extend the rubber tree farm. One of the few times that a branch has altered the decision of a central officer occurred in 1965, when the Port Harcourt branch successfully protested Ejim Akuma's permission to the Assembly of God mission members to absent themselves from Sunday meetings.[4]

The central union occasionally delegated the Port Harcourt branch to undertake a mission on its behalf, sometimes pertaining to the resuscitation of another faltering branch. In 1950 the Port Harcourt branch wrote to both the Aba branch to submit the balance of its dues, and the Opobo branch to collect its dues. In 1958 a group was sent to revive the Umuahia branch. In 1947 the central union assigned to the Port Harcourt branch the task of making one of the three gowns for the chiefs. In 1959 the central union instructed the branch to repurchase some science apparatus for Enuda College at a public auction.[5]

The central union depended on the dues collected by its branches. At no time did the central executive itself directly levy its members. Although the Port Harcourt branch did not always contribute to the fullest extent of its means, particularly in the last few years, it did have a fairly good record. When the annual dues were 24 shillings 4 pence or higher, the branch retained 2 shillings 2 pence and sent 22 shillings 2 pence to the central union. In 1962 the union reduced the annual contribution of each member to 20 shillings, from which the branch received 2 shillings.

Several prominent members and officers from the Port Harcourt branch were elected to the central executive. K. Kalu, one of the long-tenure officers with five terms in office, served as an officer for two years in the Port Harcourt branch, but he no longer lived in Port Harcourt when elected to the central executive. Two of the most active branch officers—W. N. Lekwuna, president of the Port Harcourt section of the ACIU from 1948 through 1956, and E. E. Eme, secretary of that section from 1951 through 1958 and again in 1961—became officers of the entire ACIU organization—Lekwuwa as auditor and vice-president, Eme as assistant secretary. Since Lekwuwa was an officer in 1960 and 1963, it is likely that he was also elected in 1961 and 1962, two years for which records could not be examined. Two other members of the branch served briefly as officers in the initial years of the union. Considering the size and wealth of the Abiriban community in Port Harcourt, it is surprising that so few central officers were recruited from the area.

ROLE OF THE ACIU IN THE PORT HARCOURT POLITICAL SYSTEM

It is difficult to estimate accurately the size of the Abiriban community in Port Harcourt. In 1964, 462 men were listed on the membership roles of the Port Harcourt and Diobu branches. Not all these men paid their dues or attended regularly, so the lists may be considered to include many potential rather than actual members. Probably between 1,000 and 1,500 adult Abiribans lived in Port Harcourt, with many of them not registered to vote there. In a city with a potential electorate between 100,000 and 150,000, the Abiriban community as such had little political significance. No wards included a majority or even a significant minority of Abiribans.

The most insistent demand made by the Port Harcourt branch related to its proposed meeting hall. The assignment of plots of land by the Port Harcourt municipal council was frequently associated with insinuations of bribery and corruption. Even ministers in the Eastern Region government interfered with the allocation of land in the city. One of the charges on which the Ironsi regime arraigned the former minister of town planning in the Eastern Region concerned his interference with the assignment of land in Port Harcourt. Hence, when Echerue Emole, then acting minister of justice and attorney general, visited the branch in 1965, members asked that he use his influence to change the plot allotted to them in Gborokiri for their hall to a more centrally located site.[6] Apparently Emole never used his influence on their behalf, for the union did not receive a new plot.

Occasionally the branch asked municipal authorities to regulate the behavior of its members in order to preserve the favorable reputation of Abiribans as law-abiding citizens. In 1949 the union sent a letter to the superintendent of police, magistrates, and judges asking that any Abiriban found guilty of theft or obtaining money under false pretenses be imprisoned for ten years with hard labor.[7]

As with most other groups, the primary political demand of the Abiribans was for recognition through selection for office. Despite the small size of the Abiriban community, by working in coalition with other groups from Bende and Owerri Divisions, it achieved some success in having kinsmen nominated and elected as municipal councilors. Usually two Port Harcourt Abiribans served on each municipal council —Ina Obasi and either E. E. Eme, Onwuka Aba, or Oda Kalu. In addition, the council sometimes included a third Abiriban from the Diobu branch. The ACIU did not, however, play a significant role in recruiting these men to political office.

Ina Obasi and E. E. Eme, elected respectively for four and two terms as municipal councilors, were both long-time members of the NCNC, having joined the party in 1947. Although most municipal councilors from Abiriba did not have prominent positions in the Port

Harcourt ACIU prior to their election, both Obasi and Eme served as officers of their age grades in the Port Harcourt branches and in the central body. Obasi was president of the Akahaba age grade, which built the hospital, and Eme was president of the Egwuena age grade that constructed the girls' secondary school. Eme had been an officer of the Port Harcourt ACIU but never became vice-president or president of the branch. Obasi became a vice-president after he was elected to the municipal council, although his frequent absence from meetings, which provoked criticism, probably limited his active role in the branch.

In Port Harcourt the NCNC primarily performed the function of recruitment for several reasons. As an established party with a history predating politics in the city, the NCNC had mechanisms for recruitment. Competion between groups within the NCNC for nomination had become the accepted channel for recruitment. Since virtually all potential nominees were automatically supported by their immediate kinsmen, whether or not they were officers of their unions, it was possible for the party to select its candidates on the basis of other political criteria. A nominee identified only with his own community would probably lack the broad appeal necessary for election in an ethnically heterogeneous constituency.

It is not possible to cite the precise reasons for the success of the Abiribans in gaining nominations. Other residents and observers in Port Harcourt described them as one of the most ambitious and aggressive groups. As traders, they may have had more time to devote to politics. Their affluence and cohesiveness furnished definite political assets. Also the Abiriban community at home and in Port Harcourt had a record of consistent loyalty to the NCNC; no Abiriban ever ran as an independent against a party nominee.

The ACIU contributed to the material improvement of Port Harcourt through membership on the Council for Social Services. Abiriban traders, as one of the more affluent groups, presumably paid more than the average in taxes. But in view of the ACIU's negative effect of draining resources away from Port Harcourt for twenty-five years through its demands both in finances and in time, its material support appears negligible.

Compared with its material aid, the support provided by the branch through emphasizing obedience to laws was considerable. From time to time the branch forcibly repatriated legal offenders to Abiriba in order to protect the reputation of the community. The threat of repatriation seems to have acted as a deterrent since in the ten years preceding 1966 no such repatriations took place.

ROLE OF THE PORT HARCOURT ACIU
IN THE EASTERN REGION POLITICAL SYSTEM

Frequently branches were more direct and forthright in reminding politicians of their communal obligations than were the central unions. The demands made upon kinsmen usually pertained to improvements needed at home. In 1965 the Port Harcourt branch presented Emole with a list of problems requiring his attention as recently appointed minister of justice and attorney general. This list included the absence of Abiribans on the boards of established industries in the Eastern Region and in executive positions in the civil service, as well as the denial of scholarships for higher learning to Abiribans by the Eastern Scholarship Board. They also asked him to have the Amogudu-Abiriba road tarred and to use his influence to change their plot of land in Port Harcourt.[8] Earlier in the same year the Port Harcourt branch submitted the following resolution for the agenda of the September meeting:

> In view of the fact that the entire Abiriban people are ardent followers and strong supporters of the NCNC and in view of the fact that we have been trying our level best to bring certain developments in our town to lessen Government's burden of development, and in view of the fact that we have Chief Honourable E. Emole, Minister of Finance and Honourable Nnana Kalu, MHA [Member of the House of Assembly] that we should through the foresight of the Union and the influence of these gentlemen *PRESS* on the Government to site an Industry at ABIRIBA.[9]

The representative for Bende East in the Federal House of Representatives, Kalu Ezera, a lecturer at the University of Nigeria, also met with the branch to describe his efforts to bring amenities to the constituency. He took the opportunity to thank the Abiribans for their support.[10]

The Port Harcourt branch played a part in the recruitment of candidates for regional office. When Chief Ikpe tried to block O. A. Otisi's election to the Bende Native Authority, the first step for election to the House of Assembly under the 1951 constitution, because Chief Ikpe believed that Otisi, then president of the ACIU, did not pay him proper respect, the Port Harcourt branch sent telegrams to the Calabar, Umu-ahia, Itu, and Ifiayong branches to send delegations to Abiriba along with the Port Harcourt branch to resolve the differences. In spite of the dispute, the union asked Otisi to contest the election. Chief Ikpe then sent a letter to the branch enumerating his grievances and insist-ing that I. U. Eke, the vice-president, stand for the election. In its reply the branch reiterated that the union had chosen Otisi and that no change was necessary.[11]

Both Emole and Onyeije wrote to the branch in 1953 requesting its support for their nomination to the House of Assembly. The Port Har-court branch asked Onyeije, who was then principal of Enuda College, to withdraw in favor of Emole in the interest of the school. When Emole was nominated by the NCNC, the Port Harcourt branch mem-bers actively supported his campaign.

Periodically in times of crisis the Port Harcourt branch passed resolu-tions and sent messages expressing support for members of the Eastern Region government. In 1958 when K. O. Mbadiwe challenged Nnamdi Azikiwe's leadership of the NCNC and then withdrew from the party, the branch wrote a letter to Premier Azikiwe expressing confidence in him. The branch also sent congratulatory telegrams to Premier Michael Okpara and Emole on their appointments to office.

VIII | The Mbaise Unions
in Port Harcourt

Port Harcourt was the urban center in which the most numerous Mbaise community living outside its home had settled. While the potential market in Port Harcourt for their wares attracted the Abiribans, the Mbaisans responded to the promise of employment there. When questioned, Mbaisans either refrained from approximating the size of their community or offered diverse figures, ranging from 5,000 to 10,000 persons, based on such unsubstantial evidence as the remembered number of persons attending special dances. The growth of the Mbaise community in Port Harcourt probably reflected the population patterns of the city. Like most of the other communities in Port Harcourt, the Mbaisans emigrated primarily as unskilled, uneducated laborers rather than as educated persons whose skills could not be utilized in the countryside. Fewer Mbaisans had histories of prolonged residence in Port Harcourt than did the Abiriban traders, many of whom had already taken up residence there before the 1941 ACIU census. These factors influenced the role of the Mbaise unions in Port Harcourt, and the relationships among their constituent units.

THE INTERNAL ROLE

Members of all the ethnic groups constituting the Mbaise community resided in Port Harcourt, generally in numbers proportionate to their relative size in Mbaise. After the reorganization of the Mbaise Federal Union in Port Harcourt, clan representation became proportionate to the size of each community. Ezinihitte sent six representatives, Agbaja (the three communities of Nguru, Enyiogugu, and Ok-

146

wuato) sent six, Ekwerazu five, Ahiara four, and Oke four. With the exception of the somewhat reduced size of the Ezinihitte delegation, these figures approximated the distribution of seats on the Mbaise County Council.

All of the clan unions, the Mbaise Federal Union, and some of the town unions had branches in Port Harcourt. For many of the unions the branch in Port Harcourt was among the first founded. In addition, a new union was formed in 1954, the Mbaise Youth Movement, emphasizing the common Mbaise identity. Although other branches of the Mbaise Youth Movement developed, its evolution and most of its activities reflected the particular conditions in Port Harcourt.

Despite the greater need of the Mbaise people than of the Abiribans for assistance, the Mbaise unions did not fulfill these requirements. Generally most of the Mbaise unions lacked the capabilities of the ACIU branch. Theoretically most of the clan unions and the Mbaise Federal Union met once a month, but in actuality few held regular sessions. Up to 1966 the Mbaise Federal Union had met at infrequent intervals for several years and had virtually ceased to operate for two years. By the early months of 1966 the Ekwerazu Clan Union, now renamed the Ekwerazu Assembly, had not called a meeting for five years. Although other unions had assembled more frequently than the Mbaise Federal Union and the Ekwerazu Clan Union, most unions missed at least a few meetings each year.

The suspension of operation of the Mbaise Federal Union and the Ekwerazu Clan Union resulted from specific circumstances. Some sources disclosed that the inactivity of the Mbaise Federal Union proceeded from the inability of the branch to account for its expenditure of funds, which engendered charges of misappropriation. Other sources blamed the officers, especially the president, whom they claimed was incompetent. The even worse record of the Ekwerazu Clan Union in Port Harcourt reflected the general disarray of the entire clan, which had been precipitated by competition between Umuokrika and the other villages and by the political feud between Pius Nwoga and N. D. Ukah. Unlike the Ezinihitte clan's disputes, which suspended the operation of the home chapter and the central union but not the urban units, the conflict in the Ekwerazu clan between the villages of varying affluence undermined the entire apparatus of the unions, including the urban branches.

Membership was not even theoretically mandatory in most unions.

The president of the Ahiara Clan Union explained that while most residents joined, no one was forced to do so against his will. Members were not compelled to pay dues, although they were maintained at modest rates. For example, the Ahiara Clan Union levied one shilling and the Nguru Patriotic Union six pence per year. Some unions tried to collect supplementary contributions to finance special projects. For example, many unions launched campaigns to raise the requisite payment to the government for the installation of water pipes. However, only the Nguru Patriotic Union and the Ahiara Clan Union actually collected supplementary subscriptions from most of their members.

The size of several of the communities precluded assembling all members for meetings. In addition to the Mbaise Federal Union, the Ezinihitte Clan Union had only indirect membership. Each village in Ezinihitte originally sent five delegates to the monthly meetings. The size of the delegations was reduced to two representatives in June 1963. Even with this reduction the frequent absence of entire delegations or some of the members continued to present problems. Some villages failed to elect or appoint representatives until prodded by several letters from the Ezinihitte executive body.

According to the minute books of the Ezinihitte Clan Union, the delegates spent most of their time discussing various organizational problems: the absence of representatives, the failure to collect outstanding debts, and delays in holding elections.[1] Consequently they did not originate any projects for the improvement of Ezinihitte or Mbaise. Not only did the delegates fail to promote community development, but they never even discussed the affairs of Mbaise. Some members contended that the formerly effective union had declined since the death of its first president and election of the incumbent in 1963. The unavailability of minute books for the earlier period prevented verification of the claim.

In October 1954 the guests at a wedding in Port Harcourt decided to form an Ezinihitte youth association to further the development of their clan. The founding members later agreed to transform the association from an Ezinihitte to a Mbaise youth movement with the over-all goal of fostering the unity of Mbaise. Unlike most of the other Mbaise improvement unions in Port Harcourt, the Mbaise Youth Movement continued to meet regularly and to promote purposeful activity. Approximately thirty to forty members usually attended their fortnightly meetings. In order to emphasize their Mbaise identity, all membership was direct, and no committees or executive bodies were apportioned on the basis of the members' clan affiliations. As a consequence of their higher level of education, members generally debated in a more sophisticated manner than in most unions, adhering to the finer points of parliamentary procedure.

The Mbaise Youth Movement levied dues of one shilling a month. Unlike the other Mbaise unions, individuals who failed to pay their dues lost their membership. In addition, officers often undertook special collections to finance social gatherings or to assist members of the Mbaise community. Formerly the other unions also contributed money for the marriages, funerals, or illnesses of their members, but these contributions were discontinued, probably owing to the clan unions' limited financial resources. With their superior education, the members of the Mbaise Youth Movement generally had better-paying jobs than most other residents from Mbaise in Port Harcourt and hence could more easily fulfill their financial obligations. Receptions, weddings, and funerals called for compulsory attendance by members, along with a donation from the movement's funds. When other residents from Mbaise needed assistance, the movement sometimes contributed money, even if the needy did not have any affiliation with the organization.

Although the Mbaise Youth Movement did not start as a substitute for the other clan unions, it assumed that function in Port Harcourt, particularly in relation to the Mbaise Federal Union. Branches later formed in a few other cities and in 1962 at Mbaise, where Donatus Onu and E. O. Osuagwu served as president and secretary respectively, but these branches were not nearly as active. Most members of the general coordinating executive of the Mbaise Youth Movement came from Port Harcourt. Hence, the movement originated and remained primarily as a Port Harcourt organization, filling special needs created by the failure of the other unions to operate effectively. Assisting residents of the Mbaise community in Port Harcourt financially constituted just one of the functions that the movement performed.

As the primary representative of the entire Mbaise community in Port Harcourt, the Mbaise Youth Movement undertook as one of its primary duties the preservation of Mbaise's reputation. On several occasions the executive either replied directly to newspaper articles that were considered demeaning or contacted the relevant clan union to take action. In the absence of a functioning branch of the Mbaise

Federal Union, the executive of the movement also assumed responsibility for guarding Mbaise's interests. When projects affecting Mbaise were delayed, the executive often wrote to the relevant ministry to complain. When newspapers reported that the government had decided to electrify selected villages in the Eastern Region, the executive made inquiries concerning a possible installation in Mbaise. The youth movement also refused D. N. Abii's claim to be the eze of Mbaise.[2]

In addition to the periodic conferences to which branches sent representatives and the annual December meeting at home, the Mbaise Youth Movement as a unit also held an ekpe dance during the Christmas holidays at home. Attendance at this dance, like all other functions of the movement, was compulsory for members.

The Mbaise Youth Movement periodically planned economic projects. At one time the members agreed to build a hotel in Mbaise. When they could not finance it, they decided to form a Mbaise Trade and Contract Company through the subscription of shares.[3] But few of the members donated money, and this venture failed also. Their most recent commitment was the construction of a meeting hall in Port Harcourt. When the Mbaise Federal Union ignored the requests of the youth movement to try to acquire a plot of land on which a Mbaise town hall could be erected in Port Harcourt, the Mbaise Youth Movement assumed the responsibility. The movement wrote to Pius Nwoga, then minister of town planning, asking him for his assistance. Several months later the municipal council assigned them a plot in the Diobu section of Port Harcourt, doubtless after Nwoga intervened on their behalf.[4] After the first military coup, Nwoga was arrested and charged with conspiracy, forgery, abuse of office, and false assumption of authority. He was alleged to have signed a document for the release of a plot in the Diobu Government Residential Area to a private person without proper authority. He was later cleared of the charges in the general amnesty for Eastern politicians after Ironsi's assassination.

Reflecting the nature of the membership, the officers of the Mbaise Youth Movement tended to be more educated than were those of the other improvement unions in Port Harcourt. In 1965–1966, 75 percent of the officers of the Mbaise Youth Movement at Port Harcourt had at least completed a secondary education, as compared with 19 percent of the officers of the other improvement union branches from Mbaise in Port Harcourt and 58 percent of the central union officials. Five of the eight officers had secondary school certificates, and one a bachelor of arts degree.

Mbaise was the only community in Port Harcourt that was sufficiently numerous to participate in the political system without necessarily entering into divisional alliances. An awareness of the advantages and prestige this conferred reinforced the Mbaise identity. In Port Harcourt the exigencies of participation therefore elevated the Mbaise identity relative to the predominant clan referent at home. Since outsiders failed to distinguish between the clans, the image of Mbaise projected from the residents of Port Harcourt was of a single, united community. Consequently, while the dynamics of political representation and economic lobbying maintained existing clan divisions in Mbaise, they united the clans in Port Harcourt.

The most insistent demand made by the Mbaise community was for political recognition rather than economic assistance. The potential strength of the Mbaise parliamentary delegations and the possible influence that ministers from Mbaise could exercise increased the tendency of residents in Port Harcourt to appeal directly to the Eastern government rather than work through the Port Harcourt system. The appeal to Pius Nwoga for the plot of land exemplified this pattern.

Since Mbaisans did not have to subsume their identity under the aegis of a division union, the Mbaisan politicians usually had a more dedicated group of workers than did their associates. Their electoral successes demonstrated the advantages this conferred on the politicians from Mbaise. A member of the Mbaise community represented Port Harcourt in the Federal House of Representatives from 1957 to 1966. The NCNC nomination for the other federal constituency in Port Harcourt also went to a man from Mbaise in 1964. Several residents from Mbaise usually sat on each of the Port Harcourt municipal councils.

The careers of two prominent Mbaise politicians illuminate the benefits and limitations of appeals on the basis of the Mbaise identity. D. D. U. Okay, a market trader, made his way up through the NCNC ranks in Port Harcourt until he was acknowledged as one of its leading members. However, he never actively participated in any of the Mbaise unions in Port Harcourt or overtly identified with Mbaise causes. By 1957 he had decided to seek one of the two House of Assembly seats from Port Harcourt and, after much maneuvering, was nominated by the NCNC district executive committee. Azikiwe then personally intervened and asked Okay to step down in favor of the incumbent, because he wanted all NCNC members of the Eastern House of Assembly returned. The 1958 election had been called by Azikiwe to demonstrate public support for himself as premier after the secretary of state for colonies had accused Azikiwe of improper conduct in his dealings with the African Continental Bank. A commission of inquiry specifically accused Azikiwe of instructing that public funds be deposited in the African Continental Bank while he maintained control of the bank and the bank itself did not meet minimum specifications of viability as defined by the British administration.[5] Okay agreed to withdraw, and the incumbent from Port Harcourt was reelected along with the vast majority of NCNC members of the House of Assembly in a public endorsement of Azikiwe's actions. As a consequence, in a by-election shortly afterward Okay received the nomination of the NCNC to fill the seat of the representative to the Federal House, who had died in a car accident. In 1959 the party renominated him for this post, and he was reelected for a full term.

Descriptions of Okay's activities during this period indicate that he assumed many of the techniques of the ward heelers and political bosses in American cities at the turn of the century. Okay devoted almost all of his time to politics in order to cement his network of supporters. He generously paid people's fines and bought them bicycles and other items. When he performed political favors, he did not discriminate between people on ethnic grounds. Consequently his base of political support went far beyond the Mbaise community.

In 1964, when Okay stood for reelection, other ethnic groups demanded that it was time for a change. Three contenders, all from Onitsha Division, came forward. Once more Port Harcourt politics revolved around the Owerri-Onitsha division. Despite Okay's past inclinations for avoiding Ekwerazu clan and Mbaise activities, he asked F. U. Anyanwu to call a special meeting of the Mbaise Federal Union. Anyanwu, one of the wealthiest members of the Mbaise community, had just been made a chief in recognition of his contributions to various projects in Ekwerazu. Despite his personal dislike for Okay, Anyanwu called the meeting, at which he appealed for unity in order that the nomination would not go to an outsider. When the Onitshan contenders claimed that the nomination should be withdrawn from Mbaise, they inadvertently rallied all dissident members of Okay's group to his side. Okay and other members of the Mbaise community then systematically went through the city, ward by ward, attempting to ensure that candidates sympathetic to him would be elected to the NCNC district executive committee. Apparently these efforts were successful, as Okay was renominated. According to Okay, only ten members of the nominating committee came from Mbaise.[6] Many of the other members of the district executive committee supporting his candidacy came from Bende and Owerri Divisions. Hence, Okay's primary ethnic affiliation contributed to his renomination, but was not the decisive factor. He also benefited from the fragmentation of the Onitsha Division between three and later two candidates, after one of them had withdrawn.

For the same federal election in 1964 another Mbaise man, Godfrey Elugwaraonu, was nominated by the NCNC for the other federal seat within the Port Harcourt district executive committee's jurisdiction. The nomination of Elugwaraonu for the Ahoada central constituency seat constituted an even greater political feat than Okay's engineering of his nomination. Diobu, from which he came, comprised only a small portion of the constituency, which encompassed the surrounding predominantly Ikwerre areas. According to Mbaisan informants, the Mbaise Federal Union directed a campaign for Elugwaraonu such as it had for Okay. But as with Okay, ethnic support from Mbaise did not by itself account for the nomination, because Elugwaraonu was an acknowledged leader of the NCNC in Port Harcourt and had held several high party posts. Moreover, to the extent that any fragmented, impoverished group lacking a common identity could have leadership, Elugwaraonu was reputed to be that leader for Diobu. Members of the St. Andrew's Council social welfare teams attempting to improve conditions in Diobu recognized him as one of the most important leaders in the slum and attempted to work with him,[7] so that Elugwaraonu, like Okay, had a network of supporters beyond the Mbaise community that could be mobilized on his behalf.

Prior to 1964 an Ikwerre from Ahoada Division had held the seat for which Elugwaraonu was nominated. By the time of independence the Ikwerres had awakened from their half-century of political apathy and were demanding special recognition as the indigenous inhabitants of Port Harcourt. Although an Ikwerre had won one of the Port Harcourt House of Assembly seats in the 1961 regional election, many Ikwerres refused to accept him as a legitimate representative of their community, since he supported the thesis that Ikwerres were Ibos. By 1964 many influential members of the Ikwerre community claimed that

Ikwerres were not Ibos and therefore were entitled to special minority privileges from the Niger Delta Development Board. This board, a joint responsibility of the federation, Eastern Region, and Western Region (and after its creation in 1962 the Mid Western Region in place of the Western Region), was established to promote the economic development of the Niger Delta area, which included parts of Eastern and Western (then Mid Western) Nigeria. The charges of discrimination by the governments of Eastern and Western Nigeria against the minority ethnic groups resident in the Niger Delta area and the special problems of developing this ecological zone with its mangrove swamps and many small islands prompted the formation of the Niger Delta Development Board. Each of the three governments pledged themselves to giving special consideration to the area during the 1962–1968 planning period.[8]

After Elugwaraonu had received the NCNC nomination through his superior organization and greater activism, to the consternation of the numerically dominant Ikwerres, Nwobodike Nwanodi, an Ikwerre barrister practicing in Port Harcourt, seized the opportunity to propose to the Ogbaki Ikwerre Central Executive Committee that he should run as an independent. The Union endorsed his candidacy and, like the ethnic unions in Mbaise, actively campaigned on his behalf. In the end, numbers defeated Elugwaraonu, just as they had defeated other official NCNC nominees in Mbaise.

Hence, neither Okay's nor Elugwaraonu's political successes could be ascribed solely to ethnic factors. Both candidates could unite people of diverse ethnic origins behind them. The Mbaise Federal Union legitimized the candidacies with respect to the Mbaise community and mobilized assistance for them, but in neither case did it recruit them or assure their nomination or election.

The lower correlation between political and union office also manifested the reduced role of the Mbaise unions in Port Harcourt. Okay never attended meetings or actively participated in Mbaise affairs. Elugwaraonu, however, served as president of the Oke-ovoro Clan Union in Port Harcourt. Of the three Mbaisan members on the suspended municipal council, only Elugwaraonu was an officer. One of the former councillors was also an officer of the Ekwerazu Clan Union in Port Harcourt. Hence, only one-third of the Mbaisan politicians in Port Harcourt held office in one of the clan unions. As with the ACIU in Port Harcourt, office in the clan union might have followed from rather than preceded their emergence into political prominence.

As with many other unions, the concern of the Mbaise community with preserving its image acted as a prophylactic shield impeding the involvement of residents in unlawful activities. The Mbaise community was also represented on the Council of Social Services and thus participated in the limited social reform movement. Their most significant type of support for the Port Harcourt political system, however, derived from their successful participation in it.

Had the war not intervened, residents from Mbaise probably would have assumed a Port Harcourt oriented identity sooner than residents from communities like Abiriba. A larger proportion of the emigrants from Mbaise were workers and thus likely to join trade unions. As the trade unions grew stronger, the men from Mbaise might have perceived them as an alternative organizational vehicle through which they could gain security. As workers, many might also have preferred to spend their limited resources on a house in Port Harcourt rather than one in Mbaise. Furthermore, the lower level of development in Mbaise made it a much less pleasant place than Abiriba in which to live.

Part Three | The Impact of
Ethnic Unions
on Political
Development

IX | Ibo Ethnic Unions and the Institutionalization of the NCNC

From its formation in 1944 until its dissolution in 1966 the National Convention of Nigerian Citizens (NCNC) claimed to be a national political party speaking on behalf of all Nigerians. However, while the NCNC maintained the national orientations and aspirations of its founders, its solid base of support narrowed to the Eastern Region and, after its establishment in 1964, the Mid Western Region. In the West, the North, and some of the minority areas of the East, many people came to view the NCNC as an Ibo political party.

A second factor attenuated the NCNC's claim to be a national political force: its failure to develop a strong party structure. Even in the Ibo areas of the Eastern Region, the NCNC suffered from perpetual organizational deficiencies. In some ways the NCNC resembled a loose confederation of regional and divisional groupings rather than a coherent political party. According to one scholar, "Relations between NCNC National Headquarters and its regional leaders . . . sometimes took on the appearance of foreign relations between sovereign entities, rather than the passing of messages between different levels of an established hierarchy."[1] Consequently, the NCNC frequently experienced turmoil and indiscipline. One Nigerian columnist described the NCNC as a "peculiar example of human relations whose secret of survival lies in its mania for self-suffering."[2]

The failure of the NCNC to become a more effective political party and national political force vitally affected the evolution of Nigeria. Political parties generally play a crucial role in the process of political development in transitional societies. In many parts of Africa the establishment of political parties as a significant political force preceded the Africanization of governmental institutions by several years. An ineffective political party in Africa, therefore, diminished the possibilities of political modernization and change. Since the regionalization of political power in Nigeria contributed to its disintegration, the factors accounting for the metamorphosis of the NCNC, the first mass political party there, into an allegedly Ibo political party have considerable significance.

The institutional weaknesses of the NCNC as reflected in its relationship to the other most widespread type of semimodern organization, the Ibo ethnic unions, were many. The establishment of the ethnic unions preceded in most places the efforts of the leaders of the NCNC to organize local branches based on individual membership. Although the NCNC never encountered significant opposition by another political party in its home territory, it had to reach an accommodation with the ethnic unions. According to some observers, the NCNC as a party never transcended the sum total of such supporting organizations. John Mackintosh, for example, described the NCNC as a "gathering of clan and town unions rather than a party based on individual membership."[3]

In Abiriba, Mbaise, and Port Harcourt the relationship between the NCNC and the ethnic unions proved rather complex. Moreover, the role of the Ibo State Union differed considerably from what was assumed by many political opponents of the NCNC, namely, that it was a policy-making instrument of the NCNC. In order to assess the manner in which ethnic unions affected the ability of the NCNC to institutionalize and extend the scope of its support, the relationship between the party and the unions must be evaluated in three different situations: the rural area at the village and county council levels, the urban setting in Port Harcourt, and the regional level.

In his significant pioneering study Samuel Huntington posited that the achievement and maintenance of a political community or a "regularized, stable, and sustained coming together" incarnating a moral consensus and mutual interest depends on the scope of support of political organizations and their level of institutionalization.[4] According to Huntington, institutionalization describes "the process by which organizations and procedures acquire value and stability."[5] Huntington listed four criteria of institutionalization: adaptability, complexity, autonomy, and coherence. Institutions, procedures, or political systems vary in their level of institutionalization in direct proportion to their degree of adaptability, complexity, autonomy, and coherence. Adaptability refers to the cumulative capacity to accommodate to changes as reflected by chronological age, generational age, and variations in function. Complexity measures the number of organizational subunits and the differentiation of types of organizational subunits. Autonomy indicates the degree of independence from the interests of social groups, such as a family, clan, or class. Coherence involves the attainment of unity, esprit, morale, and style.[6] The indices of institutionalization applied here to the NCNC are the four presented by Huntington along with a fifth, capability. The concept of capability alludes to the effectiveness of the NCNC in formulating or representing demands, recruiting (nominating and electing) candidates to political office, communicating party and government decisions, and through these roles, structuring political participation. A consideration of the number and type of groups that joined the NCNC, or its scope, illuminates whether the affiliation of Ibo ethnic groups with the NCNC restricted the entry of non-Ibo groups into the party.

ETHNIC UNIONS AND THE NCNC IN RURAL AREAS

The establishment of the Abiriba Communal Improvement Union in 1941 preceded both the extension of the NCNC into rural Nigeria and the decision of the colonial administration to constitute elective local government councils. Hence, the ACIU preempted the role of the local government councils and became the instrument through which the trading community maintained its cohesion and tapped the financial resources of wealthy traders for the development of Abiriba. The willingness of the ACIU to cooperate with the NCNC meant that the party could maintain a political monopoly in Abiriba without establishing a functioning chapter there. Abiriba constituted most of one constituency for the Eastern House of Assembly and was grouped with Ohafia for a seat to the Federal House of Representatives. From the inauguration of the Eastern legislative assembly in 1953 until its dissolution in 1966, an Abiriban barrister represented the Abiriban-dominated constituency. Just as Abiriba controlled the House of Assembly constituency, Ohafia determined the nomination for the seat in the House of Representatives.

Abiribans considered themselves faithful and loyal members of the NCNC and frequently reminded their political representatives of this view. After his initial election to the House of Assembly, Emole joined the NCNC and became a minister in the government. As he grew in influence in the party, leaders of the ACIU found it increasingly to their advantage to stress their loyalty to the ruling party and to recommend the reelection of Emole.

When Abiribans wanted something, they customarily looked to the ACIU or its affiliated age grade organizations to provide it. The inward-centered orientation of most demands excluded the NCNC from having a significant role in their formulation or represention. When it was not possible for the ACIU to satisfy the needs of the community, such as the construction of paved roads or the installation of water pipes, branches of the ACIU would petition Emole to remind him of his obligations to his constituency. The officers of the ACIU held Emole accountable to the community through themselves. Hence, the relationship between the representative and the community was mediated by the ethnic union. Emole had enacted a ritual of accountability by reporting the services he had performed on behalf of Abiriba at ACIU conferences. Similarly, the contacts between federal representatives and Abiribans were usually arranged by ACIU branches outside of Abiriba.

Although Abiribans elected representatives to the local council, the county council, the Eastern House of Assembly, and the Federal House of Representatives, the ACIU and the NCNC were only partially involved in the recruitment for these posts. The lack of prestige and influence accorded by membership on the superfluous local council, along with the stipulation that members must be permanent residents of Abiriba, discouraged most Abiribans, with the exception of the illiterate farmers, from seeking election to the Abiriban local council. Furthermore, in order to further weaken the local council, the ACIU passed a resolution making the teachers in the Abiriban schools ineligible for membership. As a result, neither the ACIU nor the NCNC concerned themselves with recruitment for the local council.

For similar reasons few Abiribans enthusiastically sought election to the Owuwa Anyanwu County Council. At times, however, the ACIU recruited Abiribans for membership. In 1948 the ACIU decided to elect its president to represent Abiriba on the Bende Native Authority, the predecessor of the Owuwa Anyanwu County Council. In 1951 the ACIU directed its president to submit his name as a candidate and then reimbursed him for his campaign expenses. Subsequently the ACIU did not influence the selection of candidates for the county council. Neither did the NCNC formally contest these elections, although Abiriban councilors identified with the NCNC.

Emole originally put himself forward as a candidate for election to the Eastern House of Assembly. When he returned from England in 1952 as the first Abiriban with a law degree, he sent letters to all ACIU branches to announce his availability for political office. The ACIU endorsed his candidacy and then persuaded the other candidate to withdraw. In subsequent elections the ACIU's continuing endorsement of Emole probably discouraged other Abiribans from attempting to oppose him. Consequently, while the NCNC formally designated Emole as their nominee for the constituency, the party played a minimal role in his recruitment.

Channels of communication between political representatives and the community ran through the ACIU rather than through the NCNC. Emole reported through ACIU general conferences and at meetings with branches in urban centers, as did the federal representative. The Abiriban community gained another line of communication with the House of Assembly when, after an Abiriban was elected in 1961 to represent Aba, an urban center near Port Harcourt, the union members made him their president in order to benefit from his prestige and possible political influence.

In contrast with Abiriba, Mbaise was a larger and more ethnically heterogenous community. The pattern of ethnic unions in Mbaise reflected the ethnic complexity of the county council area. Clan unions were imported into Mbaise beginning in 1937 and thus preceded the establishment of both NCNC branches and elective local councils. However, none of the Mbaise unions attained the organizational complexity or assured resource base of the ACIU. Those that did raise some funds invariably spent the money for political rather than developmental purposes.

The NCNC actually had party apparatus in the Mbaise County Council area. Branches of the NCNC were formed in each of the nine local council jurisdictions constituting the Mbaise County Council, and representatives of these branches made up a Mbaise district executive. Since these NCNC branches rarely met except before and during electoral campaigns, the party never translated its extensive support in Mbaise into a corps of active members. Owing to the ineffectiveness of the local organization and its lack of relevance, leading politicians in Mbaise did not bother to assume office in it.

As in Abiriba, the NCNC never faced a serious threat from an opposition party in Mbaise. But unlike the situation in Abiriba, NCNC candidates in Mbaise often found themselves opposed by independents, who had bolted the party after failing in their efforts to be nominated by the NCNC. The threat posed by the independents haunted the NCNC in the Eastern Region, especially in the 1961 regional election when multimember constituencies were divided into single-member electoral units. As the electoral results in Mbaise demonstrated, an independent candidate sponsored by a large, relatively well-organized union could have a decisive advantage in certain constituents over the regular party nominee. The NCNC, which did not impose lasting penalties on independents, failed to counteract the temptation to oppose official nominees. Threats of expulsion had little effect, since the NCNC felt it necessary to reincorporate independents into the party after each election.

Most of the improvement projects completed in Mbaise and the amenities distributed were sponsored and partially financed by the county council. The local councils and most of the ethnic unions lacked the resources with which to undertake ambitious schemes. As a consequence, groups directed their demands for improvement projects at the county council. However, the campaign to secure as large a slice of the development pie as possible devolved upon the clan union as the most important organized subunit in the Mbaise system. Since all participants in the competition for development resources belonged to the same political party, membership in the NCNC was irrelevant as a basis for contending for scarce funds. Although councillors were elected by and officially represented villages, the councillors considered themselves representatives of their clan. Political divisions in the county council formed around the larger ethnic divisions, with each clan attempting to ensure that it received a share of amenities at least equal to its proportion of the total population. The clan unions, not the NCNC, thus became the most important formulators of demands in Mbaise.

With ethnic nepotism a principle of politics in the Eastern political system, the larger number of constituencies represented by Mbaise— four seats in the House of Assembly and two seats in the Federal House of Representatives—enabled Mbaise to realize considerable assistance from the regional government. This form of assistance was arranged by the prominent politicians from Mbaise, who often utilized their positions within the NCNC for the advantage of their kinsmen.

Mbaisans vigorously contested elections to the Mbaise County Council, the House of Assembly, and the Federal House of Representatives.

Two factors intensified the attractiveness of these positions: political office conferred more prestige in Mbaise than did office in a clan union, educational achievement, or wealth; and the link between political influence and economic gain was clearly perceived.

Village unions or informal groups of villagers generally recruited prominent members of their community for candidacy to the county council. Sometimes would-be politicians approached kinsmen to inform them of their availability. After the county council was constituted by direct election, the members selected the chairman from among themselves. Invariably the chairman came from one of the two largest clans and held another important office in his clan union or one of the legislative assemblies. The last incumbent was the long-time chairman of the Mbaise district executive of the NCNC. According to various informants, however, he owed his election to the intervention of the most important politician from Mbaise, who was a minister in the regional government and a member of the same clan, rather than to his position in the NCNC party apparatus.

The reapportionment of the constituencies for the Eastern House of Assembly before the 1961 election precipitated a marked increase in the involvement of the ethnic unions in the process of political recruitment. Problems in Mbaise arose from the new grouping of local government areas into constituencies which either split clans or included two groups that refused to accept each other's control over the seat. In their drive for political recognition, clans first approached the NCNC nominating committee for the relevant constituency. Often the clan would hold a kind of primary to choose its candidate before petitioning the nominating committee. Since membership on the nominating committees did not reflect the exact ethnic distribution of the constituency, the candidates selected did not necessarily come from the largest clan group.[7] When the NCNC nominating committee rejected their candidates for the 1961 regional election, two clan unions decided to sponsor the campaigns of their candidates as independents by donating money and having officers canvass clan members to remind them of their ethnic obligations. Both of these independent candidates won. The official nominees in the two other Mbaise regional constituencies in that election, who were returned successfully, were ministers in the Eastern government and incumbent or past officers of the numerically dominant clan union in their respective constituencies.

Prior to the 1964 federal election only one of the five native court areas, which had been federated to form Mbaise in 1941, lacked a member in one of the legislative assemblies. The excluded clan union selected one of its prominent members and presented him before the NCNC nominating committee for one of the two federal seats. Apparently the justice of their demands to partake of the spoils of ethnic arithmetic convinced the minister in the Eastern government from the larger clan in that federal constituency to cooperate with them, and thus protect his own position, at the expense of the incumbent, who was a member of his own clan. The other incumbent member of the Federal House of Representatives from Mbaise was also refused renomination: because of a split within his own clan over the siting of certain development projects and his alleged responsibility for the new regional constituency boundaries, one section of the clan refused to support his candidacy. Ethnic bonds could thus be loosened by political stresses.

Most political representatives in high office held more than one important position. Frequently they were officers of their clan unions and also sat on the Mbaise County Council. Communication, as in Abiriba, was rarely through the NCNC apparatus. Unlike Abiriba, however, ethnic unions did not monopolize the channels of political communication in Mbaise. Because the ethnic unions in Mbaise were less institutionalized than in Abiriba, contacts with political representatives tended to be more informal. The link between the representative and his constituency and his accountability to them, however, continued to be largely on the basis of ethnic obligation.

ETHNIC UNIONS AND THE NCNC IN PORT HARCOURT

Port Harcourt, the largest city and the industrial center of Eastern Nigeria before the war, was a city of rural immigrants, virtually all of whom retained strong ties with their village of origin. Unlike many other African cities, Port Harcourt did not have ethnically homogenous or segregated neighborhoods. Hence, the hundreds of branches of the various ethnic unions operating in Port Harcourt provided a crucial physical link and communications network between the immigrants in Port Harcourt and the community at home, sustaining identity with the more parochial community in the potential urban melting pot. Village and clan unions also lent comfort, assistance, money, and support to members in order to facilitate their adjustment to urban life.

In addition to the village and clan unions commonly found in the countryside, divisional associations proliferated in Port Harcourt based on divisional administrative boundaries of the colonial period. The key function of the divisional unions was to mobilize support behind members running for political office, particularly in a direct confrontation with someone from another division. In a population of perhaps 500,000, the separate village and clan groupings in Port Harcourt remained too small to participate effectively in the political process.

As in the countryside, the NCNC established itself as the only significant political party in Port Harcourt, but as a party which could not mobilize its adherents into a disciplined political force infused with a loyalty transcending ethnic divisions. The NCNC had few ongoing activities in Port Harcourt between elections. The greater difficulties in running independent political candidates in Port Harcourt, with its large population and its ethnically dispersed residential pattern, made the official endorsement of the NCNC nominating committee more important than it was in the rural areas.

A political entrepreneur in the ethnically segmented Port Harcourt arena had to go beyond his own immediate community and weld together a coalition. Frequently divisional alliances provided the core of these coalitions, with the divisions in old Owerri Province cooperating against the divisions in old Onitsha Province in the main township, and with Owerri Division and an alliance of Orlu and Okigwi Divisions constituting the major opponents in the Diobu slum area. The methods employed to weld together the multiethnic coalitions resembled those used by men who ran the party machines in American cities at the turn of the century. Like political leaders in traditional Ibo society and American party bosses, would-be Port Harcourt politicians cemented their network of supporters by performing services for them.

The newcomers to a particular neighborhood in Port Harcourt had needs and demands relevant to the city: more schools, better roads, improved sewage disposal, and increased police protection. To secure these amenities, they had to work through their representatives on the Port Harcourt municipal council. But many people were disenfranchised in Port Harcourt because they maintained their voting registration at home. Furthermore, municipal councillors represented constituencies in which their kinsmen constituted only a small proportion of the population. With the atrophy of the NCNC at this level and with the irrelevance of ethnic unions in the ethnically pluralistic neighborhoods, the constituencies for the Port Harcourt council lacked an organizational forum in which residents could easily communicate with one another to formulate demands or petition their representatives.

Ethnic factors entered into political calculations at two levels: patronage and recruitment. Recognition through election of political office was the symbol—both for the community and for the individual—of having "arrived" in Port Harcourt society. Election to the municipal council constituted one channel of political accession, but higher political offices —namely, membership in the House of Assembly and House of Representatives—conferred even more prestige. Port Harcourt elected two members to the House of Assembly and determined the selection of one seat in the House of Representatives. The Port Harcourt NCNC divisional executive committee also nominated the candidate for a House of Representatives constituency based on the rural outskirts of the city and including Diobu, the slum section. Before elections each of the wards in the township chose a member for the NCNC divisional executive committee, which then served as the nominating body. Hence, the most effective way to ensure nomination was to place a sufficient number of supporters, through intraethnic alliances, on the NCNC executive to control its deliberations.

In such a situation ethnic unions were not the significant actors in the nominating process that they were in the rural areas. Ethnic unions rarely designated one of their members a candidate and offered his name to the NCNC in Port Harcourt. Once a member had become a contender for a nomination, through his own political skill and service to the NCNC, however, ethnic unions would attempt to mobilize support behind him. But even politicians from large cohesive communities, like Mbaise, relied more on the network of support they had built up through favors and services than on the assistance of their kinsmen. Furthermore, since candidates correctly assumed that their kinsmen would automatically endorse them, it reduced the incentive to court such support.

Political communication in Port Harcourt could potentially have operated on the basis of primary ethnic communities, residential patterns, divisional ethnic groups, or constituency boundaries. Political communication with members of the municipal council or the legislative assemblies on the basis of primary ethnic communities nevertheless had limited effectiveness and probably could secure only certain kinds of economic patronage, primarily the jobs and contracts at the disposal of the representative. Because divisional unions rarely met, they did not provide a continuing forum for communication with politicians or among members. Furthermore, in Port Harcourt all political offices were based on geographic constituencies, which did not reflect ethnic divisions. At the same time, neither Port Harcourt itself nor particular neighborhoods within it sufficiently inspired the allegiance or loyalty of the residents to prompt the formation of effective organizations based on geographical units. The absence of such organizations forestalled the evolution of a sense of community among Port Harcourt's residents and deprived them of a forum in which to express their needs, thus reducing the effectiveness of communication between the representative and his electors.

THE IBO STATE UNION AND THE NCNC AT THE REGIONAL LEVEL

Some of the problems of operating in the large and complex political arena of Port Harcourt were magnified on the regional level with its approximately twelve million people. Just as the exigencies of political competition had activated the divisional unions in Port Harcourt, the Ibo State Union claimed to be the representative of "all the Ibos" at the regional and federal levels. However, the Ibo State Union did not and could not assume similar functions on the regional level. The grandiose visions of the officers, which depicted the Ibo State Union as the spokesman, defender, and arbiter of the Ibo people, were never realized in its actual role.

Although the Ibo State Union theoretically included every branch of all Ibo ethnic unions, only a fraction of the existing Ibo unions ever registered, sent delegates to conferences, or communicated with the central chapter. The payment of a registration fee and yearly dues might have discouraged some Ibo unions from joining, because few benefits accrued from membership. The officers and executive committee of the Ibo State Union never exerted any kind of control over the unions that did affiliate. Ethnic unions, which had formed in response to local needs and goals, resisted the occasional and superficial efforts of the Ibo State Union to divert them from their parochial orientation. Besides, the small size of the staff and the character of the leadership—which was predominantly businessmen with little education—were not such as to propel the Ibo State Union toward a dynamic role. Moreover, Z. C. Obi, the businessman who was president of the Ibo

State Union during most of its organizational life, resisted attempts to politicize it for fear that he would lose his control.

By its very existence the Ibo State Union symbolized the unity of the Ibo people. Its major ongoing activity, the promotion of Ibo Day as a holiday to commemorate Ibo accomplishments, signified this unity. But the Ibo State Union did not actively work to mold a sense of Iboness, and the eventual evolution of an inclusive identity cannot be attributed to efforts of the Ibo State Union.

Political opponents of the NCNC portrayed the Ibo State Union as the director and handmaiden of that political party. When a coalition of social and political organizations constituted the NCNC in 1944, then called the National Council of Nigeria and the Cameroons, the Ibo Federal Union, the predecessor of the Ibo State Union, had signed its charter. At this time, however, the Ibo Federal Union consisted of only a few Lagos-based Ibo union branches and was only one of some hundred organizations that became charter members of the NCNC. Furthermore, at its inception the NCNC had a Yoruba president, whose political party, the Nigerian National Democratic Party, also became one of the original organizational components of the NCNC.

From 1948 until 1954 many NCNC politicians held high office in the Ibo State Union. But again it would be deceptive to infer from this that the Ibo State Union possessed political influence. Politicians joined the Ibo State Union in response to the invitation of the administrative secretary, whose intention was to gain prestige for the organization, and not as a result of calculations that they would derive political benefits from membership in the union. In fact, when the NCNC split in 1953 over whether to continue participating in the Macpherson constitutional system, the cooption of political leaders to offices in the Ibo State Union proved to be mutually embarrassing to the politicians and the union. After 1954, when the politicians resigned from the union, the Ibo State Union and the NCNC remained two autonomous associations whose general membership overlapped. The Ibo State Union was essentially a cultural organization with an independent origin, role, and source of support.

Few issues in the Eastern political system were formulated on the basis of an Ibo versus non-Ibo ethnic division. With Ibos constituting approximately two-thirds of the population, cleavages within the Ibo community on geographical or religious lines energized the political system. Because of its inclusiveness, the Ibo identity did not constitute a salient political referent. Generally an alliance of several Ibo subgroups would confront a similar coalition, with minority groups joining one or both sides in a manner not dissimilar to the dynamics of the political process in Port Harcourt.

Political configurations, which divided the Ibo community in various manners and featured shifting interethnic alliances, obviously minimized the role that could be played by an organization representing all the Ibo people. Hence, the Ibo State Union, as an apex organization distinct from its separate ethnic union components, rarely participated in politics. On two occasions, in 1953 and again in 1958, when significant splits appeared within the NCNC, both sides canvassed for support within the Ibo State Union. In neither case, however, did the union as an organization take sides or try to mediate the dispute. The Ibo State Union, along with hundreds of other ethnic associations and cultural organizations, testified before the commission appointed by the British government in 1957 to inquire into the fears of the minorities in Nigeria and the means to allay them. It submitted a memorandum opposing the creation of a separate state for the minority areas of the Eastern Region, because the only basis for such a state would be opposition to the Ibo majority rather than any principle of unity or viability.

When the Nigerian Federation began to disintegrate and the Ibo identity became more salient, the Ibo State Union participated somewhat more actively in the political system on the federal level. After the dissolution of the NCNC-NPC (Northern People's Congress) alliance and the NCNC's rejection of the questionable 1963 census results, Northern legislators made a series of statements attacking the Ibo people, rather than the NCNC. Newspapers supporting the NPC and its satellite NNDP (Nigerian National Democratic party) in the West published articles claiming that the Ibo State Union controlled the NCNC and that Ibos monopolized federal posts. These attacks politicized the Ibo State Union, which responded by denying the allegations and by publishing two pamphlets to support its case. (The NCNC may have been involved in compiling the information for the pamphlets or in subsidizing the cost of publication.) In 1965 the Ibo State Union sent a delegation to Prime Minister Balewa to request that he use his influence to end attacks against Ibos in the Northern and

Western Regions and to restore the property and jobs taken from Ibos. The Ibo State Union's limited involvement in federal politics thus came as a defensive response to discrimination and attacks.

Whereas the NCNC did not become a truly national party, it was always more than just an Ibo political party. The Nigerian orientation of the party leaders militated against a closer connection between the NCNC and the Ibo State Union. Occasionally when it might further party interests, as in the 1953 and 1958 party disputes, individual leaders sought symbolic support from the Ibo State Union, but on the whole the Ibo State Union could not confer sufficient benefits to the party to warrant risking the political repercussions of association with it.

Hence, the formulation of demands, recruitment of political leaders, and communication between party and populace took place primarily on the local level of the political system. There were no regional constituencies or interests represented in the Eastern political system. Consequently, not the Ibo State Union but the village and clan unions in the rural areas and the divisional and provincial unions in the urban areas tended to perform these political functions. At the regional level the political representatives of the local interests sought to secure their own positions by obtaining amenities for their constituents and maneuvering for important positions within the NCNC. Regional politics subsumed the melange of parochial groups without subordinating their conflicting interests to a higher principle, such as loyalty to the NCNC or Ibo unity. The most significant political competition in the Eastern Region therefore ensued within the NCNC, as representatives contended for the scarce political goods available for distribution.

ETHNIC UNIONS AND THE EVOLUTION OF THE NCNC

The brief organizational existence of the NCNC, covering twenty-two years from its inception until its dissolution by the military government, suggests that the NCNC lacked adaptability, which was Huntington's first index of institutionalization. However, since the NCNC was the casualty of a military coup and a civil war, its demise did not indicate any inadequacy on the part of the NCNC but was symptomatic of the unviability of the postindependence Nigerian political system. During its life as a political party, the NCNC experienced two changes of leadership. When Herbert Macaulay died in 1946, Nnamdi Azikiwe became its president. After Azikiwe resigned as premier of the Eastern government in 1959 to become president of the Nigerian Senate and then Governor General and President of Nigeria, Dr. Michael Okpara assumed the leadership of the NCNC. Neither of these changes in leadership constituted the coming to power of a new political generation, which is another sign of adaptability. The brief tenure of Macaulay as leader and the important position Azikiwe held even before Macaulay's death diminished the import of that uneventful succession. Similarly, Okpara worked closely with Azikiwe before the premiership passed to him and was of the same political generation as his mentor. At independence many nationalist parties face a crisis of adaptability when they must assume a new political role and functions. The NCNC did not have to undergo such a drastic transformation upon independence. Independence was sought and attained in Nigeria primarily through negotiations at a series of conferences. During the terminal colonial period, political parties focused their energies on improving their bargaining position by winning control of areas through the electoral process. Moreover, participation in the government at both regional and federal levels came early.

The operation of the ethnic unions contributed to the capabilities and effectiveness of the Eastern political system in performing crucial political functions. In Abiriba and Mbaise, for example, ethnic unions provided forums for the formulation of demands and the recruitment of candidates to political office, which are functions generally associated with political parties. Communication between political representatives and their constituents also usually occurred through the ethnic union apparatus or on the basis of ethnic bonds rather than through NCNC channels. But the question arises whether ethnic unions did not at the same time prevent the NCNC from assuming these functions and thus inhibit its institutionalization. With certain qualifications, the decisive factor limiting the NCNC's capabilities seemed to be its inadequate institutional structure at the local level of the political system rather than the activities of the ethnic unions.

The NCNC institutional apparatus was geared for only one political function at the local level, the nomination of candidates before elections. Other aspects of the process of political recruitment, as well as the formulation of demands and communication, required a more permanent organization than the NCNC had in most places. Hence, the increasing involvement of the ethnic unions in politics often constituted a kind of functional compensation for the inadequacies of the NCNC.

Apparently NCNC leaders envisaged a limited role for the party and were usually content to allow the ethnic unions to undertake other political functions. The NCNC and the ethnic unions rarely competed to perform a specific function in the same political arena. The major exception was the conflict over political recruitment in the rural areas. Yet even there, if the NCNC had possessed a more effective organization, it would have prevailed more frequently over the ethnic unions. Ethnic unions confronted the NCNC with their candidates and sometimes bolted the party with impunity. If the NCNC had imposed a meaningful penalty instead of quickly reincorporating defectors after elections, it would have discouraged ethnic unions from departing on an independent course. In 1964, after the NCNC had waited up to three years to readmit most of the independents elected in 1961, besides inaugurating new nominating procedures, only fifteen independents contested the election.

Moreover, the inability of the ethnic unions in certain situations to perform political functions effectively did not encourage the NCNC to augment its role. The NCNC was not any more effective in the rural communities without strong ethnic unions. In areas where ethnic unions were not as institutionalized as in Abiriba and Mbaise, more traditional village organizations often assumed similar roles.[8] In Port Harcourt the inability of the ethnic unions to fulfill political functions effectively left an institutional vacuum, because the NCNC did not have an ongoing party organization. The NCNC party apparatus there atrophied between elections, in much the same manner as in the rural areas. Immigrants faithfully attended ethnic union meetings and clung to their communal identities partly because of the absence of alternatives in the Port Harcourt system.

The institutionalization of an organization also varies with its complexity, which in turn depends on the number and differentiation of organizational subunits, both hierarchically and functionally. Although the unions benefited from certain organizational deficiencies of the NCNC, they did not necessarily induce them. The NCNC never expended resources on fostering a stronger party machinery, particularly in the Eastern Region, because it was irrelevant to the party's needs. A shoddy party apparatus did not jeopardize electoral prospects, since independents petitioned to rejoin the NCNC after elections, and opposition parties primarily campaigned in a few non-Ibo constituencies. The NCNC, like several other African parties, was a victim of its own success. NCNC party teams generated so much support on their initial forays into the East that the party did not have to form local branches in order to win large electoral majorities.

Despite several attempts to organize the NCNC more effectively, party leaders were unable to exert control over local communities and to centralize power in party headquarters. In part this reflected the limitations of the party headquarters, which operated without sufficient professional staff and requisite sums of money for party organizational work. Most party leaders apparently lacked the interest or aptitude for the day-to-day drudgery of party building. Another significant factor inhibiting the centralization of power in the party was the nature of the society. Neither the various administrative systems imposed on the East by the colonial government nor the organizational efforts of the NCNC sufficed to overcome radically the decentralized traditional power structure of the Ibo, Ibibio, and Rivers peoples. Moreover, the absence of strong party branches at divisional and village levels rendered the central NCNC body impotent in exerting effective local control.

NCNC leaders were opposed in principle to dependence on ethnic unions. Such ethnic unions, even when affiliated with the NCNC, did not subordinate themselves to the party. Consequently many party leaders hesitated to strengthen further a series of organizations that collectively constituted the strongest potential challenge to the party's authority. However, despite their opposition to reliance on ethnic unions, party leaders never undertook the sustained work necessary to establish ongoing local branches.

The NCNC did not rely on the ethnic unions to compile its electoral victories. In fact, the relationship was quite the reverse. Ethnic unions worked within the NCNC because of its success. Independent candidates spurned the overtures of opposition political parties for financial assistance and affiliation because such sponsorship would have excluded them from the sources of patronage. During electoral campaigns many independent candidates stressed their support for the NCNC and their intention to rejoin the party if elected. After elections, ethnic unions usually pressured their candidates to reenter the NCNC with all due haste in order to minimize the negative consequences of infidelity.

Autonomy, another dimension of institutionalization, pertains to the relationship between political organizations and social groups. The more autonomous a political organization, the more independent it will be of any particular family, clan, or class. While the NCNC was rooted in the structure of Eastern Nigerian society, it was not subordinate to any social group within that society. As an umbrella party, the NCNC included within itself a variety of ethnic groups, classes, families, and associations. Membership by any one of these groups did not preclude a similar affiliation by other groups. Formal or informal membership in the NCNC by ethnic unions, like the other NCNC ancillary elements, linked specific societal groups to the party. The plurality and diversity of such societal groups within the NCNC deterred any one of them from dominating the party.

The flexibility and pluralism of the NCNC allowed the party to accommodate to new groups as they gained political consciousness. When the Ahiara clan in Mbaise demanded equal representation by sending a member to one of the legislative assemblies, the NCNC nominated an Ahiara man for a federal constituency in Mbaise. Similarly, when the Ikwerres, the ethnic group indigenous to the Port Harcourt area, awakened from their half-century of political apathy, the NCNC adjusted to the situation by nominating an Ikwerre for a House of Assembly seat. The willingness of the NCNC to readmit successful independent candidates into the party, while reducing discipline, also supplied another channel of access for politically active groups. As new groups became involved in politics, they identified with the NCNC and its procedures.

The more coherent and unified an organization, the more highly institutionalized it will be. At first glance the NCNC seemed extremely disunified. Yet the party also had unity and esprit. After cataloguing the problems of the NCNC, Richard Sklar appraised it as being, "a vanguard party in a tumultuous era. Most struggles for power within the NCNC have reflected conflicts of interest that run deeper than personality conflict and would have occurred in another form if they had not erupted within the party. By any fair standard the NCNC is distinguished by the quality of stable leadership and by the loyalty of the rank and file of the party to its elected officers."[9] The somewhat unwieldy operation of the NCNC reflected the pluralistic nature of Eastern society. Because the NCNC attained only a moderate degree of centralization, political action depended on the coordination of several power centers. Such coordination required more political skill and appeared less tidy than a hierarchical chain of command. At the same time, the relative decentralization of power localized disputes within the NCNC, which prevented them from disrupting the party apparatus.

Despite the pluralism within the party, there was loyalty to the NCNC apart from and transcending ethnic identification. The NCNC did not merely survive as a holding company for a gathering of ethnic unions. Membership in the ethnic unions did not constitute a prerequisite for membership or leadership in the NCNC. Within most of the local units there was a tacit understanding that groups would attempt to resolve disputes while maintaining affiliation with the NCNC. Office in the ethnic unions often followed from and reflected the political success, rather than the reverse.

ETHNIC UNIONS AND THE SCOPE OF SUPPORT FOR THE NCNC

The relationship between the Ibo ethnic unions and the NCNC did not necessarily limit the appeal of the NCNC to other ethnic groups. Since the NCNC incorporated groups into the party on a locality basis, affiliation of Ibo communities did not preclude a like relationship with associations in another area. In the relatively decentralized political party, what the NCNC did in one area had little affect on its activities in another area. In fact, the NCNC sometimes enlisted non-Ibo ethnic support through cooperation with ethnic associations. In the predominantly non-Ibo Ogoja and Ikom Divisions of the Eastern Region, the NCNC collaborated with various clan committees. In the Mid Western Region, the Urhobo Renascent Convention, the Warri People's party, and the Otu Edo were among the associations affiliated with the NCNC. Other communities in the East, Mid West, and West rallied to the NCNC without being linked through the medium of an intermediary instrument.

Although the NCNC did not attain the status of a national party in Nigeria, no other political party had a more national base of support. The NCNC was always more than an Ibo party. When the party formed in 1944, it had a Yoruba president. In the 1951 election its president, Nnamdi Azikiwe, ran from a constituency in Lagos rather than one in the Eastern Region. Three years later in the federal election of 1954 the NCNC defeated the Action Group, the political party based on the Yorubas, in its heartland of the Western Region. At that time the NCNC concluded a permanent alliance with the most important opposition party in the North, the Northern Elements Progressive Union. By exploiting traditional Yoruba rivalries and by affiliating with local parties, the NCNC secured a following in certain areas of the Western Region that it retained even during Action Group electoral

victories. The voters of the Mid Western Region rewarded the NCNC
for its consistent support of the creation of a new region out of the
minority areas of the West when in their first election they chose an
NCNC government, making the NCNC the first and only political party
in Nigeria to control more than one region. In 1964 the NCNC joined
with the Action Group and several opposition parties in the North to
form the United Progressive Grand Alliance (UPGA), which attempted
to campaign actively in every Nigerian constituency for the federal
elections. In 1958 less than half of the officials in the national NCNC
party apparatus were Ibo, and this proportion held for ministers in the
Eastern and federal governments overall. For example, in 1960 only
three of the ten NCNC federal ministers were Ibo.[10]

Even within the Eastern Region it was misleading to describe the
NCNC as an Ibo political party. In the four elections held in the region
between March 1957 and March 1965, the NCNC vote in the minority
Calabar-Ogoja-Rivers area ranged from a low of 48 percent to a high
of 67 percent. The NCNC always won more than half of the seats in
these areas, going from a low of 52.5 percent of the seats to a high of
84 percent.[11]

Several factors blocked the NCNC from achieving a more national
endorsement: relations between political leaders, the distribution of
power in the Nigerian Federation, and the punitive sanctions available
to political opponents. When Herbert Macauley and Nnamdi Azikiwe
joined to form the NCNC in 1944, they virtually ensured the alienation
of most of the educated Yoruba leaders because of the previous record
of mutual political opposition and personal animosity. Prior to the
formation of the NCNC, Macaulay had led one protopolitical party,
the Nigerian National Democratic party (not to be confused with the
party of the same name formed by Samuel Akintola in 1964), and
various educated Yorubas supported the Nigerian Youth Movement
(NYM) as their political vehicle. Azikiwe, who joined the NYM on his
return from the United States and Ghana, broke with their leaders in
1941, primarily over their alleged discrimination against Ibos and Ijebu
Yorubas. Consequently, the leaders of the NYM never countenanced
affiliation with the NCNC and in 1951 established their own party, the
Action Group.

The NCNC never had a firm base in the North, largely because the
animosity of most Moslem Northerners to Southern "infidels" precluded
establishing branch organizations of a Southern political party. In the

Moslem emirates the fusion of traditional and Northern People's Congress (NPC) leadership virtually conceded political paramountcy to the NPC. In that conservative area, the NCNC depended on its rather weak ally, the reform-oriented Northern Elements Progressive Union. In the predominantly pagan lower North or Middle Belt, when groups decided to express their opposition to the ruling NPC, they tended to support the Action Group rather than the NCNC.

The distribution of power in the Nigerian Federation permitted the NPC to exclude the NCNC from the North and allowed the Action Group to weaken the NCNC's position in the West. With the exception of three brief years, 1951 to 1954, British colonial policy promoted the evolution of strong regions rather than a unitary state. Nigeria's independence constitution vested most functions of government and residual powers in the regions. The advantages that accrued to a party from its control over the regional government enabled it to consolidate its position within the region. In all regions the political party in power strengthened its position considerably by the generous use of patronage through the networks of regional banks, marketing boards, and development corporations. People commonly believed, often with justification, that regional governments would refuse to allocate development funds to areas that voted for opposition parties. Conversely, constituents expected rewards in the form of more amenities for their faithfulness in continuing to return party candidates to the regional and federal legislatures.

Another important device used in consolidating power, particularly in the North, was coercion, together with related sanctions. Native authorities in the North, which had powers far exceeding those of local councils in other regions, refused to give opposition political parties permits for political meetings and rallies and denied food and sleeping accommodations to them during campaigns. Political opponents of the entrenched NPC frequently found themselves sentenced to prison terms on trumped-up charges by native authority courts, particularly before elections. In the West the Action Group and then the Nigerian National Democratic party sometimes resorted to manipulating chieftancy laws, customary courts, tax assessment committees, and local government police to harass opponents. The Western Region government suspended many NCNC-dominated local government councils on grounds of alleged irregularities. (It should be noted that the NCNC was less able to engage in such tactics, because Eastern customary courts lacked criminal jurisdiction and there was no local government police.) Once other political parties had gained control of the Northern and Western Regions, the NCNC was foredoomed to the political wilderness.

Relative to most other African political parties, the NCNC established a fairly competent political organization. Other African political parties have espoused more radical policies and adopted constitutions calling for complex, hierarchical, and disciplined organizational structures, but the attainment of a significant level of institutionalizaton has eluded all parties in sub-Sahara Africa. Reevaluations of the nature of political parties in Africa have called into question the typologies that magnify contrasts between supposedly mass and elite political parties. In contrast with earlier assumptions that mass or radical political parties had more institutionalized organizational structures with a greater ability to mobilize the population than did the elite parties, recent studies have depicted political parties in Ghana, the Ivory Coast, Senegal, Mali, Guinea, and Tanzania, which are often cited as examples of mass parties, as actually operating in much the same manner as the so-called elite parties.[12] For all African states, mobilization through a political party remains more of an objective than a reality. Local party branches have languished, while the chains of communication and command between the local, intermediate, and national political bodies have eroded. Somewhat ironically, the affiliation of the ethnic unions with the NCNC might have brought about a more permanent form of local organization than has characterized political parties that have attempted to establish more direct local control through branch organization.

The high level of economic and political expectation in the Eastern Region, combined with the scarcity of political goods, and not the existence of ethnic unions precipitated the dynamics of Eastern politics. Political affiliation could not provide a basis for the formulation of demands, because virtually everyone belonged to the NCNC. Hence, competition between groups within the NCNC, rather than common membership in the party, became the salient dimension of politics in Eastern Nigeria. The pluralistic nature of the society promoted ethnicity as the structuring principle of political competition. Ethnic unions served as convenient organizational appendages, but did not themselves inspire the politics of ethnic confrontation and compromise.

The unwieldy appearance of the NCNC caused many observers to underestimate the level of institutionalization attained by the party.

Although the relative lack of centralization in the party somewhat reduced its coherence, it enabled the NCNC to accommodate to the traditional political fragmentation of the society. Furthermore, the pluralism of the NCNC allowed for meaningful political participation and competition within the one-party regional system. Ethnic unions provided the institutional media for certain subgroups to maneuver within the political system. If the NCNC had been less able to absorb the subgroup maneuvering, it might have fragmented into two or more parties. Had such formal opposition parties formed, the political competition would have been more intense and less contained.

Although there were occasional bursts of ideological and organizational energy, the leaders of the NCNC conceived of the party primarily as a recruitment agency. In association with ethnic unions, the NCNC performed the function of political recruitment effectively in the Eastern Region. It incorporated almost the full range of politically conscious groups in the East. On a local level the party-cum-independent recruitment process sensitively reflected changes in political power among various groups and furnished a channel through which communities could enter politics as they gained political consciousness. On the regional level, the NCNC was able to balance and aggregate the many local interests into a workable coalition. In its decentralization of power, its emphasis on recruitment, and the coalition nature of the party, the NCNC resembled American political parties.

There usually was no direct correlation between the roles played by ethnic unions in particular localities and the effectiveness of the NCNC. Hence, ethnic unions rarely affected directly the institutionalization of the NCNC. When the NCNC failed to take advantage of opportunities to strengthen its organization, factors other than the existence of ethnic unions occasioned this negligence. However, the viability of the NCNC, operating as it did in a complex and formidable political enviroment, should not be underrated. The organization and procedures of the NCNC acquired some value and stability. Finally, the NCNC machine managed to work within the Eastern Region, a complicated transitional political system, which was no minor accomplishment.

X | Ethnic Unions and the Institutionalization of Local Government Councils

The foundations of the local council system, which was dissolved by the military accession to power in 1966, dated from 1950 when the colonial government put into effect the Eastern Regional Local Government Ordinance. This ordinance established a three-tier network of local government councils patterned on the English county council, urban or district council, and parish council system. The impetus leading to the adoption of this ordinance in Eastern Nigeria was the failure of the three earlier systems of administration imposed by the British. It later became the model for local government reforms in Western Nigeria, Ghana, and various other British dependencies.

Because of the special difficulties encountered by the British in Eastern Nigeria, they regularized the administration there later than in the other regions. Until ten years after World War I, there was a perfunctory system of direct rule based on a series of native court areas, presided over by a colonial officer, with a bench of warrant chiefs, who had been created by British administrative decree. This administrative experiment was terminated shortly after the women's riots of 1929. The riots clearly demonstrated the refusal of the highly individualistic Ibos to accept the centralization of authority, especially when it was concentrated in a person who was not accountable to the community.

British administrators then introduced a native authority system ensconcing the Lugardian principle of indirect rule and supposedly reflecting traditional ethnic divisions. Again the administrative innovation met with defeat. As a result of the frequently inadequate anthropological surveys and the very small scale of some Ibo communities,

182

many of the native authority areas did not parallel traditional bound-aries. Moreover, Ibo village-groups had neither a specific set of tra-ditional leaders to serve on the native authority councils, nor a traditional practice of delegating authority to representatives in place of the village meeting of all adults. Colonial authorities, however, ascribed the insufficiencies of the native authorities to their small size, which according to the British was inadequate to undertake requisite services.

Less than ten years after the native authorities had been constituted, colonial officers began to encourage the federation of the small councils to form larger units with a common treasury. In 1941 five native author-ities in Owerri Province voluntarily joined to form one such federation and took the name of Mbaise, which means five groups. In like manner, other native authorities became associated throughout the Eastern Region. But the enlarged native authorities still did not become the progressive development agencies that the colonial government had envisaged. As the native authorities were constituted, their members lacked the understanding and skill for complex development efforts. The residents' annual administrative reports for the period attest to the criticisms made of the nominated native authorities by educated men and their occasional refusal to cooperate with these authorities.[1] When the heady winds of constitutional reform began to blow after World War II, the native authorities came to seem anachronistic, both for their composition and for their ineffectiveness.

Elected councils also did not prove to be a panacea in Eastern Ni-geria.[2] Colonial administrators could not transplant the British system of local government to rural Nigeria at one stroke. Moreover, the original intention of the government to implement the reform gradually in selec-tive areas soon gave way to the unrestricted execution of the 1950 act throughout the Eastern Region. Almost overnight the newly elected councilors, practically devoid of supervision by administrative officers, had to operate a complex system of local government. In such a situa-tion the ineffectiveness of most councils and the excesses of others were predictable.

Framers of the 1950 ordinance amalgamated the existing native authority units in order that the new district and county council areas would be sufficiently populous to sustain social welfare services and development schemes. By introducing such inclusive local government units, administrators anticipated that they would be able to concentrate power in fewer bodies and would also be able to centralize and streamline the decision-making process in Ibo villages.[3] Instead, the 1950 scheme generated unending demands for secession on the part of groups who were unwilling to subordinate themselves to the alien county councils.

In response to these demands, the 1958 and 1960 local government laws discarded the inclusive counties in favor of smaller council jurisdictions. Under the 1960 act the 17 county councils envisaged under the 1950 ordinance were partitioned into a total of 107 authorities, approximately the size of the 1950 middle-level district councils. Both laws restored the supervising powers of the district officers in order to eliminate or at least reduce abuses of authority. The two acts provided for the direct election of both the local councils and the county councils in the new two-tier scheme.

Changes in local government laws and the passage of time did not extirpate the problems inherent in establishing democratic local self-government in a transitional political system. In order to assess and understand the institutional weaknesses of the local council, it is necessary to analyze the relationship of the local councils with the Ibo ethnic unions. Being the most prevalent form of organization in Eastern Nigeria, Ibo ethnic unions confronted both the local and the county councils at their inauguration as their most likely competitor for authority. The impact of the ethnic unions on the institutionalization of local councils is evaluated in light of the experiences in Abiriba, Mbaise, and Port Harcourt. Again, the dimensions of institutionalization applied are adaptability, capability, complexity, autonomy, and coherence. To ascertain capability, the following functions of government are appraised: receiving and processing information, making and implementing decisions, ensuring compliance with policies, extracting resources, providing for participation, and resolving disputes.

ETHNIC UNIONS AND RURAL COUNCILS

Doubtless the operation of the ethnic unions in Abiriba and Mbaise served to increase the capabilities of the local political systems in certain ways. But the question arises as to whether this came about at the over-all expense of decreasing the prospects for institutionalization of the local councils.

Abiriba had a local council, which along with those of several other clans and the provincial town of Ohafia constituted the Owuwa Anyanwu County Council. There were nine local councils under the jurisdiction of the Mbaise County Council. Because Abiriba was a rather large Ibo clan, the dominion of the Abiriba local council correspondingly covered a greater number of people than did many other local councils. With 900 local councils in Eastern Nigeria for a population of approximately 12,000,000, before secession, the population per council averaged about 1,333, in contrast with the 40,000 in Abiriba. In like manner, local council areas in Mbaise encompassed about 24,000 people, and the Mbaise County Council area included more inhabitants than did most other county councils. The unusually large population of Abiriba did not make the local council any more effective, but in Mbaise it seemed to enable local councils to undertake more significant projects, when asked to do so by the Mbaise County Council, than most local councils. On the county level the size of Mbaise prompted the regional government to review requests for assistance sympathetically, but it did not contribute directly to the effectiveness of the county council.

The brief period of existence of the local and county councils makes it difficult to evaluate their adaptability over time. It is relevant, though, to measure their adaptability in terms of changes in leadership and the acceptance of new functions. Even during the short tenure of the councils the level of education in the community increased and relative status positions of some groups altered sufficiently to effect a possible change in leadership. Although the local government statute listed about ninety-six functions, the councils decided which of them would be executed.

The Abiriba local council did not adapt to the potentialities for new leadership offered by Abiribans becoming better educated. In part this resulted from the strictures on membership in the local council that either evolved in the community or were imposed by the ACIU. With a few exceptions, illiterate farmers continued to predominate in the composition of the local council. For some reason Abiribans accepted the convention that all members of the council should be permanent residents of Abiriba and that the president should never have lived outside of Abiriba. This convention automatically eliminated the traders from membership on the council, along with most of the educated elite. Furthermore, the ACIU passed a resolution, to which the community adhered, excluding teachers in the Abiriban schools from serving on the local council.

Neither the community nor the ACIU placed similar restrictions on membership in the county council. The Abiriban delegation regularly included several educated members of the community. One of the Abiribans, whose higher education was sponsored by the union, even became chairman of the Owuwa Anyanwu County Council for several years on the basis of his ability.

The ACIU thus restricted the adaptability of the leadership of local government councils. It actively blocked improvement of the quality of members, probably in order to assure the impotence of the local council. Moreover, by attracting many of the civic-minded and educated men to positions in the unions and by convincing Abiribans that activities of the ACIU were of foremost importance to the community, it discouraged qualified individuals from turning their attention to local government councils. The ACIU nevertheless did not coopt many of the most educated Abiribans, particularly the university graduates, to leadership positions in the union. Hence, these men were theoretically free to focus their efforts on improving the quality of local government, but most of them failed to be induced to serve on the county council.

Ethnic unions in Mbaise did not pose an obstacle to the recruitment of qualified individuals to the various councils. For one thing, none of the components of Mbaise had the ability to gain its objectives by acting autonomously. Therefore none of the ethnic unions in Mbaise had the prestige and central position in their communities that the ACIU held in Abiriba. Furthermore, the relative inactivity of the ethnic unions in Mbaise meant that participation in them did not consume the high proportion of a leader's time that a similar position would in the ACIU. Consequently the same men in Mbaise who held office in ethnic unions were likely to seek membership on the local government councils. Even major politicans sometimes secured a place on the county council, to augment their other bases of influence.

County councils concerned with Abiriba and Mbaise abjured most of the ninety-six possible functions listed in the local government statute and concentrated on education, health centers, local roads, markets, bridges, and the maintenance of local courts. Their pattern of expenditure did not vary fundamentally from the general trends in outlays by county councils. According to a 1964 survey, rural county councils spent £4 million in the following manner: 36 percent on education, 24 percent on public works, 12 percent on health services, and 10 percent on courts. In 1964 local authorities in the Eastern Region maintained 14 teacher training colleges, 16 secondary schools, and 1,800 primary schools; subsidized 90 scholarships to universities, 56 to technical colleges, and more than 3,000 to secondary schools; operated 63 health centers, 146 maternity centers, and 278 dispensaries; supported 351 customary courts; and had constructed 963 bridges and 15,000 miles of road.

Yet the Owuwa Anyanwu County Council rendered few services for Abiriba. With almost half of the members from Ohafia, it directed most of its energies and resources there. It maintained four local junior elementary schools in Abiriba and allotted a yearly subsidy of £500 for the hospital in lieu of operating a medical dispensary. The only public works project it sponsored in Abiriba was the construction of new market stalls.

The Abiriba local council performed even fewer functions. Occasionally it acted as the agent of the ACIU vis-à-vis governmental agencies. When the county council decided to build market stalls in Abiriba, it directed the local council to buy and clear the land. But even then the ACIU deemed the local council accountable to the union as well as to the county council.

In contrast with the minimal role of the Owuwa Anyanwu County Council with respect to Abiriba, the Mbaise County Council sponsored most of the development projects in all parts of Mbaise. It originated the schemes for the creation of the Mbaise County Secondary School and the Mbaise County Joint Hospital. At one time it loaned money to students to finance university education. When it discontinued these loan scholarships, it instituted a secondary school scholarship program. The county council awarded small grants to secondary schools in Mbaise managed by voluntary agencies. At the time of its dissolution the Mbaise County Council was about to assume management of the thirty-five primary schools constructed under the Eastern Region's universal primary education scheme. The county council constructed four health centers and a post office. It maintained most of the roads in Mbaise as well as the water supply installations. It assisted the local councils in building several small bridges.

Both the hospital and the secondary school, however, could be completed only after the regional government had contributed substantial sums of money toward their construction. After they were built, the county council turned over management to the Bishop of Owerri, despite objections of the Protestant minority in the community. Like the ACIU, the Mbaise County Council lacked the competence to administer its most important projects.

Financial considerations rather than activities of the ethnic unions limited the scope of the local councils. More than half of the funds for the county councils came from the regional government in the form or rebates and grants-in-aid. Most county councils hesitated to raise the rates of the local taxes they could levy above 20 shillings. The Mbaise County Council, in fact, imposed a lower tax rate than did most other county councils in Owerri Division. Consequently there was a rigid ceiling on expenditures for county councils. The framers of the various local government statutes had intended the local councils to be agents for the provision of services rather than agencies to sponsor large-scale economic development projects, but even so, the poverty of the region greatly restricted the number of schools, dispensaries, and maternities that local communities could afford, given the high cost of building and the recurrent expenses of operating them, relative to the resources available.

The concept of capability refers to the manner in which the political system operates. Most transitional political systems have relatively ineffective institutions, particularly at the local level. Therefore, most new states have low capabilities. For the most part the activities of the ethnic unions contributed to the well-being of the micropolitical units by increasing their level of capability.

The effectiveness of government depends to some extent on the amount and quality of information available to the governors. The structure of the ethnic unions provided a communications link between the community at home and the emigrants residing in other areas of Nigeria. Branches submitted certain kinds of information at the request of the central unions in Abiriba and Mbaise and usually forwarded proposals from their members. Annual conferences to which each branch sent delegates allowed for direct communication among members.

In both Abiriba and Mbaise the local councils lacked such an elaborate communications network with important opinion leaders living outside of the home community. However, the ethnic unions did not prevent them from soliciting information. Furthermore, in Mbaise the ethnic unions actually increased the information flow to the county council by disclosing to it the demands and reactions of their members.

The possibility of an ethnic union assuming a general decision-making function depended on the willingness of its potential constituents to accept the union in this role. Such acceptance was forthcoming only within the context of a relatively homogeneous local community. Hence, the ACIU fulfilled this function for Abiriba in lieu of the local council, while the ethnic unions in Mbaise were more restricted in the scope of their decision making. This limitation reflected the lower level of integration within the clans in Mbaise, relative to the Abiriban clan, and the inability of most clans to achieve their goals without working through Mbaise institutions. The integration of Abiriba enabled the ACIU to supersede the more particularistic traditional organization in Abiriba and become the spokesman for the community. Later this paramount position enabled the ACIU to monopolize decision making at the expense of the local council, which was left to languish as an irrelevant appendage to Abiriba. In contrast, in Mbaise the activities of the clan unions reinforced the status of the Mbaise County Council as the premier institution.

The irrelevancy of the local council in Abiriba cannot be completely attributed to the ACIU. Local government statutes called the local councils into being without according them funds to engage in constructive projects and without clearly defining the role they were supposed to play. Local councils could levy a financial precept of four shillings per head, which would be collected and accounted for by the county council, but they did not receive grants-in-aid. Nor could they hire a staff. At most they looked after village markets and bush roads or occasionally acted as agent for the county council in local transactions.

Both the unions and the local government councils lacked effective sanctions to enforce their decisions. Even the local government councils did not have direct access to physical coercion, because there were no local government police in the East. The weapons that the unions employed were subtle ones—humiliation, embarrassment, communal disapproval, and ultimately ostracism. The ACIU attempted to use force and seize the property of recalcitrant levy evaders after a conference resolution had conferred this power on the union, but these measures, along with requests to make the payment of dues enforceable through the courts, never gained the approval of the colonial administrative officers. In the final analysis the strength of the sanctions available to the unions and councils depended on the desire of any individual or group to maintain association with their community of origin by fulfilling their civic duties. This weapon was wielded more effectively by the unions.

One of the greatest contributions that the unions made to the development of the micropolitical system was to increase the ability to extract resources. Estimated revenues of the Mbaise County Council for 1965–1966 were £110,972, compared with £64,989 for the Owuwa Anyanwu County Council.[4] Calculations of per capita revenue, using these estimates and the 1953 census figures, show that the Owuwa Anyanwu County Council had a slightly higher extractive capability. Although the Mbaise County Council raised fewer resources per capita, it still dispensed far more money than did any other organization in Mbaise. The total value of the projects completed by the ACIU, in conjunction with its affiliated age grades, exceeded £100,000, according to estimates of costs made by various officers of the ACIU. Over many years the ACIU probably collected more resources per capita from dues, donations, and special levies than the Owuwa Anyanwu County Council received per capita from its local taxes and rebates. In Mbaise the unions did not enhance the extractive capability of the system to the same extent. With the exception of the Nguru Patriotic Union, none of the clan unions completed a community development project. Yet even in Mbaise when a need arose to raise the one-eighth share of the mandatory contribution of the local community toward the cost of installing water pipes, the communities entrusted the various ethnic unions with the task.

The extractive capability of the ethnic unions did not divert potential resources from the local councils or from the regional government. The governmental bodies would not have received the funds tapped by the unions either through taxes or as a voluntary donation. The willingness of the community to make sacrifices and divert funds from private use, such as business investment or consumption, derived from the sense of legitimacy accorded to the unions as the embodiment of the unity of the community. An additional factor was the realization that projects made possible by these funds would probably directly benefit the donor or some member of his extended family. Only those projects that the regional government or the councils undertook to benefit a specific local community, such as the installation of water pipes or electrification, could fulfill the above conditions and thus call forth additional locally generated funds.

The contribution of the ethnic unions to the extractive capabilities of the political system, which was not made at the expense of the resource base of any other organization, is particularly crucial because of the frequent absence of alternative fund raisers on the local level. Transitional political systems suffer from a general inability to raise resources commensurate with needs. The government employs most of the resources that are extracted from the revenue-producing international trade and urban industries to finance the operation and projects of the central and intermediate levels of the political system. Consequently, the local level, which has the most limited resource base, generally remains the most starved for funds.

With rising expectations for social welfare services and amenities, the flow of resources in many transitional countries has shifted. The provision of amenities in rural areas has often come at the expense of freeing resources for more economically lucrative development projects. For example, in Colin Ley's study of Acholi, Uganda, the evidence suggests that the improvement of the standard of life in Acholi between 1962 and 1965 curbed the net outflow of resources from Acholi to the rest of Uganda.[5] As the government allocated increasing sums for social welfare benefits in Acholi, other parts of the Ugandan system were neglected. In contrast with this resource diversion tactic, the ethnic unions collected slack funds.

Ethnic unions helped to preserve the legitimacy of the local political system by maintaining the integration of the community. If members living away from home were not linked through the unions, the operation and evolution of the local political system would have ceased to be meaningful for them, and the potentially most valuable members would have been lost to the community. Unions also stressed the obligations of individuals to their community and sometimes to the political system. Branches encouraged members to pay taxes and to obey laws. It was unlikely, though, that the ACIU promoted more than a superficial tolerance of the county council. Furthermore, the ACIU attempted to inculcate the notion that membership in the ACIU constituted the foremost civic obligation, which operated to the detriment of the local council.

By providing citizens with an elaborate vehicle for political participation, the ACIU consumed the time and energy of many of its members, which diverted them from participating in local councils. In Mbaise, by contrast, the ethnic unions helped to structure participation on the councils, which enabled them to be more relevant and rewarding for members. Factors other than the operation of the ethnic unions also affected participation in the micropolitical systems. The Abiriban local council was so unobtrusive that many Abiribans though it had been dissolved years before. County council proceedings usually took place in English and followed parliamentary procedure, which reduced the ability of the less educated councilors and many villagers to follow their deliberations. Finally, councilors often failed to inform their constituents about pending council decisions on questions of concern to them.

In Abiriba and Mbaise disputes sometimes arose among individual members or subgroups within the community. Ibo society seemed particularly prone to internal dissensions. According to one anthropologist, "Ibo society is a delicately balanced compromise between the two principles of mutual dependence and mutual antagonism."[6] Sometimes these disputes temporarily disrupted part or all of the community. Although the various ethnic unions could not always resolve the conflicts among members immediately, they served as moderating agencies to which opponents could turn for conciliation. On several occasions the unions were instrumental in ending festering controversies. By containing many potential disputes and moderating others, unions decreased the potential burden of the councils and the courts. Furthermore, the county councils were noticeably reluctant to involve themselves in internal clan controversies or conflicts between constituent clans.

The level of complexity is another criterion of institutionalization. The structure and procedures of the councils were prescribed by law. In addition, the divisional administrative officers inspected and supervised the operations and expenditures of the councils. Hence, the level of complexity of the councils did not evolve in response to internal needs but was imposed from above on the communities. In contrast with this pattern, the frequently greater complexity of the ethnic union structures represented an indigenous development. Consequently the more complex ethnic unions sometimes operated more smoothly than the artificially grafted councils.

Autonomy, another index of institutionalization, assesses the relationship between the relevant organization and its community. The composition of the local councils as dictated by law included all segments of a community proportionate to their size. In at least a formal manner, therefore, the councils represented all the various groups and were autonomous of any one of them.

An even more valid measure of autonomy in this context would the councils' vulnerability to nonpolitical influences within the society, thus making them easily subject to disruptions. In Abiriba the ACIU shielded the local councils from the society to the point of virtual isolation. Perhaps this situation constituted the counter excess of subordination or an absence of autonomy. The perspective of the ethnic unions in Mbaise, in contrast with Abiriba, enhanced the relevancy of the local councils to the point that the activities of the county council could itself generate conflicts among subgroups. In 1964 alleged discrimination by one chairman of the Mbaise County Council in favor of his own clan virtually disrupted the council. The willingness of the larger clans to compromise and the lure of greater political prizes at higher levels of the political system somewhat stabilized the operation of the local councils. Furthermore, subgroups did not always remain united behind their objectives but were prone to internal dissension themselves from time to time. On balance, the ACIU shielded the local councils and thus increased their autonomy at the expense of severely restricting their relevance, while the unions in Mbaise promoted the pertinence of the local councils by forfeiting some of their autonomy.

The impact of the ethnic unions on the coherence of the councils should be measured in terms of both their internal operations and the manner in which the councils fit into the over-all Eastern political system. Available indicators seemed to manifest a low level of coherence. In some ways the low level of coherence of the councils was a reflection of the internal divisions of the society. It also suggested that the imposed institutions of alien procedures rested uneasily on the predominantly illiterate population. At council meetings the fixation on procedural issues pertaining to prerogatives, which often disrupted substantive discussions, testified to the councilors self-consciousness and discomfort. Yet despite this concentration on Western rules of procedure, the chairman often could not maintain order, as everyone attempted to speak simultaneously in a typically Ibo fashion.[7]

The prevalence of corruption in local councils also attested to the failure of many councilors to recognize their obligations to the community and to the council as an institution. Although a rise in the incidence of corruption afflicts most transitional societies, in Nigeria and Ghana it attained the proportions of a plague. To the extent that the clash between traditional values and the imported principles underlying the system of local councils gave rise to the corruption, this deviation from British-inspired norms of conduct provided one more indication of the failure to assimilate a foreign cultural standard. But the causes of corruption were far more complex.[8] Enough information exists to evince that corruption was endemic in the local councils, as on all levels of the political system in Nigeria. In Eastern Nigeria, according to Simon Ottenberg, "Almost every council position, whether of elected councillors or appointed staff, has its salary and also its additional income through corruptive activities. Persons in the council see these two as important aspects of their position. . . . Corruption and bribery fit into internal and external political conflicts in the councils. In fact they form a major political aspect of local government."[9] Though councillors did not often internalize norms of parliamentary procedure and conduct, they apparently had no difficulty adjusting to the almost institutionalized system of corruption.

The general prevalence of corruption at all levels of the political system relieves the ethnic unions in Abiriba and Mbaise of major responsibility for this integral but lamentable aspect of the political process. Officers of ethnic unions seemed more honest in handling funds and other responsibilities than council members were in executing their charges. The same people who at least passively countenanced corruption in the local councils were scandalized by hints of irregularities in ethnic union accounts. The contrasting performances of ethnic unions and local government councils in this respect prompted R. E. Wraith's assessment that, "In the East, moreover, the tribal unions have demonstrated that there are other, simpler, and more economical ways of promoting public welfare at the local level."[10]

The system of local councils in the East was consonant with the framework of the political system. The Eastern Region moved from quasi-indirect rule to a political system based on layers of representative bodies. These reforms did not eliminate the supervisory powers of the administrative officers, but at the same time the regional government never increased significantly the density or proportion of civil servants to population. Hence, the basic line of authority in the Eastern Region went through the two layers of elective councils rather than through a hierarchy of civil servants. In some areas an exceptional administrative officer was able to exercise power directly through the sheer force of his personality.

There are advantages to decentralizing certain functions to the local level of the political system, as they were in the East. By investing local communities with the responsibility for providing particular goods and services for their members, the regional government freed itself for other tasks that it alone could adequately perform. In Abiriba the role of the ACIU and in Mbaise the predominance of the county council diverted demands that might have overloaded the capabilities of the higher levels of the political system. In both Abiriba and Mbaise people became reliant to a great extent on the local rather than the regional political system for the fulfillment of their demands.

Despite their many inadequacies, the local councils in Eastern Nigeria compared favorably with similar local bodies in Western Nigeria and in other transitional political systems. Moreover, the councilors benefited from their experience, and the standard of operation in many communities improved. Both the Owuwa Anyanwu and the Mbaise County Councils were among the most successful in Eastern Nigeria.[11] From another perspective, the cost of this civic education was very expensive relative to the total resources available. Any cost-benefit appraisal of this investment in the local council would depend in part on one's vision of the goals that a political system should pursue and in part on an assessment of the degree of improvement of the local councils. One would also have to consider the feasibility of alternative modes of organizing the political system and whether the participant-oriented Ibos would have assented to administration through civil servants.

ETHNIC UNIONS AND THE PORT HARCOURT COUNCIL

As a new city originating in the colonial era, Port Harcourt was planned and governed by a British local authority (civil servant) and a township advisory board rather than by a native authority. Reforms in 1949 made Port Harcourt the first town in Nigeria to have a council with an elected majority. The uniqueness of Port Harcourt's administration was retained through subsequent local council reforms, during which the status of a municipality was conferred on it alone in the

Eastern Region. However, the Port Harcourt council was exceptional operationally only in the inglorious sense of being one of the most corrupt local council bodies in Eastern Nigeria.

Democratic urban authorities throughout Nigeria shared a deserved reputation for ineffectiveness and corruption. The four major urban authorities in Eastern Nigeria—Port Harcourt, Aba, Enugu, and Onitsha —all were dissolved by the regional government at one time for maladministration compounded by corruption. Moreover, several members of the Port Harcourt council were prosecuted on charges of bribery and the misuse of public funds.

Out of fairness to the frequently maligned urban councils, it should be pointed out that the complexity of the problems they faced and the lack of funds commensurate with the magnitude of the needs were not conducive to effective local government. For example, in the ten years preceding the 1966 dissolution, the population of Port Harcourt more than doubled, according to official estimates, and may have tripled or quadrupled if all the immigrants were counted. Immigrants arrived without funds, homes, jobs, and often skills. Since the rate of immigration into Port Harcourt far outstripped the rate of economic growth, the municipality could not have provided these immigrants with welfare benefits to cushion the adjustment, homes, and occupational training without a budget probably equal to that of the entire Eastern Region. Furthermore, the municipality confronted the task of constructing the physical infrastructure for a growing community. Its residents and the foreign companies, whose activities sustained the economy of the city, called upon the municipality to build and maintain roads, to provide schools and medical facilities, to improve the primitive sewage disposal system, to extend the water and electric systems, and to furnish police protection.

With its growing pains and other urban afflictions, Port Harcourt suffered from many of the same problems that trouble cities throughout the world. In the case of Port Harcourt, the magnitude of these dilemmas of urban life were aggravated by the exceptional rate of population growth, the absence of many elements of the needed physical infrastructure, and the pressures on the city as the center of the Eastern oil industry. Under these circumstances only a municipal council of urban specialists might have been able to cope effectively with the problems. Few municipal councillors had more than a secondary education, and many had attended only primary school. Residents of

Port Harcourt even elected a few councillors who had never attended any school.

Just as many people now consider New York City ungovernable, most residents of Port Harcourt apparently did not expect the municipal council to effect miracles of urban transformation. Their expectations and consequent demands were limited by their lack of urban experience and by their inability to identify with Port Harcourt. With all of Port Harcourt's deficiencies, many of its residents probably lived in conditions that were physically better than in their former villages. Some slum dwellers in Diobu, with their abject poverty, constituted the major exception to this premise. Many members of the Port Harcourt community, particularly the less educated, seemingly viewed the Port Harcourt municipal council as a dispenser of patronage, particularly in the form of contracts and market stalls, rather than as a problem-solving agency. Many elected councillors similarly sought membership for the benefits that would accrue to them as distributers of patronage and not for the services that they could perform for the community. Though some councillors were service oriented, and others concerned themselves with the conditions in their constituency, these seemed to be in a definite minority. Most councillors were either overwhelmed by the complexity of governing Port Harcourt or interested only in what council membership could do for them.

The financial resources available to Port Harcourt were grossly inadequate for the magnitude of its problems. The twelve urban county councils and the municipality of Port Harcourt together spent approximately £1 million, as compared with the approximately £4 million allocated yearly to ninety-seven rural county councils. Although the regional government rebated a larger sum per person to the urban authorities than to the rural county councils, in light of their greater needs and costs, a smaller percentage of the urban budgets came from recurrent grants than did the rural county council's. The regional government paid Port Harcourt six shillings per person, in comparison with two shillings and ninepence it granted to the rural county councils. However, the regional government based its calculations on the official census estimates, which grossly undercounted the Port Harcourt population. Since the Port Harcourt population was probably at least twice as large as the census figures, the actual allocation to Port Harcourt per person was almost equal to that given to the county councils. Recurrent grants constituted 23.6 percent of the total budget of Port

Harcourt and the urban county councils, while they paid for 50.2 percent of the expenses of rural county councils.[12]

Port Harcourt had the largest revenue of any local government authority in the East, some £275,000 in 1963–1964. In that year only thirty-six other local authorities had budgets in excess of £50,000, Wraith's dividing line for financial viability.[13] Lest the relative affluence of Port Harcourt dazzle the reader, he should compare the resources of Port Harcourt with Mbaise both absolutely and in terms of the tasks that their two local councils faced. With a population probably half that of Port Harcourt's, the 1963–1964 estimated revenue for Mbaise was £108,748. Moreover, Mbaise could not even complete construction of a secondary school and a hospital without considerable assistance from the regional government, in addition to its annual grant. Furthermore, the deficiencies of Mbaise never attained the crisis proportion that they did in Port Harcourt.

To further compound the scarcity of financial resources, corruption probably drained a greater proportion of the Port Harcourt council's funds than similar abuses cost the rural county councils. The greater incidence of corruption in Port Harcourt reflected the more frequent exposure of councillors to tempting offers and the opportunities to make larger sums than in the rural areas. In addition, residents probably scrutinized council dealings even less than inhabitants of rural areas concerned themselves with the financial transactions of their county councils. The ethnic heterogeneity of constituencies might have decreased the residents' interest in the conduct of their representatives and reciprocally reduced the councillors' sense of accountability to their constituents.

The sorry performance of most of the democratic urban councils led to their dismissal and the appointment of caretakers by the regional government. Their record also induced analysts like Wraith to dismiss the hope of their improvement. Wraith concluded, "there is no evidence in Nigeria that local government councils are necessary in urban areas."[14] Certainly direct administration by civil servants would have brought about a more efficient use of resources in Port Harcourt and a stronger problem-solving orientation. Since most of Port Harcourt's residents considered themselves only temporary urban dwellers, they probably would have accepted a more bureaucratic system of urban administration as well.

The ethnic unions played only a peripheral role in recruiting members and affecting the proceedings of the municipal council. The village and clan unions concentrated on rural affairs, and the divisional and provincial unions mobilized for regional and federal elections. At the constituency level residents lacked a permanent and operative institutional forum. By reenforcing rural referents, ethnic unions indirectly contributed to the urban malaise. One prerequisite for any fundamental improvement of the political life and material situation in Port Harcourt was a greater sense of responsibility on the part of participants in Port Harcourt politics, and this sense of responsibility would have been a product of a more explicit urban frame of reference. However, the very ineffectiveness of all urban institutions militated against the transferral of identity. Immigrants clung to their rural frame of reference and attended clan union meetings in large part because of the absence of alternatives in the Port Harcourt system.

It is not possible to delineate authoritatively the impact of ethnic unions on the institutionalization of local councils in Eastern Nigeria. As the Abiriba and Mbaise cases have shown, ethnic unions varied considerably in their level of institutionalization and in the consequent role that they played in the micropolitical system. Moreover, within the context of a specific micropolitical system, ethnic unions both contributed to and detracted from the process of institutionalizing the local councils.

By insulating the Abiriban community from the Abiriban local council and the Owuwa Anyanwu County Council, the ACIU inhibited the institutionalization of these bodies vis-à-vis Abiriba. The effectiveness of the ACIU in fulfilling the needs of Abiribans relegated the governmental councils to a position bordering on irrelevance for the community. On the other side of the balance sheet, the ACIU significantly increased the capabilities of the Abiribian political system. By doing so, it reduced the level of potential demands that Abiribans might have made on the county council, which freed it to concentrate on other areas within its jurisdiction.

In Mbaise the ethnic unions enhanced the institutionalization of the local councils, particularly the Mbaise County Council. By promoting the Mbaise County Council as the primary institution in Mbaise, the ethnic unions channeled constructive energy primarily to it, whereas in Abiriba community service was directed through the ACIU. Ethnic unions in Mbaise functioned frequently as adjuncts to the county council. On the other side of the evaluation, the intensity of concern with the activities of the county council reduced significantly its autonomy in the society, which made it more susceptible to disruptions.

The differing roles of ethnic unions in Abiriba and Mbaise derived primarily from two factors: the relative resources available and the level of community identity. Abiriba could afford to abjure from a more active concern with local government councils since it was fairly self-reliant in providing for its needs. The poverty of Mbaise, compared with the relative affluence of Abiriba, gave rise to a dissimilar pattern of relationships between ethnic unions and local government bodies. Ethnic unions in Mbaise approached the county council as supplicants on behalf of their members. Even though the Owuwa Anyanwu County Council had a larger resource base per capita than the Mbaise County Council, the funds of the Mbaise County Council loomed more prominently in its micropolitical system. To put it simply and starkly, for many ethnic groups in Mbaise who could not internally generate resources for improvements, the county council constituted the only hope, the sole alternative.

The ethnic homogeneity of Abiriba, which was based on a common clan allegiance, also strengthened the position of the ACIU as the agent and protector of all Abiribans. Moreover, without the ACIU, the dispersed Abiriban traders could not have renewed their Abiriban identity so easily. The heterogeneity of Mbaise, however, and the dependence on a Mbaise-wide pool of resources prevented any one ethnic union from assuming a position similar to that of the ACIU. Transactions at the county level in Mbaise were facilitated by the evolution of an allegiance to Mbaise as a unit. At least on the part of the Abiribans, such a loyalty to the Owuwa Anyanwu unit did not exist.

The difficulties of inferring a direct cause-effect relationship between the role of ethnic unions and the institutionalization of local councils is intensified by the absence of a correlation between the activities of unions and the effectiveness of councils. Weak ethnic unions did not necessarily lead to strong councils. Inversely, some county councils institutionalized in the face of institutionalized ethnic unions. To spell out these observations in more detail, village level councils virtually never became meaningful political institutions in the East, irrespective of specific local conditions. In some more traditional areas, like Udi Division, neither the ethnic unions nor the local government councils attained much effectiveness. Instead, villagers depended on the traditional meeting of all adults to make important decisions.[15] Abiriba's lack of involvement did not unduly affect the operation of the Owuwa Anyanwu County Council with respect to its other constituents. The Port Harcourt municipal council languished despite the peripheral role of the ethnic unions.

In the wider context of the general quality of life, the ethnic unions significantly augmented the potential for a meaningful and materially improved life in most areas. The ACIU channeled the wealth of Abiriban traders into constructive projects for the benefit of the community. Without the ethnic unions, Port Harcourt might have been characterized by widespread anomy and suffering. Ethnic unions at least made politics more meaningful in Mbaise.

Finally, even if ethnic unions, like the ACIU, somewhat inhibited the institutionalization of local councils, their communities probably gained over-all from their role. For instance, officers of ethnic unions tended to be more honest and civic-minded than local councillors. Ethnic unions, unlike official governmental bodies, were able to inspire self-sacrifice and thus divert resources from consumption to community development. Dependence on local councils decreased the total amount of resources available for improvements. Moreover, such dependence, when it transformed ethnic unions into supplicants, as in Mbaise, caused the unions to fritter away funds that might otherwise have been used for scholarships on political campaigning. Therefore, the Abiriban model comprises a testimonial to the benefits of decentralization and to the potential for rapid development that once existed in Eastern Nigeria.

XI | Ethnic Unions and
Political Integration

The political boundaries of Africa endure as an infamous memorial to the scramble for African territory at the end of the nineteenth century. Most new states in Africa lack historical roots reaching beyond the brief colonial interlude. Moreover, during the period of colonial control in Africa, administrators did little to foster a sense of identity with the new territorial entities among the diverse unrelated, and sometimes hostile groups they governed. Hence, in many of the new states citizens acknowledge an allegiance only, or at least primarily, to their immediate ethnic, linguistic, racial, or religious community. Leaders of these states cannot assume a residual national loyalty or even an awareness and concern with national affairs in a time of crisis.

For these reasons national integration looms as one of the most significant problems in Africa. Political integration refers to the process through which identification with a more universal community is super-imposed over parochial loyalties. As a general concept, political integration can allude to the formation of an identitive community on any level of a country's political system or for a supranational political entity. National integration specifically refers to a condition in which the commitment to the national community has become paramount for a majority of the people. The ability to command the overriding loyalty of its citizens constitutes one of the distinguishing characteristics of a modern nation; unless the state has become the primary focus of political identification for its citizens, the state has not yet become a nation. National integration does not presuppose a radical displacement of existing commitments; ties to smaller, more primary units need not be dissolved. An individual member of a relatively integrated community may still identify with his clan, family, linguistic group, or race. However, when conflicts arise between the parochial and the more general community that could potentially weaken or undermine the unity of the nation, the more universal commitment must prevail.

The only viable policy for the ethnically and culturally pluralistic states of Africa is to embrace the principle of "unity in diversity," that is, to accept the existence of subordinate subcultures and to impose a common nationality over them. As long as culturally diverse peoples agree that they constitute one nation, it does not matter which language or languages they speak, whom they recognize as their ancestors, or which religion they profess. After all, ethnic groups still exist in the most developed nations, including the United States. Many nations have survived without cultural homogeneity, including Switzerland, the United States, and the Soviet Union.

Contrary to many assumptions, ethnic identity is not a given, dictated by tradition, with immutable boundaries. Immediate circumstances structure and determine the nature of the ethnic group. As conditions in the social, economic, and political environment change, ethnic boundaries ebb and flow to accommodate them. The contingent aspect of ethnic identity contradicts the rigidity of the theoretical formulations that conceive of the encounter between parochial ethnic and national identities as a struggle between two fixed and irreconcilable forces.

The relevant question is which factors, conditions, and agents promote transformations in ethnic identity that will be conducive to the formation of a national political community. More specifically, under what circumstances does ethnic identity become generalized? Do ethnic unions inhibit the molding of more inclusive identities by locking ethnic loyalties at a more primary level? Do expressions of ethnic identity necessarily indicate the absence of a national community?

ETHNIC IDENTITY

There is nothing vastly original in the assertion that ethnic identity is a contingent variable. Other scholars have argued this point, some very eloquently. Aristide Zolberg pointed out that, "Primordial ties constitute a moving rather than a static pattern of identities; interaction between various identities does not occur once and for all when 'tradition' encounters 'modernity,' but goes on throughout the process of change." Paul Mercier emphasized the relative character of ethnic reality: "An ethnic map never reflects factual complexity." Clifford Geertz wrote about the aggregation of primordial groups into larger, more diffuse "ethnic-blocs" as a response to partial modernization and political independence.[1]

Some scholars view the process of ethnic generalization beyond the confines of traditional groups as specifically an urban phenomenon. Immanuel Wallerstein and Richard Sklar, for example, stressed differences between the nature of ethnic identity in rural and urban areas. Wallerstein suggested that the term "ethnicity" should be used to refer to loyalty to the new, more diffuse solidarity communities in the urban areas. According to Wallerstein, this "ethnicity" may aid rather than inhibit integration in Africa by assuming certain roles of the extended family and thus diminishing the importance of kinship. Among urban immigrants the ethnic groups serve as a major media for resocialization into patterns suitable for the city environment. By providing an alternate form of social stratification and by facilitating social mobility through communal improvement, ethnic groups help to keep the class structure fluid and prevent the emergence of fixed castes. Finally, ethnic groups furnish an object on which tensions can be displaced, diverting them from the state or the political party.[2]

Richard Sklar employed the expression "communal partisanship" to refer to ethnic loyalties in the rural areas where traditional values and ties of authority are still binding. In contrast with communal partisanship, "pantribalism" emerges in modern urban environments as an expression of ethnic group activity by those who are the most politically conscious. He considered pantribalism to be consistent with the affirmation of nontraditional values.[3]

A study of the Ibos demonstrates the fruitfulness of the concept of the contingent nature of ethnic identity. Moreover, it shows that nontraditional ethnic communities form in rural as well as urban areas. Not only do the cases studied illustrate the continuous process of transformation of ethnic boundaries, but they also indicate that groups can simultaneously adhere to different types of identity. The salience of an identity for a group depended on its usefulness in a given situation.

Prior to the imposition of colonial rule, the effective sociopolitical unit among the Ibos, the autonomous village, incorporated members of the same clan, who by tradition were descendants of a common ancestor. Confrontation with the forces of modernity unleashed by the colonial administration precipitated the formulation of a new and more inclusive identity, the Ibo people. Educated elements first embraced this new identity in the late 1920's and early 1930's; villagers readily acknowledged themselves as Ibo only in the 1950's. The acceptance of an Ibo identity did not, however, displace the more parochial clan identities. In most transactions the older identity remained more relevant. In units in which all people were Ibo, the acceptance of a common identity did not transform their relationships. Divisions still occurred on the basis of more particular commitments. Although ethnic minorities existed in the Eastern Region, they were rarely juxtaposed in daily contact with Ibos, except in certain border areas, because their home territories were geographically separate. Even in the most important border city, Port Harcourt, commitments associated with one's primary community of origin and economic considerations structured social relationships. In Port Harcourt the overwhelming predominance of Ibos made the issue of Ibo versus non-Ibo politically irrelevant in most situations.

In addition to identification as members of a clan and as Ibos, the administrative units created by the British furnished a third area for commitment. Divisional boundaries in the East varied only slightly through the region's several administrative reorganizations. In the larger, more complex political arenas of the cities and the Eastern Region, the divisions became significant foci of identification. The size of these political arenas relegated clan and village units to political impotence.

The evolution of Mbaise demonstrated the dependence of ethnic identification on the nature of participation in the political and economic systems. Mbaise, an artificial unit, was formed as a result of the administrative policy of the British to federate small native court areas, in order to establish more effective local government bodies. Only one of Mbaise's five court areas was actually a clan at the time of federation. By the end of the colonial period Mbaise, and to a greater extent four of the five former native court areas, had become endowed with many of the characteristics of ethnic groups.

Each resident of Mbaise had several different units with which he could identify: his village, his local government council area, his clan, his native court area, Mbaise, Owerri Division, and the Ibo people. At any one time he belonged to all of these groups. Which one became relevant for him depended on the exigencies of competition for political and economic assets. Within Mbaise the former native court areas evolved as the most relevant units for four groups. The fifth court area,

Agbaja, a union of three mutually hostile groups, remained solely an administrative unit. These native court areas were the largest units through which assets could be divided and hence participation organized. They directed their activities at the primary dispenser of economic amenities in Mbaise, the Mbaise County Council. Although councilors officially represented villages, they formed ethnic blocs to contest the allocation of resources. Gradually residents of the area accepted the former native court areas as clans with which they identified. When the clan-native court area occasionally became too large for the effective distribution of economic and political assets, other more local units, such as the local council areas, became salient for their members. For example, the local council areas in Ezinihitte and the villages in other clans sometimes contested existing arrangements, even though their action destroyed the effectiveness of the clan as a bargaining agent.

Outside of the home area, the more inclusive Mbaise identity increased in importance relative to the otherwise predominant clan divisions. In the more complex, heterogeneous political arenas of Port Harcourt and the Eastern Region, persons assumed the Mbaise identity. Just as the exigencies of political participation divided the clans in Mbaise, it united them in the larger arena, where Mbaise's position as the largest cohesive community in the Eastern Region eliminated the necessity for joining a divisional alliance and thus conferred certain advantages.

The evidence of the Ibos indicates that when all other factors are equal, the ethnic identity assumed in a particular situation is the one most relevant for political participation. The unit most relevant for such participation is the most inclusive level at which the assets of the system can still be shared. Consequently, in any political system integration depends in part on increasingly inclusive units becoming functional for participation. In Mbaise the native court areas gradually assumed the dimensions of the clans, because they became the most relevant units for political participation in the local political system. Members of the various villages constituting the native court areas learned to cooperate with one another and to communicate on political matters when political utility provided the incentive. Although administrative efficacy had called Mbaise into being, individuals and groups within this county area latched on to the Mbaise identity when it became politically expedient. In Abiriba the ACIU performed adequately most functions of government in the local political system. As a consequence, the more inclusive unit of government, the Owuwa Anyanwu County Council, did not assume a similar role to the Mbaise County Council. For this reason, no incentive arose for the Abiribans to subordinate their identity to the more inclusive one in the rural area. In Port Harcourt, Abiribans allied with other groups from Bende Division or old Owerri Province. Immigrants almost automatically coalesced according to divisional origins in political contests in urban areas, because this was the suitable unit for participation. Iboness rarely became a salient referent within the Eastern political system owing to its lack of relevance for political purposes. On the regional level, just as in Port Harcourt, groups usually allied on the basis of divisional and provincial origins, with coalitions of Ibo and minority groups confronting similarly constituted alliances.

Other studies of Nigerian and African political systems have also demonstrated a correlation between political expediency and the nature of political identification. In Enugu, the capital of the Eastern Region, the division between locals or native sons and outsiders or strangers was the politically most significant distinction both in city politics and in the Nigerian Coal Miners' Union. However, the definition of what constituted a local man or a stranger changed in response to political circumstances. The same man from Awka who organized a protest by the local people against their neglect by the stranger-dominated NCNC, a few years later set up the Enugu Strangers' Organization.[4] In his study of a rural district in the Saloum region of Senegal, Jonathan Barker observed that the integration occurring among groups of contiguous villages resulted primarily from administrative requirements and the pressures of commerce and transport rather than from ties of custom and kinship. Joan Vincent's study of Bugondo, a town in the Teso District of Uganda, indicated that individuals employed an ethnic frame of reference only in situations that rewarded such an emphasis. The hostility and ethnic competition among immigrants from the Malawi, Lozi, and Bemba areas of Zambia in Luanshya, a town in the Copperbelt which A. L. Epstein studied, followed from efforts by members of these groups to secure or defend positions in the mines. Although the immigrants from Malawi had no traditional unity, they described themselves and were referred to by their national designation (then Nyasaland) rather than by their ethnic one, since they constituted an economic elite.[5] As the number of micropolitical studies increases, more cases of conscious manipulation of ethnic identity in accordance with political expediency should be discovered.

POLITICAL INTEGRATION

The mere creation of an ethnic union did not necessarily contribute to either the integration or the enhanced relevance of the community represented by that union. Ethnic unions formed on all levels of the political system to further the interests of villages, clans, counties, divisions, and regions. Many of them operated side by side, with an individual eligible for membership in several of them. Some people, as in Mbaise, actually joined several unions and participated in their activities. Obviously, then, another factor besides the mere existence of an ethnic union determined the salience of a particular ethnic identity and dictated the individual's and group's selection of one kind of ethnic union as a suitable political instrument in any situation.

One should not infer a cause-and-effect relationship when a new union appeared during the same period that an identity assumed greater relevance for a group. The Ibo State Union, for example, originated just as people began to proclaim their allegiance to this inclusive community. Officers of the Ibo State Union asserted that the activities of the union encouraged the formation of the local Ibo unions and the acceptance of an Ibo identity. Despite these elaborate claims, however, no evidence exists to substantiate the contention that the Ibo State Union significantly advanced the cause of Ibo unity. The assumption of an Ibo identity ensued from the social, political, and economic changes accompanying colonial rule. Furthermore, the Ibo State Union never controlled or directly influenced local level Ibo unions. No matter what campaigns or activities were undertaken by the Ibo State Union to promote Ibo unity, it would have failed to undermine the prevalence of more parochial identities. In fact, the very weakness of the Ibo State Union vis-à-vis other, more particular Ibo unions reflected the relative lack of importance of the Ibo/non-Ibo division within the Eastern political system.

Similarly no correlation existed between the salience of the Mbaise identity in Port Harcourt, relative to the rural home community, and the effectiveness of the two Mbaise Federal Union branches. Despite the ongoing involvement of several Mbaisans in Port Harcourt politics and the acknowledgement there of the Mbaise identity, the Port Harcourt branch of the Mbaise Federal Union virtually ceased operating. Even in its weakened organizational state, though, it could occasionally be reactivated in Port Harcourt when political conditions made this advantageous.

Although residents commonly grouped according to divisional origins in Port Harcourt politics, the divisional unions there, like the Mbaise Federal Union in the years prior to the suspension of elective politics, were activated only during electoral campaigns. Something resembling a division of labor evolved in Port Harcourt between the village and clan unions, on the one hand, and divisional and provincial unions on the other. Moreover, primary ethnic unions served as mutual aid associations and as links with the community of origin. Divisional and provincial unions operated as political vehicles within the NCNC organization. Thus, aside from politicking, members of the same division shared few common activities. This relatively low level of social integration on the divisional level did not, however, impede their political cooperation.

The strength and influence of a particular ethnic union depended on a number of factors. The same forces of social change that activated the desire for economic amenities and for political recognition also called the ethnic unions into being. As long as acquisition of these goals could be facilitated by participation in or through a specific union, the union flourished. No correlation existed between the traditional unity of an area and the political relevance of the union. Other factors, like the size of the political arena and the needs of individuals in particular environments, determined to a great extent both the relevance of an identity in a specific situation and the resulting suitability of an ethnic union as an instrument for political participation.

Ethnic unions in Mbaise, for example, grew in importance as the clan unit was perceived as a valuable unit for political competition. Since the village was too small and the county too inclusive for partitioning political spoils, their corresponding ethnic unions tended to languish in Mbaise. On those occasions when the clan itself was too inclusive for the distribution of amenities, the clan unions could not prevent dissident ethnic groups from undermining the unity of the clan and immobilizing the clan union.

Ethnic unions cannot be entirely discounted as forces for unity and integration. Out of the five constituent court areas of Mbaise, only one, Agbaja, failed to develop a clan identity. Significantly Agbaja was also the only court area without a clan union. For a few years an Agbaja Clan

Union did exist in name, but in fact it was merely the Enyiogugu Clan Union operating under the more inclusive title. Again it is difficult to infer a cause-and-effect relationship. No one in Mbaise could recall any attempt to establish a genuine Agbaja union embracing all parts of the unit, so that the nonexistence of such an organization may just have been owing to a lack of initiative or the decision of Joseph Iwunna, one of the earliest clan union and political leaders in the area, to constitute a Nguru Patriotic Union in preference to an Agbaja union.

Perhaps the same factors that inhibited the evolution of an Agbaja identity also deterred the establishment of an Agbaja union. The history of Agbaja provided several divisive influences. Both Nguru and Enyiogugu had attained a greater degree of unity as traditional clans prior to their inclusion in the Agbaja native court area than had most other constituent units of Mbaise. The third section of Agbaja, the three towns of Okwuato, traditionally felt closer ties with Ezinihitte than with Enyiogugu or Nguru and thus was invited to participate in the Ezinihitte Clan Union. People in both Nguru and Enyiogugu resented their incorporation in Agbaja. Leaders of the Nguru clan contended that their inclusion in the Agbaja unit represented a form of punishment for the destruction of the original court building at Nguru, which had been razed during the women's riots. To complicate matters further, the meeting hall and treasury for Mbaise were briefly located in Enyiogugu, which was affronted to the point of excluding itself from many Mbaise activities when the buildings were transferred to Aboh. Both Enyiogugu and Nguru constantly petitioned the Mbaise County Council and Mbaise Federal Union for recognition as independent and equal components of Mbaise. Moreover, Nguru by itself was almost as large as Ahiara and thus relatively able to compete as a separate political unit.

In other cases the formation of an ethnic union actually helped to unify the group involved, at least in a minimal manner. In Mbaise clan unions fostered assimilation to the clan identity by sponsoring festivals, ceremonies, and other activities. At the county level the Mbaise Federal Union served as the symbol of unity for the entire community, even while at home. Activities of the Abiriba Communal Improvement Union reinforced the unity of the clan.

In most situations when other social, political, and economic factors made the unity of a specific group advantageous, the operation of an ethnic union for that group probably facilitated its political integration. Ethnic unions could not, however, by their mere existence, call a vital identity into being and foster its salience in a political context. The political strength of ethnic unions, like ethnic identity itself, operated as a dependent variable.

Ethnic unions did not by their activities turn Port Harcourt into a cauldron of communal tension.[6] Indeed, for a city afflicted with so many pressing social and economic needs, Port Harcourt remained amazingly free of violence and political tension. In 1966 when residents of the Diobu slum finally rioted, the issue that provoked their confrontation with the police and the military was police brutality. Also in the aftermath of the massacre later in 1966 of about thirty thousand Easterners in the North, with others returning home often mutilated and devoid of property, residents arose and murdered a few Hausa traders, but this event must be evaluated in the context of the initial massacre.

Divisional ethnic unions operated as political subgroups within the NCNC to maximize positions and nominations for their members. The intensity of the political conflict was mitigated by the common NCNC allegiance and by the need even for divisional groups to cooperate with similar units to gain their political objectives. If ethnic unions prompted ethnic competition and confrontation, they also induced political compromise and accommodation. Ethnic unions commonly traded support from one another for a specific political goal. Individuals also held multiple allegiances, and those with the strongest emotional appeal were not necessarily the units through which the individuals competed politically. Therefore, participation in politics through the more inclusive divisional union, rather than through the primary village or clan unions, actually increased the ability of groups to compromise and accommodate.

CULTURE AND INTEGRATION

The evidence from the case studies in Abiriba, Mbaise, and Port Harcourt indicates that political integration often correlates with units of political cooperation. These units of political cooperation frequently coalesce on the basis of political expediency and therefore do not reflect previous traditional clusters. Hence, integration seems to require an ability to communicate on political matters and an incentive to do so in ever-widening associations, but does not depend on general cultural homogeneity. Ethnicity as a political factor operates more as an ordering mechanism under normal circumstances than as a value system. Since loyalty to a parochial community does not relate directly to the subject of political acculturation, the two are mutually compatible. To clarify these statements, it is necessary to distinguish more clearly between culture, society, and political relationships.

Karl Deutsch's model of the foundations of nationality differed with this prognosis because he identified culture and community with nationality. Deutsch defined a nationality or a people as a large group of persons linked by complementary habits and facilities of communication. Membership in a people depended on the ability to communicate more effectively on a wide range of subjects with other members than with outsiders. This ability to communicate rested on a similarity of economic and social preferences and values, along with the existence of unbroken chains of connection. In Deutsch's view, a people was a large community rather than a large society. In fact, for Deutsch culture and community described a single complex of processes, with culture referring to the configuration of preferences and values, and community emphasizing the aspects of communication. A society, in contrast, denoted a group of people who had learned to work together on a more limited range of subjects primarily relating to the division of labor and the distribution of goods and services. Although Deutsch posited that both communities and societies develop through a process of social learning in which people learn to communicate with each other more effectively, he also believed that a national community, not a national society, provides the only stable foundation for a nation.[7]

But communication need not be an all or nothing proposition, and the level of communication need not relate only to economic matters or to the entire range of the values and preferences that constitute a culture. Theoretically, a moderate degree of acculturation can take place when an ability to communicate increases faster than necessitated by economic relationships and yet embraces a more limited range of subjects than an entire cultural panoply. Such political acculturation has occurred historically and seemed to be taking place within the political system of Eastern Nigeria.

In many ways the development of the United States' political system constitutes the best historical example of the formation of a political community without social assimilation or complete historical acculturation. After all, the United States is "a nation of nations," a composite of many different ethnic groups.[8] Furthermore, as Aristide Zolberg indicates, social science tends to recognize two models of national integration, one of which is a pluralistic pattern based on an idealization of the

American experience, and the other an assimilationist version derived from an idealization of French experience. The pluralistic model assumes "the creation of cross-cutting affiliations by superimposing non-coincidental cleavages over primordial ones, culminating in hyphenated identities."[9] Recent research on the persistence of ethnic voting and ethnic loyalties, despite several generations of residence in the United States, demonstrates that considerably less assimilation and acculturation has occurred than previously assumed and that primordial loyalties here retain their resilience.[10] As Michael Parenti convincingly argued, "The question of why ethnics continue to vote as ethnics despite increasing assimilation focuses on a false problem because minority groups are not assimilating." According to Parenti, despite occupational, educational, and geographic mobility in the United States, "residual ethnic cultural valuations and attitudes persist; . . . the vast pluralistic parallel systems of ethnic social and institutional life show impressive viability; . . . psychological feelings of minority group identity, both of the positive-enjoyment and negative-defensive varieties, are still deeply internalized."[11]

In spite of its imperfect structural assimilation and acculturation, the United States became politically integrated, at least sufficiently so to maintain a stable national political community among the descendants of the nonblack immigrants. Without structural assimilation and despite the retention of some aspects of cultural distinctiveness, immigrants soon came to share a political community based on an ability to cooperate politically. Or as Lawrence Fuchs put it, "while most of the newer immigrants did not assimilate, they did acculturate to the dominant values, attitudes, and behaviors which comprise the American political culture.[12] Political acculturation, as distinct from general acculturation or assimilation, took place rapidly in the United States. Because black Americans were prevented through slavery and then political discrimination from participating in the political system on the same basis as other immigrant groups, their political acculturation was less complete. Political expediency thus did not intervene to the same extent to motivate black Americans and various white immigrant communities to develop mutual patterns of political communication.

Ethnic affiliation generally operates as an ordering device in American politics. As in rural Eastern Nigeria and Port Harcourt, ethnicity in American politics primarily revolves around issues of recruitment and the distribution of amenities and patronage. In the United States ethnicity has become the substance of politics when gross inequalities have prevented an ethnic group from participating on an equal basis and when the barriers can be removed only by governmental intervention. Similarly ethnicity became the substance of Nigerian politics before independence on two occasions: when minorities contended that their inclusion in one of the three existing regions would relegate them to permanent political impotence, and later when the political discrimination and abuses of the North, culminating in the 1966 pogroms of the Ibos living there, seemed to threaten the political future of the Southern regions.

When Nigeria disintegrated in anti-Ibo conflagrations, the Ibo identity assumed greater relevancy, although widespread cultural differences still existed among Ibo-speaking groups. In fact, certain Ibo dialects remained mutually incomprehensible, so that large Ibo gatherings including several Ibo subgroups generally conversed in English. An attitude survey conducted among sixteen Ibo villages and eight minority villages early in 1966 showed more differences than similarities in the patterns of response in the eight relatively traditional and the eight more acculturated Ibo villages. Sometimes the answers of one Ibo group resembled the minority villagers more than the other Ibo sample.[13] The Ibo identity was clearly superimposed on a culturally heterogeneous people; the acceptance of a more inclusive identity did not transform the distinct linguistic and cultural preferences resulting from their traditional isolation. The increasing salience of the Ibo identity in the final years of the first Nigerian Federation resulted from political factors and not from a growing cultural homogeneity.

Integration thus depends on political allegiance, not cultural uniformity. Theorists who contend that cultural uniformity must precede or accompany integration fail to observe empirically the pluralism maintained in many nations that are considered politically integrated. Even in the most advanced nations men separate personal from economic and political relations. In any political system integration hinges on increasingly inclusive units becoming functional for participation, which induces communication beyond narrow ethnic confines. Ethnic group membership prevents complete structural assimilation in the social system, but pluralistic societies by definition have such substructures. Ethnic loyalties also help to preserve distinctive cultural elements. This cultural uniqueness does not thwart political integration if compensatory incentives within the political system foster intraethnic cooperation.

Eventually such political cooperation can lead to political integration, whereby the national identity becomes a meaningful referent.

ETHNIC IDENTITY AND NATIONAL INTEGRATION

Individuals and groups can and often do maintain multiple social and political levels of identity. Consequently the competition among various political referents for allegiance is not an all or nothing proposition. The more relevant question is under what circumstances does an individual or group consciously or unconsciously adopt a particular identity. Ethnic identity is no more incompatible with national loyalty than any other particularistic attachment—class, locality, occupational group, or ideological fellowship—and is no less legitimate than any of them. Furthermore, when genuine needs and common interests are shared by members of an ethnic group, as is often the case in many political systems, there is no reason to consider that actions on the basis of this ethnic identity are any less modern than are those which follow an economic rationale. Under such circumstances ethnically inspired political actions result from a rational perception of self-interest and not from an emotional response or from a traditional pattern of action. Ethnic competition within a participant political framework constitutes a modern rather than a traditional political phenomenon. In a predominantly agricultural country lacking a rigid class structure, ethnic competition has a more meaningful basis and provides a way to accommodate more groups than any other form of political differentiation.

Other scholars have stressed the compatibility between parochial attachments and national loyalty. Paul Mercier and Aristide Zolberg agreed that ethnic politics in African states often represent a search for equilibrium within the national political system. The absence of such ethnic competition in a pluralistic society often results from a low degree of political consciousness or the prevalence of a nonparticipant political culture. Clifford Geertz combined his generally pessimistic appraisal of the impact of primordial attachments in new states with the analysis that "primordial and civic sentiments are not ranged in direct and implicitly evolutionary opposition to one another in the manner of so many of the theoretical dichotomies of classical sociology."[14]

Ethnicity and nationality, or primordial and civic sentiments, are not fundamentally different, as Geertz implied, but nationality is simply an extension and more inclusive variation of ethnicity.[15] The reading of any newspaper with international coverage or a contemporary history shows that for most people nationality can also become a "given" of social existence. Nationality seems no more inherently secular or rational than subethnic allegiances. In relation to the world community, both represent manifestations of particularisms that have potential for constructive and destructive inspiration. In both cases, allegiances that may originally accrue from political expediency have a tendency to strike emotional roots. Hence, it seems more justifiable to consider ethnicity and nationality as two alternative forms of group identity, distinguishable by their level of inclusiveness.

As for the conditions under which ethnicity can be transformed into nationality, the Abiriba, Mbaise, and Port Harcourt cases do not furnish the entire answer, but they do attest to the significant contributions made by economic and political incentives. Economic and political expediency can motivate groups toward learning to communicate and to cooperate with one another. The institutional arrangements of a political system can foster such learning by making increasingly inclusive units necessary for participation and thus encouraging political cooperation across limited ethnic boundaries. In Africa a political system that combined either functional devolution to a provincial level or micropolitical decentralization with a politically strong center would tend to maximize the capabilities and the integration of the political system at this stage of development.

The Nigerian political system, as it existed prior to the first coup in January 1966, comprised one of the worst alternatives for political integration. The independence constitution in Nigeria strengthened the regions at the expense of the central level and thereby limited the relevance of the national identity for most political participants. While it failed to promote the formation of strong transregional organizations, it also made control over the federal level increasingly important. A confederal system of government would have allowed the regions to coexist autonomously without many points of conflict. Until the federal government violated the sanctity and autonomy of the Western Region in 1962 through its politically inspired declaration of emergency and dissolution of the government, an adherence to the "rules of the game" by all major participants shielded the dominant political party in each region from political interference.[16] From 1951 until 1962, during which period the first Nigerian Federation resembled a confederation of autonomous, regional political systems, Nigeria remained fairly stable.

After 1962, as the participants came to realize the increased importance of gaining control over the federal government, two national alliances gradually crystallized. However, by the time that the alliances were formed, the Northern People's Congress had secured a majority in the Federal House of Representatives by virtue of its unshakable political domination over the Northern Region. Ironically, realization of the potential role of the federal government as arbiter of the regions' fortunes dawned for most participants only after they had lost the opportunity to block the hegemony of the Northern People's Congress. Thus, the inherent imbalance in the Nigerian political system, with the Northern Region more populous than all others combined and yet significantly less developed, educationally and economically, along with the potentially influential role of the Northern dominated federal government, doomed Nigeria to instability and probably to disintegration.

One question that cannot be answered by this study is whether political cooperation and eventual political acculturation can occur between two ethnic groups whose attitudes toward political participation, governmental authority, change, and the social structure are as diametrically opposed as, for example, the Ibo and the Hausa-Fulani in Nigeria. Even the disintegration of Nigeria did not offer a conclusive answer, since in the North the more liberal and reformist political parties, such as the Northern Elements Progressive Union, never had a fair opportunity to establish themselves. In the United States immigrants from political cultures in Europe which stressed many of the same orientations toward the political system as the Hausa-Fulani very quickly seized the opportunities for political participation in an egalitarian framework. Studies of political culture in India, traditionally one of the least egalitarian and participant-oriented societies, show the evolution of an emerging mass political culture, many of whose characteristics seem adaptive for democratization, political stability, and perhaps modernization. In fact, the emerging mass political culture in India, as described by Myron Weiner, is remarkably similar in many ways to the mass political culture in Eastern Nigeria.[17] If both immigrants from Russia and peasants in India can become political participants, there would seem to be no inherent reasons to exclude the possibility of some form of political cooperation emerging among other very different cultural groups. Unless this political cooperation leads to the evolution of a shared political culture, or at least to some agreement about the fundamental rules under which the political system will operate, a stable national community will not develop. History offers inspiration for hope as well as reason for despair.

Ethnic identity as a contingent phenomenon often adapts itself in accordance with the political opportunities offered by a specific environment. As political arenas become larger in scope and more heterogeneous, ethnic identification adjusts by becoming more inclusive. Hence, individuals and groups often have multiple allegiances. Conditions under which political participation occurs usually determine which of these identities shall become the salient one. Integration, or the imposition of more generalized sets of political loyalties over more particular ones, can take place on any level of the political system—a village, a clan, a county, a city, a region, or a nation.

General cultural homogenization or structural assimilation do not seem to be prerequisites for political integration. Political cooperation can cement ties between diverse cultural groups sufficiently to foster a political identity among them. Although political expediency often motivates such alliances, in time they may develop stability and emotional connotations. Groups with somewhat diverse cultures can apparently acculturate to similar political orientations. Whether such acculturation to a pragmatic, participant political system can reach across and integrate such traditionally diverse people as the Ibo and Hausa-Fulani is a question that cannot be answered conclusively, but the evolution of the American and Indian political systems offers hope that significant traditional differences can be overcome.

Contrary to many assumptions, ethnic unions do not deter political integration. The role and strength of ethnic unions depends on the same factors that determine the salience of political identities in particular political arenas. For the most part, ethnic unions operate as social welfare organizations or as ordering media to facilitate political competition and cooperation. While ethnic unions may reinforce primary identities, this strengthening of parochial ties does not preclude the establishment of more inclusive networks of loyalty. The Abiriban identity had little relevance in Port Harcourt, so Abiribans living there operated politically within the Bende Divisional and the old Owerri Provincial alliances. The activities of the Abiriba Communal Improvement Union, which was a highly institutionalized and active ethnic union, therefore did not impede the adoption of a more inclusive political identity when circumstances warranted it. Politically ethnic unions promoted compromise and accommodation as well as confrontation.

By making increasingly inclusive units functional for participation and thus by encouraging political cooperation among ever-widening groups, political institutions can encourage integration. When political systems disintegrate, as in the Nigerian case, the major responsibility often rests with the institutional arrangements and imbalances and with the persons responsible for their formulation and perpetration, rather than with ethnic selfishness and exclusiveness. In contrast with the institutional arrangements on the federal level, the Eastern Region political system offered inducements for intraethnic cooperation and thus eventual political integration. On the regional level Ibo subgroups often allied with other Ibo or minority subgroups against similarly constituted political coalitions. If ethnicity had continued to be the form rather than the substance of political competition in the East, political integration would have proceeded on a regional level.

XII | Ethnic Unions and Cultural Modernization

Political development has subjective as well as objective attributes. Along with the creation of more effective political institutions and procedures, the process of political development depends on the evolution of certain cultural perspectives. The concept of political culture embraces those elements of the general culture which have political relevance, that is, all the values, beliefs, and norms which condition political action. Some attitudes foster political development more than others. Since these attitudes are generally associated with people acculturated to modern rather than traditional ways of life, Gabriel Almond and G. Bingham Powell, Jr., suggested that the emergence of such attitudes be referred to as cultural secularization. Most new states are clothed in the institutional garb of modern industrial nations; at first glance their sophisticated political and administrative institutions seem to be replicas of those existing for their former colonial masters. However, these borrowed institutions generally do not operate so effectively in a fundamentally different environment. Almond and Powell interpreted this institutional ineffectiveness as deriving in large part from an incompatibility between the modern institutions and the predominantly traditional cultures in most new states. In other words, they did not believe that the values, attitudes, beliefs, and norms adhered to by most citizens in the new states were congruent with the needs of a relatively developed political system.[1]

The processes of political integration and cultural modernization or secularization, as defined in this study, are primarily subjective in nature.[2] Political integration is measured by the level of political identity assumed by participants in specific situations. Political culture relates to the kinds of attitudes and orientations that political actors have about themselves; the purpose, nature, and proper goals of the political system; the manner in which power and influence are conferred on social and political leaders; and the means of pursuing political objectives. Although political integration and cultural modernization are primarily subjective, both directly influence the evolution and operation of the political system. The dimensions of political development can only be isolated analytically. The degree of unity or integration achieved by a political system affects in some ways the manner in which its institutions function and the propensity to adopt different perspectives and orientations. Similarly, a relatively modern political culture should facilitate institutionalization and integration. No explication of the nature of political development has as yet, however, presented verifiable statements of the precise relationships between specific dimensions.

Unlike many traditional or precolonial societies, the separate Ibo villages held orientations, values, and attitudes toward the sociopolitical system that were often remarkably modern in content. Although their simple and almost "primitive" institutions were like those of other political systems at the earliest stages of evolution, the norms infusing their operation had much in common with the standards that social scientists cite as constituting a modern political culture.[3] For instance, precolonial Ibo society was egalitarian, achievement motivated, participant oriented, pragmatic, innovative, and instrumental in its approach to politics.

The political attitudes and standards of conduct for the precolonial Ibos were, however, tied to the small, intimate, autonomous village-group. Colonial penetration undermined the insularity of these village groups and linked them to a wider political system. Consequently the Ibos had to adjust to politics in an environment totally different from the one in which their orientations first evolved. The ability to accommodate to political involvement in the wider political system depended in part on learning about the world outside the village and about the operation of the new political system. A successful transition also demanded acquiring the organization and skills for representative government in place of the traditional direct involvement. The metamorphosis was fraught with difficulties, and the result by no means assured. As David Smock's study of coal miners in Enugu showed, Ibo villagers did not necessarily transfer their precolonial orientations when faced with modern organizational needs for strong leadership and quick action.[4] It is necessary to assess some of the values, attitudes, and orientations to politics in Abiriba and Mbaise in order to evaluate how successfully the people there made the transition to a wider, representative political system. In this context, the role of the ethnic unions is significant.

POLITICAL AWARENESS

Traditionally Ibo social and political institutions were not clearly delineated. The political unit was also a kinship group, with all members descendants of the same man. Patrilineages and age groups regulated members, often to the exclusion of any wider authority. Village assemblies of all adults, or all male adults, did not meet on a regular, continuing basis and had no political figure to whom to delegate authority or to implement the agreed upon policy. As a result, villagers probably did not have a perception of politics as a distinct sphere of activities.

By at least 1966 the vast majority of villagers were linked to the world beyond the primary kinship unit, and with that awareness came a recognition of the new political institutions impinging on them. For the Ibo villager the political sphere consisted of the NCNC, which had a nominal or sometimes an active branch in the immediate vicinity, local councils, and representatives to regional and federal legislative bodies. His perception of the political focused primarily on aspects of the larger system, which had been imposed on his village, rather than on politics as a distinct sphere within his own village. In places like Abiriba from which many residents regularly traveled, political ties between the home and the wider political system probably seemed natural because of their broadened perspective. In remote and traditional areas, the political nexus appeared more intermittent and the dichotomy between the village and the wider political system more rigid.

Consequently, the less autonomous a village remained and the greater the number of bonds between it and a more inclusive political unit, whether that unit was a county council area, a division, or the regional political system, the more likely it was that members of the primary community would concern themselves with politics. Since local councils rarely became vital institutions, politics involved an awareness of and a willingness to become involved in a political unit beyond the confines of the precolonial community. Politics per se related to the activities and needs of the modern, representative political system emanating from Enugu, the regional capital.

For at least a significant proportion of the population in both Abiriba and Mbaise, participation in the wider political system was accepted as beneficial. Abiribans generally ignored the political proceedings of the Owuwa Anyanwu County Council, not because they were political parochials but because the county council did little on their behalf. A large number of Abiribans were politically sophisticated and attuned to the activities and potentialities of working through the regional level. In Mbaise people commonly accepted their integration into the county political unit and the Mbaise frame of reference. Although fewer people than in Abiriba assumed a regional perspective, leaders of the various subgroups in Mbaise followed some regional decisions and policies, as they affected Mbaise, through the reports of political representatives.

Ethnic unions helped orient people toward involvement with a more inclusive community than their traditional kinship units. Through their activities, ethnic unions acquainted people with modern procedures and organizations. They provided an informational link with the wider world. They also constituted an organizational vehicle through which people could participate in a meaningful manner in the modern political system.

One of the greatest contributions of ethnic unions to the process of transformation from political parochialism to political awareness was the role they played in bridging the psychological and political gap between rural and urban areas. This gap constitutes one common characteristic of transitional societies. It often leads to what Samuel Huntington called the "green uprising," which involves a late mobilization of rural peasants for political participation, often at the price of instability and abandonment of many modern values and practices.[5] Ethnic unions alleviated the need for a "green uprising" by preventing such discontinuities in the political system. The pattern of politics in urban centers like Port Harcourt resembled political interactions in rural communities like Mbaise, but adjusted for the larger, more heterogeneous political arena. Unlike many other transitional societies, urban areas in Eastern Nigeria did not comprise oases of political participation in an environment of political parochialism and apathy.

Ethnic unions accomplished this linkage between urban and rural Eastern Nigerians by making urban residents available for leadership in rural communities. Ethnic unions evolved as the instrument for urbanites to transform the countryside. Urban branches continued to control most ethnic unions by virtue of their greater representation at general conferences, which enabled them to elect central officers having urban experience. By reenforcing rural identities, ethnic unions deterred members from adopting an urban frame of reference. Though this contributed to the problems of urban centers, it also encouraged urban residents to take an active developmental and political role in their home communities. On balance, the countryside benefited far more than the urban centers suffered.

By virtue of their urban experience and usually greater education, the leaders of the ethnic unions viewed politics in a wider perspective than most other members of the community at home. They had the political skills needed for operating within the modern political system, which enabled them to gain advantages in the form of political offices or amenities for their communities. The possibility of securing these objectives provided an incentive for participating in the modern political system to members of the rural branches at home.

Most Eastern Nigerians viewed the wider political system through the perspective of their local community rather than perceiving it as a complex, interconnected system. In other words, few Eastern Nigerians appreciated and were concerned with the regional political system apart from its interactions with their primary community. This limitation on political awareness probably characterizes many people in more developed political systems as well.

ORIENTATION TOWARD POLITICS

The participant orientation toward politics has been emphasized as one of the central components of a modern or secular political culture. According to this view, as individuals in a modern society learn about the political system, they come to see themselves as competent political actors, capable of influencing its decisions. Along with this participant orientation, citizens with modern cultural attitudes are supposed to have a pragmatic, empirical, and instrumental approach to politics, which is sometimes called a "marketplace attitude." The "marketplace attitude" exists when participants bargain for limited objectives by exchanging support with other groups. The desire to participate in politics, and to some extent the willingness to compromise, according to this analysis, derive from a positive attitude toward the political system and its role vis-à-vis the society.

In the precolonial Ibo political system members had a participant and pragmatic political style. The Ibo village was governed by a kind of direct democracy. Moreover, the segmented nature of society meant that political leaders, to survive, had to be negotiators and accommodators who could unify fractional groupings. While participants did not distinguish between political and other forms of activity, the relish with which they attended village meetings and contributed to political decisions implied a favorable attitude.

Although the theoretical distinction between a participant and a nonparticipant seems valid, the practical problem is to determine how much participation constitutes a participant orientation toward politics. In both transitional and developed political systems, governments sometimes herd citizens to voting booths. Even when voting is voluntary, if it constitutes the only form of political involvement within a time period of several years, it does not seem sufficient to warrant a participant label. A participant orientation toward politics obviously necessitates an active involvement in politics but few people can take part simultaneously in politics at all levels of the system.

Abiribans and Mbaisans understood that elections gave them the chance to determine their political representatives. Many took an active interest in selecting their representatives and voted regularly. They also realized that political representatives could make the government responsive to their needs and desires. To ensure the election of a favorable candidate, Abiribans and Mbaisans, as well as members of other communities in Eastern Nigeria, supported the role of their ethnic unions in recruitment and elections.

Once elections were over, however, people thought that the selection of a representative from their primary community alleviated the need for further political involvement. In most cases neither the electorate nor the representative comprehended the need for continuing relationships with each other. Electors often naively assumed that a kinsman would automatically look after their interests without additional scrutiny. Moreover, representatives often did not understand their obligations to constituents in an elective political system, beyond a vague awareness that they should work to gain amenities for them. Aside from notices from ethnic unions reminding representatives of their obligations to their kinsmen and occasional reports by representatives at ethnic union conferences, little communication occurred between a politician and his constituents. As a result, many politicians employed their offices primarily for their own advantage without suffering electoral retribution. Citizens remained ignorant about matters that various political bodies discussed and how decisions were reached. A sense of responsibility toward kinsmen, to the extent that it existed, often operated as the only check on the representative.

Strong ethnic unions with officers who were not also politicians often comprised the most effective postelectoral political forum and restraint on the representative. The ACIU fit this model. In contrast with the Abiriba model, officers of ethnic unions in Mbaise often either were politicians, who had been seconded to union leadership for the prestige, or held political ambitions and therefore sought a post in the ethnic union as a political stepping stone. When ethnic unions coopted politicians for union office, the unions substantially forfeited the opportunity to act as a political monitor.

Though people in Abiriba and Mbaise had a participant orientation toward politics, they perceived this participation more in a group context than as an individual activity. Both in Abiriba and in Mbaise most groups seemed fairly optimistic that they could obtain their goals through political action, specifically by working to elect the correct man and then reminding him constantly of his obligations to them. None of the groups was as effective in actuality as it estimated. Of the two communities, Abiribans had more success since their objectives were often more limited. Members of both communities did not keep sufficiently informed about the ongoing deliberations of their respective county councils or the Eastern House of Assembly to ascertain when they should act to ensure that their interests were being protected. Many people probably lacked the political sophistication to foresee the implications of certain policies. Furthermore, many of the most critical decisions affecting local communities were made by the ministers or civil servants, to whom few people had political access. Despite their participant orientation, few Abiribans or Mbaisans were really competent political actors.

To describe Ibos as political pragmatists would be an understatement. The central motif in the Eastern political system was the bargaining for political offices and amenities. Politics was the great marketplace where political skills were invested; support was negotiated and exchanged; and through the political bargains elections were won and goods and services attained. In this political marketplace bargainers forgot political principles, lost sight of broader political objectives, and undermined rational, economic development programs. In other words, political actors were pragmatically and instrumentally oriented to politics to the exclusion of other considerations. Occasionally individuals with ideological proclivities did band together within the NCNC to reform the party and set it on a socialist course. Before elections the NCNC also published policy papers and proclaimed its adherence to certain political principles, even socialism. In the heat of political battle, however, principles gave way to calculations on how to succeed, or ideologically oriented groups found themselves outside the political mainstream. Thus pragmatism, when not tempered by a commitment to higher principles or goals, such as the preservation of a political party or the furtherance of political institutions, can inhibit political development.

Most participants viewed the political system primarily as a distributor of political goods rather than as an instrument to regulate or change society. If an increase in the capabilities of the political system would enhance the access to resources, then they favored it. Many of the participants favored social and economic development, but they were not willing to forego personal and community benefits to attain that change. Of course, many of the amenities that communities clamored for—the schools, water pipes, and electricity—had an economic payoff, as well as making life more pleasant. However, the limited financial resources were often used unwisely or even squandered through corruption. Moreover, as the history of many ethnic unions demonstrated, including the ACIU, when properly inspired, communities would make tremendous sacrifices on behalf of development and change. Unfortunately the dynamics of the Eastern political system encouraged a manipulative self-seeking response rather than prompting a mobilization on behalf of social, economic, and political development.

When the Institute for International Social Research took a survey in Nigeria in 1962 and 1963, its results showed that Nigerians generally, and Easterners and Ibos specifically, had the highest expectations for governmental action in providing education, public health facilities, modern amenities, and agrarian assistance of any country it had studied. At least half and sometimes many more Ibos indicated their desire for governmental action in each of these fields.[6] This expectation for distribution of benefits continued until the dissolution of representative institutions.

The relative scarcity of resources prevented the Eastern political system from meeting the expectations of many of the participating groups. In an environment of economic scarcity and high demands, competitive localism has more pernicious consequences than in a more economically developed political system. Ethnic nepotism pervaded the regional political system. Each member of the Eastern House of Assembly and each minister sought to advance the interests of his community, sometimes to the exclusion of other areas.

As a consequence, an attitude survey of twenty-four villages including one from Ezinihitte and one from Ahiara, Mbaise in 1966 indicated that half of the Ibo informants thought that the government was run for the benefit of those in power, while only 34.1 percent answered that the government was run for the people. Similarly only 18 percent of the Ibo informants believed that they had a good chance of receiving justice in a court case. In contrast with the Ibo scores, the non-Ibo villagers had more positive attitudes toward the government. Some 63.5 percent of the non-Ibo informants replied that the government was run for the benefit of the people, and 53.5 percent thought they had a good chance of receiving justice.[7] In the years prior to the survey, the Eastern government had discriminated on behalf of minority areas when distributing certain types of resources, as part of its strategy for strengthening the NCNC's support among non-Ibo groups.[8] Hence, more Ibo groups with a high expectation of favorable governmental actions probably met with disappointment than did non-Ibo groups. While communities like Abiriba and Mbaise had positive attitudes toward government, the governmental responses that engendered these favorable images came at the expense of other communities. Every graded road, water system, and special subsidy for Abiriba or Mbaise brought in its wake governmental rejection of a request from a less influential community, and along with this refusal a negative reaction to the political system.

Although access to political resources on the county level often was not cumulative, on the regional level powerful men employed their influence immoderately on behalf of their constituencies and themselves. Groups usually had representation on county councils proportionate to their size, which enabled any moderately large group to bargain successfully for benefits. On the regional level, though, few primary communities had direct political representation by a kinsman in the House of Assembly, and even fewer could count on a voice in ministerial and cabinet deliberations. Moreover, relative to the number of petitioning groups, the Eastern government had less ability to apportion equally its costly electrical facilities, water pipes, roads, and other forms of assistance than the county councils had of siting medical dispensaries, post offices, and small bridges among its constituent groups.

Therefore, if the expression "those in power" in the 1966 attitude survey is construed in a broad manner to mean the communities with influential political representatives, as well as the representatives themselves, the opinion of the majority of Ibo informants that the Eastern government benefited "those in power" more than the "people" was generally correct. However, the government did not benefit "those in power" to the exclusion of the "people." After all, the preponderant proportion of funding for the county councils came as a rebate from the regional government. Moreover, the Eastern government financed schools, agricultural extension, and some public works projects without reference to patronage considerations. Furthermore, the number of groups "in power" with access to government-sponsored amenities was quite large and diversified. Even influential ministers found themselves circumscribed in what they could produce for their communities by the counterveiling force of similar political entrepreneurs.

It is difficult to evaluate the contribution made by ethnic unions to the marketplace political ethos, because unions differed in the roles they assumed. While the ACIU encouraged self-reliance, the Mbaise unions accentuated the tendency in Mbaise to depend on political handouts rather than on internal resources. Economic factors contributed to the diverse orientations. Yet several clans in Mbaise did raise funds, which were then spent on politics, and other clans could have extracted resources for developmental purposes. Ironically, by facilitating political participation and by linking individuals with the larger political system, ethnic unions in Mbaise simultaneously virtually assured that political actors would look to the county council and the regional government for the satisfaction of their needs and desires. If the ethnic unions in Mbaise were less successful politically, communities might have foregone such a concentration on political manipulation. Without ethnic unions, political participation and representational accountability would have been less meaningful for most villagers. Consequently their accommodation to the modern political system would have been slower and less complete. However, ethnic unions often reenforced group selfishness and in so doing vitiated a more inclusive developmental perspective.

LEADERSHIP QUALIFICATIONS

In precolonial Ibo society men gained status and became recognized as leaders by virtue of their wealth and their skill as conciliators. In the context of the segmented society, ability to reconcile opposed factions was crucial to the society's preservation. To operate successfully in the modern political system, however, would-be leaders needed other qualifications as well: knowledge about the workings of the system, contact with many aspects of modern life, some education, and organizational skills.

An analysis of the officers of the unions in both the Mbaise and the Abiriba communities revealed the importance of "modernists," educated men who lived in urban areas, as leaders in rural Eastern Nigeria. Every officer of the ACIU spent a substantial portion of his adult life residing outside of Abiriba. Seven of the long-tenure officers of the ACIU were educators and five were traders in a community in which approximately three-fourths of all adult males were traders. Although only two of the five presidents were educators, they served for a total of eighteen terms, as compared with the eight terms of the traders. This preponderance of educators probably reflected the emphasis on education that characterized the ACIU at its inception. The officers also had higher educational qualifications than was standard in the community; six of the eleven long-tenure officers had at least the equivalent of a secondary school education, holding either a higher elementary teacher's certificate or a professional teacher's certificate. In 1965, 58 percent of the central union officials elected in Mbaise had at least the equivalent of a secondary education. Their occupational structure was more varied than that of the officers of the ACIU, including one doctor, twelve teachers, three administrators, one clerk, eight traders, and one manual laborer.

In both Abiriba and Mbaise the occupational and educational qualifications of the officers of the central unions, charged with the responsibility for coordinating their activities, were higher than those of the branch officers. Nineteen out of the twenty members of the Port Harcourt executive of the ACIU engaged in trading. Almost half of the members of the Port Harcourt executive had not even completed primary school. In contrast to the 58 percent of the central officers who had completed the equivalent of a secondary education, only 13 percent of the Port Harcourt officers had attained so high a standard of education. The officers of the Port Harcourt branches of the Mbaise unions received somewhat more education than did their Abiriban counterparts, since 19 percent of them had attained at least the equivalent of a secondary school education. Had the officers of the Mbaise Youth

Movement branch also been included, the percentage for Mbaise would have risen. More branch officers of the Mbaise unions engaged in trading than did members of the central executives. Half of the branch officers serving in 1965 were traders. Of the remaining thirteen, three were laborers, seven clerks, two administrators, and one an educator.

In the beginning, many of the long-tenure Abiriban officers were elected from among the most qualified Abiribans. However, in the last ten years conference delegates did not elect the best educated or the most highly qualified professionals. They almost completely excluded university graduates from office in the ACIU, including the five students educated on scholarships sponsored by the union, who began to return to Abiriba in 1951. Apparently the conduct of the first principal of Enuda College, who failed to disguise his contempt for the less educated officers, caused such a reaction among entrenched members of the executive committee that no university graduate was elected after the end of his term as secretary in 1954 until 1965, when another of the original scholarship recipients became joint treasurer.

The Mbaise unions utilized the skills of their university graduates somewhat better. In addition, many Mbaise unions invited their graduates as special observers and advisers to the conferences. Also it was likely that a smaller proportion of Mbaise people received university educations than did Abiribans, and at a later date. At least one clan, the Nguru, did not have a university graduate until 1960.

As a group, politicians possessed higher educational qualifications than did either central union or branch officers. The representative from Abiriba in the Eastern House of Assembly was the first Abiriban to receive a law degree. Abiribans, along with other members of the federal constituency, elected a lecturer at the University of Nigeria from Ohafia in 1965. All politicians from Mbaise serving in either the House of Assembly or the House of Representatives held at least a higher elementary teacher's certificate; one held a diploma in education, one a law degree, and one a medical degree. Hence, all the politicians from Mbaise received at least the equivalent of a secondary school education, since the higher elementary teacher's certificate required four years of study after the completion of primary school.

In light of this survey of educational qualifications, and thus experience with facets of modern life, it seems warranted to assert that leadership in Abiriba and Mbaise was based on achievement. Just as the precolonial Ibo society required and sought out conciliators as leaders, the postcolonial Ibo community favored organizers and political entrepreneurs, who were capable of mobilizing members for community development and extracting benefits from the wider political system. The high rates of stability in the selection of leaders in Abiriba and Mbaise attested to the political skill of the officers of the ethnic unions and some of the politicians. During its first twenty-five years a self-perpetuating elite tended to monopolize central union office in the ACIU. The eleven long-tenure officers averaged nine terms each; the 110 terms they served in toto equal two-thirds of the total number of officers elected during the period. Eight men by themselves accounted for almost half of the union offices filled. Stabilization of leadership in Mbaise occurred through having the same men simultaneously hold several different offices. To overcome the fragmentation of authority in Mbaise, which lacked one central institution such as ACIU to control various spheres of activities, ambitious men who had acquired a position on one of the four organizational bases of influence—the Mbaise County Council, the regional or federal Houses, the NCNC executive and nominating committees, or the improvement unions—attempted to pyramid their assets by seeking office in one of the other organizations. The irreverent manner which which some political leaders were unceremoniously dismissed underscored the fact that skills on the part of other leaders, not the awe of their followers, kept them in office.

Though education and urban experience certainly contributed to an ability to organize and lead, they did not automatically guarantee such an aptitude in Abiriba and Mbaise, any more than they do in other societies. In some cases when Abiribans refused to elect university graduates to high office in the union, this policy derived from an accurate perception that experienced union officers were better suited. Experience in managing ACIU affairs over a period of years conferred certain skills and insights. Moreover, some university graduates, like the first principal of Enuda College, probably would have represented disruptive influences, and many other university graduates failed to demonstrate an interest in assuming the demands of union office. There were a number of university graduates, however, who showed a willingness to serve the community and manifested an ability to do so, but were not elected to union office, probably because they were blocked by existing officers. As happens everywhere, the democratic political systems failed to call upon some of their best qualified citizens for political leadership.

ATTITUDES TOWARD AUTHORITY

One of the central characteristics of precolonial Ibo society was a negative attitude toward political authority. Individuals refused to countenance centralization of authority in the village or the inclusion of the village in a wider political unit, because both would have conferred power over them to an individual or group. As a consequence, Ibo villages generally had an egalitarian society and a dispersed power structure. The requirements of a modern political system, however, undermined the autonomy of the village, at least for some purposes, and effective political action within that system called for a degree of centralization of authority.

While retaining an egalitarian social orientation, residents of Abiriba and Mbaise accepted the centralization of political authority. An uneducated farmer or laborer considered himself to be the equal in most ways of a lawyer, a doctor, or an important political leader, but for some purposes he acknowledged the need for leadership and the special qualifications of the lawyer, doctor, or politician to lead. At branch union meetings all members contributed to discussions. Similarly at central union conferences delegates participated and sometimes criticized the policy of union officers. At the same time members of the unions continued to elect the same men and grant them considerable power, and political representatives were accorded prestige and prerogatives.

Authority in Abiriba was substantially centralized in the central union officers of the ACIU. The greater size and ethnic complexity of the Mbaise area hampered a comparable degree of centralization in one organization. In Mbaise authority was shared by the Mbaise County Council, the ethnic unions, the political leaders, and to some extent, the Roman Catholic Church.[9] The structural pluralism in Mbaise derived from objective characteristics of the community, primarily its size and heterogeneity, and not from the attempt to maintain a precolonial dispersion of power.

Evidence indicates that not all Ibo communities made so successful a transition as Abiriba and Mbaise toward accepting the centralization of political authority. In Udi Division, which was less economically and educationally developed than either Owerri or Bende Divisions, the communities studied by David Smock in 1962 and 1963 continued to rely on the traditional village assembly of all adults to determine most issues. Ethnic unions there had not become effective vehicles for community development or political recruitment. A mélange of traditional and modernistic organizations often operated within the same village. Few of these organizations attained any degree of centralization even within their own structure. The villages in Udi Division thus manifested an unwillingness to centralize authority within any single organization or organizations. Instead, they adhered generally to the precolonial disposition that political authority should be dispersed. Minute books of several ethnic unions in the Enugu area and Simon Ottenberg's analysis of the fortunes of an ethnic union in an Afikpo community, another more traditional area, exemplify these same tendencies.[10]

In Onitsha, however, the abortive attempts to form ethnic unions among the indigenous community, described by Richard Henderson, suggest that the centralization of power traditionally achieved there and the ability of precolonial organizations to assume new functions made the ethnic unions somewhat irrelevent.[11] Therefore, negative attitudes concerning the centralization of authority did not account for the weakness of ethnic unions in Onitsha, as they seemed to do in certain less developed Ibo areas.

Perhaps the willingness to accept a substantial degree of centralization within a community constituted a reliable index of the degree of cultural modernization. At least this hypothesis seems verified by the limited information available. The trauma and uprooting of entire communities as a consequence of the pogroms in the North and the war will probably transform the attitudes toward authority, as well as other political orientations.

UNIVERSALISM OR PARTICULARISM

Although modern political cultures supposedly are characterized by the application of codified, universalistic rules in political processes, the most developed states still exhibit manifold tendencies toward particularism. While participants may more or less adhere to the rules and procedures of the wider political system, as in Eastern Nigeria, they continue to favor some groups more than others. As political systems develop, the bases for these particularisms change from kinship and custom alone to geographical, economic, ideological, and occupational considerations. Consequently, the predisposition to prefer certain groups over others does not of itself manifest the absence of universalistic norms.

In an attempt to evaluate the degree of universality or particularism in the cultural orientations of Mbaise and Abiriba, the absence of empirical indicators again presents problems. Although a competitive localism loomed as one of the central characteristics of the prewar political system, a similar competitive localism typifies other representative political systems, where representatives are not subject to strong party discipline and thus act only on behalf of their constituency. While the basis for this localism in Eastern Nigeria resembled the situation in the United States, the consequences in an economy of scarcity were more pernicious. Nevertheless, if localism and universalism can inhere in the American political system, they could coexist in the Eastern Nigerian framework.

Localism in Eastern Nigeria provided the most viable basis for political competition and for distribution of amenities. Participants perceived that desired amenities could be obtained from the government by pressuring it. Economic, occupational, and ideological cleavages did not offer promising foundations for political organization because people were not yet sufficiently bound together by these considerations, especially in rural areas. Moreover, the things people wanted —roads, schools, hospitals, medical dispensaries, water pipes, electrical facilities—could be allocated only to geographical units. Consequently, in many cases competing groups were divided on geographical rather than ethnic criteria. For example, in Mbaise within the county political system people competed according to the nontraditional clan-court areas or local council groups. In Port Harcourt and on the regional level participants divided on county, divisional, and provincial lines, all of which lacked traditional counterparts. Hence, competitive localism derived from rational political calculations and not from traditional loyalties.

Particularism entered politics in two more limited ways. Political representatives sometimes favored a part of their constituency, the section that coincided with their kinship group. In both Ezinihitte and Ekwerazu, for instance, the first villages to have water pipes installed were the home villages of members of the Eastern House of Assembly. The degree to which politicians specifically represented their kinship units in preference to the rest of the constituency was difficult to ascertain. In Mbaise other villages eventually received water pipes also, because Mbaise politicians usually pursued benefits for the entire constituency and sometimes for the whole of Mbaise. Some politicians, like the member of the Federal House of Representatives whose constituency encompassed Abiriba, cultivated all parts of their political domain. Ethnic favoritism by a portion of the representatives did affect the political system by causing other ethnic groups within the constituency to consider themselves politically impotent. In a sense, when this favoritism occurred, sections of a constituency were disenfranchised since they did not have a political representative. However, cases of extreme ethnic partisanship on the part of political representatives did not seem to be common. More frequently representatives used their influence to have a facility for the use of an entire constituency sited in their home village or to have the first of a series of installations constructed there.

Particularistic orientations may also have contributed to the incidence of corruption. People reacted negatively to instances of known corruption when they thought that the corruption came at their own expense. If they reasoned that the corruption primarily affected others, however, they sometimes passively condoned it. This pattern of behavior implicitly derived from a double standard, differentiating norms that were acceptable within the context of the immediate community from those that were permissible in relation to outsiders. For this reason misuse of the funds of an ethnic union evoked an uproar from members, while blatant manifestations of misappropriation of tax money by ministers only prompted the observation that all politicians were corrupt. This willingness to accept corruption as a fact of political life had complex origins, as did the set of factors giving rise to the omnipresence of corruption in all aspects of political and commercial activities.

In his study of Udi Division, David Smock asked villagers whether they would respect a man from their town who went to Enugu or another city and made a great deal of money by illegal means and cheating people. About two-thirds of the villagers answered that they would respect him, but that they would resent him if he cheated people from his own town. Smock concluded that this sort of double standard encouraged the misuse of funds in the Nigerian Coal Miniers' Union, whose members came predominantly from Udi Division.[12]

Members of the Mbaise community in Port Harcourt actively solicited Pius Nwoga, the minister for town planning, to use his influence on their behalf, legally or illegally. Eventually he was arrested for illegally changing title to a land plot in Port Harcourt. When this occurred, people from Mbaise expressed sympathy with his plight rather than deprecating it. However, when officers of the Mbaise Federal Union branch in Port Harcourt could not account fully for their expenditure of funds, the flood of criticism was so great that it inundated the union. From that point, the Mbaise Federal Union ceased operating on a regular basis. Apparently members of the Mbaise community viewed abuse of power or instances of corruption by their own politicians as another manifestation of influence and one more demonstration of the status and importance of a man from Mbaise. Unlike the misuse of ethnic union funds, they did not conceive the misappropriation of public property as depriving themselves.

In many ways Ibo communities like Abiriba and Mbaise successfully made the transition from a small precolonial political unit based on direct participation to a modern representative political system. The attitudes, values, and orientations infusing and determining political activities, at least in Abiriba and Mbaise, were relatively modern. Aspects of their modernistic political culture included a perception of politics as a separate sphere within the context of the wider political system, a positive attitude toward the political system, a participant orientation in politics with some confidence in group competence, an extremely pragmatic and instrumental approach to politics, the selection of leaders on the basis of ability, an acceptance of a degree of centralized political authority, an egalitarian societal perspective, and an adherence to universalistic criteria in relation to the general operation of the regional political system. Adherence to modern cultural norms, however, was not necessarily conducive to political and economic development. Preoccupation with the manipulative and distributive dimensions of politics, sometimes referred to as a marketplace attitude, interfered with development planning and inhibited appeals to work and sacrifice for the regional or national community. Moreover, some groups did not share equally in the political spoils and thus might have become alienated from the political system.

Ethnic unions facilitated the accommodation between tradition and modernity in the Eastern political system by conserving those elements in the traditional political culture that were conducive to political development and then by harnessing them on behalf of the development of the primary community. The role of ethnic unions in the Eastern Region often allowed them to link traditional commitments with the modern political and administrative structures. This nexus transformed traditional communities to make them more consonant with modern institutions and modified the modern institutions to make them more meaningful to individuals operating primarily within the confines of the traditional society. This rapprochment generally prevented the emergence of the widespread discontinuities that characterize many transitional political systems. According to Lucian Pye, political development "involves less the gross elimination of old patterns and values and more the successful discovery of how tradition can contribute to, and not hamper, the realization of current national goals."[13] Ethnic unions selectively employed traditional obligations and values for the realization of modern goals.

Ethnic unions often transformed those aspects of the preexisting values and beliefs that were not consonant with modern politics. They helped to overcome the traditional isolation and autonomy of the village. They facilitated the adjustment of the villagers to life and politics in an urban environment. By transforming religious facets of traditional culture into expressions of communal loyalty, the unions prevented communities from fragmenting as they went through the process of Christianization. The unions utilized commitments to local communities to mobilize members for development without impeding immersion in a wider political system. To a great extent this configuration of loyalties encouraged the evolution of a generalized identification without undermining parochial units, which thus conferred the benefits of both integration and pluralism on the political system.

Denis Goulet asked the relevant question, "development for what?" Because Goulet was disturbed by the dehumanizing consequences of the process of development, as currently conducted in many countries, he advocated a normative approach. According to Goulet, transitional societies were paying an unnecessarily high price for development by unquestioningly sacrificing traditional values on the altar of modernization. Goulet suggested also that development should enhance the possibilities for "the good life," three components of which were sustenance, esteem, and liberty.[14] Development in Eastern Nigeria was not dehumanizing. Ibo and other ethnic groups traditionally held many values that proved to be compatible with rapid development. Furthermore, ethnic unions cushioned the transition. The process of development in prewar Eastern Nigeria did not come at the expense of the sustenance, esteem, or liberty of the citizens.

The maintenance and invigoration of certain parochial units also came as a consequence of the operation of ethnic unions. By linking this parochialism with the wider political system, ethnic unions contributed to development and insulated the discomforts that often accompany change. The retention of a parochial or local frame of reference provoked a great deal of criticism from observers who wrongly assumed that it retarded integration or inhibited the acceptance of a modern outlook. As Lucian Pye remarked, even in a modern political culture "there is a constant place for particularism, for diffuse identifications, and for attaching importance to nationality and place of birth."[15] Hence, it was unrealistic to expect and actually unproductive to want to eradicate political localism. Localism could be embodied in a kind of group selfishness or it could precipitate tremendous sacrifices that promoted development. As for the eruption of group selfishness, politics inherently arises in conditions of scarcity. Competitive localism, as it was practiced in the Eastern Nigerian political system, probably resulted in a fairer distribution of political and economic resources than is achieved in most transitional or developed states.

It is difficult to predict the ways in which the recent nightmarish experiences of the Eastern Nigerian people will affect their political culture. In addition to its many tragic consequences, the war between Biafra and Nigeria called into being a greater unity, a higher degree of political mobilization, and a greater inclination to make fundamental sacrifices on the part of the Biafrans than ever before in Africa. The type of political system that follows from a constitutional conference may determine future orientations at least as much as the trauma of the war years. More specifically, the future opportunities for reconstruction, development, and meaningful political participation may be crucial factors. One can only hope that the resolution of the conflict will inaugurate an era that preserves the positive dimensions of the prewar political culture while nourishing a greater willingness to work for and sacrifice on behalf of the larger political community.

Notes

Bibliography

Index

Notes

NOTES TO INTRODUCTION

1. On the need for this kind of study, see Aristide A. Zolberg, *Creating Political Order: The Party States of West Africa* (Chicago: Rand McNally and Co., 1966), p. 153; Harvey Glickman, "Dialogues on the Theory of African Political Development," *Africa Report*, XII (May 1967), 38–39, and his "Regionalism and Micropolitics," *Africa Report*, XII (June 1967), 31–32. For other rural and urban micropolitical studies of Africa, see Jonathan S. Barker, "Local Politics and National Development: The Case of a Rural District in the Saloum Region of Senegal," unpub. diss. University of California, Berkeley, 1967; David Brokensha, "Anthropological Enquiries and Political Science: A Case Study from Ghana," presented at African Studies Association Annual Meeting, 1965, p. 11; Fred G. Burke, *Local Government and Politics in Uganda* (Syracuse: Syracuse University Press, 1964); Lloyd A. Fallers, *Bantu Bureaucracy: A Century of Political Evolution among the Basoga of Uganda* (2nd ed., Chicago: University of Chicago Press, 1965); Norman N. Miller, "The Political Survival of Traditional Leadership," *Journal of Modern Africa Studies*, VI (August 1968), 183–203; Colin Leys, *Politicians and Politics: An Essay on Politics in Acholi, Uganda, 1962–1965* (Nairobi: East African Publishing House, 1967); Gene Andrew Maguire, "Toward Uhuru in Sukumaland: A Study of Micropolitics in Tanzania, 1945–1959," unpub. diss. Harvard University, 1966; David R. Smock, "From Village to Trade Union in Africa: A Study of Power and Decision-Making in the Nigerian Coal Miners' Union and in the Villages from which the Coal Miners Migrated," unpub. diss. Cornell University, 1964; Howard E. Wolpe, "Port Harcourt, A Community of Strangers: The Politics of Urban Development in Eastern Nigeria," unpub. diss. Massachusetts Institute of Technology, 1967. For a reevaluation of nationalism and decolonization, see Martin Kilson, *Political Change in a West African State: A Study of the Modernization Process in Sierra Leone* (Cambridge, Mass.: Harvard University Press, 1966).

2. Clifford Geertz, "The Integrative Revolution: Primordial Sentiments and

Civil Politics in the New States," in Geertz, ed., *Old Societies and New States: The Quest for Modernity in Africa and Asia* (New York: The Free Press of Glencoe, 1963), p. 109.

3. Use of the term tribe is avoided in this study in favor of the more general label of ethnic group or, more specifically, clan or people. "Tribe" is misleading because it was artificially imposed by foreign administrators and scholars on a variety of cultural clusters and therefore refers to many kinds of groups. Anthropologists define a clan as the largest kinship group acknowledging the same historical ancestor and participating in common activities. Larger, more amorphous communities, distinguished by cultural characteristics or an accepted joint historical tradition, constitute a people.

4. Paul Mercier, "On the Meaning of Tribalism in Black Africa," in Pierre L. van den Berghe, ed. and trans., *Africa: Social Problems of Change and Conflict* (San Francisco: Chandler Publishing Co., 1965), pp. 483–501, esp. p. 488.

5. For this estimate, see Daryll Forde and G. I. Jones, *The Ibo and Ibibio-Speaking Peoples of South-Eastern Nigeria* (London: Oxford University Press, 1950), p. 7.

6. For studies of relations among precolonial Ibo communities, see K. Onwuka Dike, *Trade and Politics in the Niger Delta, 1830–1885* (London: Oxford University Press, 1956); Simon Ottenberg, "Ibo Oracles and Intergroup Relations," *Southwest Journal of Anthropology*, XIV (Fall 1958), 294–317. The interpretation of Robert F. Stevenson, *Population and Political Systems* (New York: Columbia University Press, 1968), that there was a state formation among the Ibo based on the Aro dominance derives from a misreading of previous sources.

7. Karl W. Deutsch, *Nationalism and Social Communication: An Enquiry into the Foundations of Nationality* (2nd ed., Cambridge, Mass.: Massachusetts Institute of Technology Press, 1966), 196.

8. Some Ibo dialects are still mutually unintelligible.

9. For caste associations in India, see Lloyd I. Rudolph, "The Modernity of Tradition: The Democratic Incarnation of Caste in India," *American Political Science Review*, LIX (December 1965), 975–989; Lloyd L. Rudolph and Suzanne H. Rudolph, "The Political Role of India's Caste Associations," *Pacific Affairs*, XXVIII (Spring 1955), 235–253; Myron Weiner, *Politics of Scarcity* (Chicago: University of Chicago Press, 1962), pp. 36–72.

10. For the rise of African voluntary associations and ethnic unions, see Thomas Hodgkin, *Nationalism in Colonial Africa* (New York: New York University Press, 1956), pp. 84–92; Kenneth Little, *West African Urbanization* (London: Cambridge University Press, 1965); Immanuel Wallerstein, "Voluntary Associations," in James S. Coleman and Carl G. Rosberg, Jr., eds., *Political Parties and National Integration in Tropical Africa* (Berkeley and Los Angeles: University of California Press, 1964), pp. 318–339.

11. For references to ethnic associations in Africa, see Ione Acquah, *Accra Survey* (London: University of London Press, 1958), pp. 104–107; Michael

P. Banton, "Adaptation and Integration in the Social System of Temne Immigrants in Freetown," *Africa*, XXVI (October 1956), 354–367; Henry Bienen, *Tanzania: Party Transformation and Economic Development* (Princeton: Princeton University Press, 1967), pp. 24–26; Kilson, pp. 260–263; René Lemarchand, *Political Awakening in the Belgian Congo* (Berkeley and Los Angeles: University of California Press, 1964), pp. 175–176; Little, pp. 26, 33; Maguire, pp. 103–114, 211–249; Ruth Schachter Morgenthau, *Political Parties in French Speaking West Africa* (London: Oxford University Press, 1964), pp. 126, 144, 151, 221; Robert Rotberg, "The Rise of African Nationalism: The Case of East and Central Africa," *World Politics*, XV (October 1962), 77–82; Crawford Young, *Politics in the Congo: Decolonization and Independence* (Princeton: Princeton University Press, 1965), pp. 246–247, 292–293; Aristide A. Zolberg, "Mass Parties and National Integration: The Case of the Ivory Coast," *Journal of Politics*, XXV (February 1963), 36–48; Aristide A. Zolberg, *One-Party Government in the Ivory Coast* (Princeton: Princeton University Press, 1965), pp. 62–65.

12. Richard L. Sklar, "The Contributions of Tribalism to Nationalism in Western Nigeria," *Journal of Human Relations* VIII (Spring-Summer 1960), 407–415.

13. See, for example, W. T. Morrill, "Immigrants and Associations: The Ibo in Twentieth Century Calabar," *Comparative Studies in Society and History*, V (July 1963), 424–448.

14. The ethnic unions formed by other ethnic groups within Eastern Nigeria were most similar to the Ibo unions in terms of origins and role.

15. G. I. Jones, "From Direct to Indirect Rule in Eastern Nigeria," seminar paper, Institute of African Studies, University of Ife, 1964, p. 4.

16. See, for example, S. N. Eisenstadt, "Primitive Political Systems: A Comparative Analysis," in William J. Hanna, ed., *Independent Black Africa* (Chicago: Rand McNally and Co., 1964), pp. 73–74. A "primitive" political system denotes the simplest kind without clearly differentiated structure and role.

17. For more detailed studies of Ibo society, see Forde and Jones; M. M. Green, *Ibo Village Affairs* (2nd ed., New York: Frederick A. Praeger, 1964; G. I. Jones, "Ibo Age Organizations with Special Reference to the Cross River and North-East Ibo," *Journal of the Royal Anthropological Institute*, XCII (1962), 191–211; G. I. Jones, *Report on the Position, Status, and Influence of Chiefs and Natural Rulers in the Eastern Region of Nigeria* (Enugu: Government Printer, 1956); C. K. Meek, *Law and Authority in a Nigerian Tribe* (London: Oxford University Press, 1937); Simon Ottenberg, "Ibo Receptivity to Change," in William R. Bascom and Melville J. Herskovits, eds., *Continuity and Change in African Cultures* (Chicago: University of Chicago Press, 1962), pp. 130–143; David R. Smock, "From Village to Trade Union"; David R. Smock, "Changing Political Processes among the Abaja Ibo," *Africa*, XXXVIII (July 1968), 281–292; Victor C. Uchendu, *The Igbo of Southeast Nigeria* (New York: Holt, Rinehart and Winston, 1965).

18. My analysis is based on interviews with officers of the Ibo State Union, documents in its files, and discussions with other Ibo political actors.

19. The first Ibo Union was formed in 1934 in Lagos. After several organizational transformations it became the Ibo State Union in 1947. Up to 1947 the Ibo Union and its direct successor, the Ibo Federal Union, consisted primarily of a few branches of Ibo unions in Lagos.

20. The dissident faction that founded the UNIP included both Ibos and members of other ethnic groups. Most of the Ibos, however, eventually rejoined the NCNC.

21. For the Ibo State Union's views on the creation of more states from the old Eastern Region, see "The Ibo State Union Memorandum to the Willink's Minority Commission" (Port Harcourt: Nigeria Popular Printing Press, n.d.).

22. The title "One North or One Nigeria" refers to the fact that the North dominated the Federation by virtue of constituting a majority of the population. Many advocates of Nigerian unity then believed that the Northern Region should be divided into more regions to produce a greater balance. The statements of the Northern legislators are quoted in this pamphlet, pp. 11–24.

23. Decree Number 33, *Federal Republic of Nigeria Official Gazette* (Lagos: Governmental Printer, May 24, 1966).

24. Robert A. Dahl, *Who Governs? Democracy and Power in an American City* (New Haven: Yale University Press, 1961).

NOTES TO CHAPTER I

1. This estimate of 40,000, while substantially higher than the 1953 census figure of 21,036 or even than the 1963 count of 33,187, nevertheless represents a conservative approximation, because a very high proportion of Abiribans—perhaps four times the number remaining at home—go abroad to trade. It is extremely unlikely that most of these traders could return for the census, since a substantial number remain away even for the important celebrations at Christmas. Some educated Abiribans estimated the population at 50,000.

2. Amaeke, Amaogudu and Agbaji are sometimes referred to as villages by Abiribans. However, their territories are contiguous, their borders ill defined, and their independent functions presently almost nonexistent. Hence, the term division is preferable to village. According to the 1963 census, the population of Amaeke was 18,577, Amaogudu 11,014, and Agbaji 3,596.

3. C. J. Mayne, "Intelligence Report on the Abam Clan and the Towns of Abiriba, Umuhu, and Nkporo," Bende Division, Owerri Province, 1933.

4. Although Ibos did not have chiefs, an Eastern House of Chiefs, similar to those existing in other regions, was established in 1959 as a concession to minority groups. It became an arena of competition among the Ibo communities, as in the case of Abiriba, despite the general absence of traditional rulers. The Eastern House of Assembly, the elected parliamentary body, continued to exercise the legislative functions.

5. Ejim Akuma, "History of Abiriba," unpub. ms., n.d.

6. The Aros were the dominant slaving and trading Ibo community.

7. A. L. Weir, "Assessment Reports, Bende Division," 1927, p. 11.

8. Ejim Akuma, "Administrative Report of the Abiriba Improvement Union," 1942 (mimeo.).

9. Akuma, "History."

10. The names of several Abiriban organizations are not structured in good English.

11. Akuma, "History."

12. Akuma's manuscript made no mention of the Abiriba Homestars, but their role in interesting the traders was described in interviews with past and incumbent officers on the origin of the ACIU. Since Akuma was not a member, he may have wanted to minimize their role.

13. The continuity between the two organizations was so great that many people considered the branches of the Abiriba Youth League to be the first branches of the ACIU.

14. "Constitution of the Abiriba Communal Improvement Union" (mimeo.). It has since been revised, but informants claimed the aims remained unchanged.

15. "Minutes of the General Meeting of the Abiriba Communal Improvement Union" (cited hereafter as "Minutes"), August 1944 (mimeo.).

16. "Minutes," August 1948.

17. Ohafia is a large town slightly north of Abiriba.

18. "Minutes," December 1956.

19. "Minutes," January 1948.

20. "Minutes," August 1948.

21. "Minutes," December 1960.

22. Interview with Ejim Akuma, Abiriba, 1966.

23. Interview with Akuma.

24. "Minutes," April 1956.

25. "Minutes of the Meeting of the Port Harcourt Branch of the Abiriba Communal Improvement Union" (cited hereafter as "Minutes, P.H."), October 5, 1959.

26. This does not mean that all projects were placed on the priority list as a delaying tactic, for the union's financial problems did limit the acceptance of new projects.

27. "Minutes," April 1956, September 1960.

28. "Minutes of the Joint Meeting of the Central Executive of the ACIU and the Board of Governors, Enuda College," September 2, 1964. The board of governors and the central executive had overlapping memberships.

29. "Minutes," December 1964.

30. "Minutes," December 1964.

31. Interview with Akuma.

32. "Minutes," January 1942, August 1944, August 1945, June 1954, April 1956, April 1959, September 1957.

33. "Minutes," February 1959, February 1957.

34. "Minutes," August 1950, April 1959, May 1960; Ejim Akuma, "Financial Report of the Acting Administrative Secretary," February 1963 (mimeo.).

35. Ejim Akuma, "Financial Report of the Acting Administrative Secretary," February 1965 (mimeo.).

36. "Minutes," September 1960.

37. "Minutes," December 1956.

38. "Minutes," September 1962.

39. "Minutes," August 1950.

40. *Eastern Nigeria, Local Government Estimates, 1965–1966* (Enugu: Government Printer, n.d.).

41. This figure was obtained by totaling the revenues of the ACIU, Enuda College, and Egwuena Girls' Secondary School.

42. R. E. Wraith, "Local Government," in John P. Mackintosh, *Nigerian Government and Politics* (London: George Allen and Unwin, Ltd., 1966), pp. 220–223.

43. "Minutes," August 1947, September 1960.

44. "Minutes," August 1948, December 1956.

45. "Minutes," September 1954, December 1956, September 1957.

46. Information on the construction of the Egwuena Girls' Secondary School was pieced together from interviews with prominent members and officers of the Egwuena age grade.

47. Interview with an officer of the Akahaba age grade.

48. "Minutes," August 1955, September 1960.

49. Interview with an officer of the Okezie age grade.

50. The Bende Native Authority was one of the federated clan councils created by the British administration in the hope that larger council units would perform more effectively than the smaller, more traditional clan-native court areas. The failure of the federated councils led to the adoption in 1950 of a system of local government councils based on the British pattern.

51. Divisional councils were the intermediate level in the three-tier system adopted in 1950.

52. "Minutes," January 1948; August, January 1951; August 1953.

53. "Minutes," January 1948, January 1956.

54. "Minutes," August 1949.

55. Arbitration took place in June 1965 by a board constituted by the Abiriban chiefs and the Abiriba local council, which were deemed the proper authorities to rule on matters pertaining to tradition.

56. "Minutes," January 1950, "minutes, P. H.," April 1, 1951.

NOTES TO CHAPTER II

1. Dahl; Edward C. Banfield, *Political Influence* (New York: The Free Press of Glencoe, 1961), p. 3.

2. The following years were used: 1941-1945, 1947-1948, 1952-1960,

1962-1965. The other years were omitted mostly because the minute books unaccountably failed to present a complete list of officers.

3. "Minutes," January 1950; "Correspondence File of the Port Harcourt Branch of the Abiriba Communal Improvement Union," April 1951.

4. This was the only time the court enforced the payment of dues. At all other times the union was unsuccessful when resorting to legal action for the payment of dues.

5. "Minutes," September 1958.

6. "Minutes," May 1956; May, September 1960.

7. The professionals included one pharmacist, an accountant, and an optician.

8. "Minutes," August 1948, June 1964.

9. "Correspondence File, Port Harcourt Branch," 1965.

10. By 1966, six doctors, five lawyers, and eight educators had returned to Abiriba; one scientist with a doctorate was teaching in the United States; and about thirty Abiribans were studying outside Nigeria.

11. "Minutes," May 1956.

12. Kalu Ifegwu, last elected in 1956, received a law degree in 1965. In 1966 two former officers, N. M. Okafor and K. O. Uche, were studying at the University of Nigeria, Nsukka.

13. "Correspondence File, Port Harcourt Branch," December 1952.

14. A federal system was agreed on at a 1953 constitutional conference and, after elections in December of that year, was introduced in 1954.

15. "Minutes," August 1953.

16. "Minutes, P. H.," November 15, 1965.

17. "Minutes," January 1959.

18. *Eastern Nigeria Development Plan, 1962–1968,* Official Document No. 8 (Enugu: Government Printer, 1962), p. 39.

19. "Minutes," December 1956.

20. Emole's role was described by an officer of the age grade.

21. "Correspondence File, Port Harcourt Branch," 1965.

22. Constitutions of Enuda College and Egwuena Girls' Secondary School (mimeo.).

23. "Minutes, May 1956.

24. "Memorandum Submitted to the ACIU Conference, September 1962, by the Abiriba Youth Movement" (mimeo.).

25. Information about the administration of the schools was derived from a series of interviews with participants and observers.

26. "Minutes," September 1965.

27. "Minutes," December 1956.

28. For the classic statement on the "iron law of oligarchy," see Robert Michels, *Political Parties,* trans. Paul and Cedar Eden (New York: Dover Books, 1915).

29. O. A. Otisi, "Presidential Address to the General Meeting of the ACIU," August 1952 (mimeo.); "Minutes," January 1958.

30. Data for this section is taken from the minute books.

NOTES TO CHAPTER III

1. For the early administrative history of Mbaise, see E. M. Dickenson, "Intelligence Report on Ezennehitte Clan," Owerri Division, Owerri Province, 1931.

2. For a discussion of this period, see Jones, "From Direct to Indirect Rule."

3. Assistant District Officer, "Report on the Nguru Court Area with Regard to the Formation of New Native Courts at Obohia and Itu," 1929.

4. "Annual Report Owerri Province," written by senior residents, 1931–1950.

5. E. N. Mylius, resident, "Annual Report, 1941: Owerri Province," p. 7.

6. The names Oke and Oke-ovoro are interchangeable.

7. For information on the clans, see Edwin Ardener, "Lineage and Locality among the Mba-Ise Ibo," *Africa*, XXIX (April 1959), 113–133. According to this source, p. 121 a village-group is "the largest local unit, named, and based on a patrilineage or a segment of one, whose members claim to be regarded as independent of other groups, even of those sharing a common ancestry, this claim being recognized by other comparble groups, but not necessarily connected with any true independence of function."

8. Inferred from an interview with Ardener. In his "Interim Report on a Social and Economic Survey of Mba-Ise," unpub. ms., 1952, p. 9, Ardener referred to the Oke as acknowledging a common ancestor.

9. "Report on the Nguru Court Area," p. 5.

10. A. Ibe, "Our Precious Cultural Heritage," in "Ezinihitte Newsletter," no. 2 (December 1965/January 1966), pp. 4–5.

11. Dickenson, pp. 9–10.

12. The 1963 census figures were not available for all of Mbaise and were widely discounted there as being invalid. Most people interviewed in Mbaise believed that the 1953 survey was more accurate.

13. Ardener, "Interim Report," pp. 5–7.

14. An estimate of the Mbaise County Council chairman. See Donatus O. Onu, "Address to the Conference of Mbaise Leaders of Thought on Behalf of the Mbaise County Council," November 21, 1965 (mimeo.).

15. The reapportionment was in actuality undertaken by an independent commission.

16. N. C. Perkins, "Annual Report, Mbaise County District Council for period from 1st April 1956 to 31 March 1957."

17. *Eastern Nigeria, Local Government Estimates, 1965–1966* (Enugu: Government Printing Office, n.d.).

18. The projections of Mbaise's development program and itemization of expenditures are from Onu.

19. Perkins.

20. "Minutes of the Mbaise County Council," January 5, 1959; February 4, 1959; July 1, 1959 (mimeo.).

21. "Mbaise County Council Given Ultimatum," in Mbaise Spokesman," I (February 1964), 6.

NOTES TO CHAPTER IV

1. Gabriel A. Almond, "A Developmental Approach to Political Systems," *World Politics*, XVII (January 1965), 192, 193.

2. "Minutes of the Mbaise Federal Union," October 1951; C. O. Onuoha, "Administrative Report to the Mbaise Federal Union," April 1955.

3. B. Amadi, "Annual Report of the Secretary-General to the Conference of the Mbaise Federal Union," Nigeria, November 1953.

4. "Minutes of the Mbaise Federal Union," December 1956.

5. No palm trees were cut for a designated period of time. Then on a certain date the entire community gathered to cut palm trees, with the proceeds from the oil going to a communal project.

6. For an intelligence report on the Agbaja clan that includes fundamental misconceptions, see "Report on the Nguru Court Area." The punishment theory was the popular belief related by many members of the Nguru clan.

7. This charge had no substance, since the constituency delimitation committee was immune to such political pressures.

8. The "Ezinihitte Newsletter's" third issue (March 1966) was devoted to a discussion of the dispute and its settlement. Since the military government had suspended the electoral apparatus along with the other civilian representative institutions, the petition to Ojukwu was meaningless.

9. Information on the political involvement of the clan unions came from interviews with officers of the relevant unions and prominent educated members.

10. Interviews with members of the Ekwerazu clan.

11. Interviews with members of the Ezinihitte clan, including some of the participants.

12. Interview with an educated member of the Nguru clan.

13. Interview with officers of the Mbaise Youth Movement.

14. "Minutes of an Emergency Meeting of the Mbaise County Council," October 6, 1964.

15. "Minutes of the Mbaise Federal Union," August 1965.

16. Interview with an officer of the Mbaise Federal Union.

17 "Minutes of the Mbaise Federal Union," October 1951, December 1952; Amadi.

18. "Minutes of the Mbaise Federal Union," August 1956, July 1959. In 1956 the secretary of state for colonies had accused Premier Azikiwe of improper conduct for instructing that public funds be deposited in the African Continental Bank, while Azikiwe controlled the bank. The bank also did not meet certain minimum specifications of viability. When the secretary of state

for colonies appointed a commission to investigate the charges, Azikiwe dissolved the legislature and sought a new mandate. He was overwhelmingly reelected, canceling the critical aspects of the report of the commission when it was later issued. The second incident, in 1958, involved K. O. Mbadiwe's 'Zik must go' campaign, when Mbadiwe attempted to depose Azikiwe from the leadership of the NCNC.

19. "Minutes of the Mbaise Federal Union," emergency meeting, August 1964; interview with an officer of the Mbaise Federal Union.

20. "Minutes of the Mbaise Federal Union," February 1955; "Minutes of a Select Committee of the Mbaise Federal Union," November 4, 1956.

21. Interviews with officers of the Mbaise Federal Union.

NOTES TO CHAPTER V

1. "Minutes of the Mbaise County Council," January 30, 1958.

2. "Minutes of the Mbaise Federal Union," April 1961, December 1961.

3. "Minutes of the Mbaise Federal Union," July 1957.

4. A. N. Awiya, "Who Shall Lead Ezinihitte," in "Ezinihitte Newsletter," no. 3 (March 1966), pp. 8-9.

NOTES TO CHAPTER VI

1. Daniel Lerner, *The Passing of Traditional Society* (New York: The Free Press of Glencoe, 1958); Karl Deutsch, "Social Mobilization and Political Development," *American Political Science Review,* LV (September 1961), 493.

2. Emile Durkheim, *The Division of Labor in Society,* trans. George Simpson (New York: The Free Press of Glencoe, 1933).

3. Interview with Howard Wolpe. Wolpe arrived at this estimate by adding together the population of the wards in which the Ikwerres dominated. Since other groups lived in these wards, the figure may be overestimated.

4. Deutsch, "Social Mobilization," p. 494.

5. Daniel Lerner, "Toward a Communications Theory of Political Development," in Lucian W. Pye, ed., *Communications and Political Development* (Princeton: Princeton University Press, 1963), pp. 327–350. Lerner originally argued in his *The Passing of Traditional Society* that exposure to the mass media would induce rapid modernization.

6. See, for example, P. C. Lloyd, A. L. Mabogunje, and B. Awe, *The City of Ibadan* (London: Cambridge University Press, 1968); Leonard Plotnicov, *Strangers to the City: Urban Man in Jos, Nigeria* (Pittsburgh: University of Pittsburgh Press, 1967).

7. Ferdinand Tonnies, *Community and Society,* ed. and trans., Charles P. Loomis (New York: Harper and Row, 1957); Max Weber, *The Theory of Social and Economic Organizations,* ed. and trans. Talcott Parsons (New York: Oxford University Press, 1947); C. S. Whitaker, Jr., "A Dysrythmic Process of Political Change," *World Politics,* XIX (January 1967), 190–217.

8. See, for example, David W. Brokensha, *Social Change at Larteh, Ghana* (London: Oxford University Press, 1966); A. L. Epstein, *Politics in an Urban African Community* (Manchester: Manchester University Press, 1958); Plotnicov; Smock, "From Village to Trade Union"; High H. and Mabel M. Smythe, *The New Nigerian Elite* (Stanford: Stanford University Press, 1960).

9. Howard E. Wolpe, "Port Harcourt: A Community of Strangers"; and his "Port Harcourt: Ibo Politics in Microcosm," presented at African Studies Association Annual Conference, 1968.

10. Wolpe, "Port Harcourt: Ibo Politics in Microcosm," p. 25.

11. *Memorandum and Estimates of Local Government Expenditures for 1963–1964* (Enugu: Government Printer, n.d.). All urban authorities received a higher rebate than did rural local councils, owing to the greater magnitude of their problems.

12. This information on trade unions came from an interview with an industrial relations adviser. See also Smock, "From Village to Trade Union."

13. Wolpe, "Port Harcourt: Ibo Politics in Microcosm," pp. 26–27.

14. Wolpe, "Port Harcourt: A Community of Strangers," pp. 459–500.

15. Raymond E. Wolfinger, "The Development and Persistence of Ethnic Voting," *American Political Science Review,* LIX (December 1965), 895.

16. This figure was attained by adding together the 1963 census estimates for the 40 wards in Port Harcourt. Since many of the residents returned to their home communities for the census or did not report, the figure is an underestimation.

17. Nwobodike Nwanodi's victory in the Ahoada Central constituency was one of the two seats won by independents in the East in the revoting of March 1965 after the boycott.

18. William Kornhauser, *The Politics of Mass Society* (New York: The Free Press of Glencoe, 1959), pp. 142–150.

NOTES TO CHAPTER VII

1. "Minutes of the Abiriba Youth League, Port Harcourt Branch," October 1939.

2. "Minutes, P.H.," September 5, November 2, 1965.

3. "Minutes," August 1948; "Minutes, P.H.," August 30, 1964.

4. "Minutes, P.H.," May 17, June 28, August 16, 30, 1964; March 21, 1965.

5. "Minutes, P.H.," October 26, 1950; July 7, 1958; "Minutes," August 1947; "Minutes, P.H.," May 5, 1959.

6. "Minutes, P.H.," November 15, 1965.

7. "Minutes, P.H.," April 9, 1949.

8. "Minutes, P.H.," November 15, 1965.

9. Correspondence between Port Harcourt Branch and central secretariat, August 2, 1965.

10. "Minutes, P.H., July 24, 1960.

11. "Minutes, P.H.," April 1, 29, 1951.

NOTES TO CHAPTER VIII

1. "Minutes of the Ezinihitte Clan Union," January 1964–April 1966.
2. "Minutes of the Mbaise Youth Movement, Port Harcourt Branch," February 21, July 11, 1963; February 25, 1965; August 8, March 2, 1963.
3. "Minutes of the Mbaise Youth Movement," August 2, 1962.
4. "Minutes of the Mbaise Youth Movement," August 8, 1963.
5. *Report of the Tribunal Appointed to Inquire into Allegations Reflecting on the Official Conduct of the Premier of, and Certain Persons Holding Ministerial and Other Public Offices in the Eastern Region of Nigeria* (London: HMSO, 1957).
6. Interview with D.D.U. Okay, which took place about two years after the events.
7. Interview with members of the social welfare team of St. Andrew's Council.
8. *Eastern Nigeria Development Plan,* pp. 9, 35.

NOTES TO CHAPTER IX

1. K. W. J. Post, "The National Council of Nigeria and the Cameroons and the Decision of December 1959," in Mackintosh, p. 413.
2. Peter Pan (Peter Enahoro) of the *Daily Times,* as quoted in "The State of Nigerian Political Parties," *West Africa,* January 25, 1964, p. 91.
3. John P. Mackintosh, "Electoral Trends," in Mackintosh, p. 522.
4. Samuel P. Huntington, *Political Order in Changing Societies* (New Haven: Yale University Press, 1968), p. 10.
5. Huntington, p. 12.
6. Huntington, pp. 612–624.
7. The NCNC was often plagued by the composition of its district executive committees because they were not fully representative. In the Agbaja constituency the three ethnic components had equal representation, despite the fact that one of them, Nguru, constituted a majority of the population.
8. For an example of localities with weak ethnic unions, see Smock, "Changing Political Processes among the Abaja Ibo," pp. 281–292.
9. Richard L. Sklar, *Nigerian Political Parties: Power in an Emergent African Nation* (Princeton: Princeton University Press, 1963), p. 412.
10. Richard L. Sklar and C. S. Whitaker, "Nigeria," in James S. Coleman and Carl G. Rosberg, Jr., eds., *Political Parties and National Integration in Tropical Africa* (Berkeley and Los Angeles: University of California Press, 1964), pp. 612–613.
11. Mackintosh, p. 531.
12. See particularly Zolberg, *Creating Political Order,* pp. 1–39; Bienen, pp. 4–5. For models of African political parties, see Coleman and Rosberg, p. 5; Thomas Hodgkin, *African Political Parties* (Baltimore: Penguin Press, 1961), pp. 68–75; Ruth Schacter, "Single Party Systems in West Africa," *American Political Science Review,* LV (June 1961), 294–307.

NOTES TO CHAPTER X

1. See "Annual Reports, Owerri Province"; L. Gray Cowan, *Local Government in West Africa* (New York: Columbia University Press, 1958), pp. 12–34.
2. I rely heavily throughout this chapter on R. E. Wraith, "Local Government" in Mackintosh, pp. 200–265.
3. See David Smock, "Changing Political Processes," p. 291.
4. *Eastern Nigeria, Local Government Estimates, 1965–1966.*
5. Leys, *Politicians and Policies,* p. 103.
6. Ardener, "Lineage and Locality," p. 130.
7. For description of a county council meeting in Abaja-Ngwo, see David Smock, "Changing Political Processes," pp. 289–290.
8. See, for example, Huntington, pp. 59–71; Colin Leys, "What Is the Problem about Corruption," *Journal of Modern African Studies,* III (September 1965), 215–230; M. G. Smith, "Historical and Cultural Conditions of Political Corruption among the Hausa," *Comparative Studies in Society and History,* VI (January 1964), 164–196; Simon Ottenberg, "Local Government and the Law in Southern Nigeria," *Journal of Asian and African Studies,* II (January and April 1967), 26–43; Ronald Wraith and Edgar Simpkins, *Corruption in Developing Countries* (New York: W. W. Norton and Co., 1964).
9. Ottenberg, "Local Government," p. 29.
10. Wraith, "Local Government," in Mackintosh, p. 260.
11. Evaluation based on interviews, reports, and the amount of revenue available to them.
12. Wraith, "Local Government," in Mackintosh, p. 223.
13. Wraith, "Local Government," in Mackintosh, p. 219.
14. Wraith, "Local Government," in Mackintosh, p. 259.
15. David Smock, "From Village to Trade Union," p. 91.

NOTES TO CHAPTER XI

1. Aristide R. Zolberg, "Patterns of National Integration," *Journal of Modern African Studies,* V (December 1967), 451; Mercier, p. 489; Geertz, pp. 110–112, 119–128.
2. Immanuel Wallerstein, "Ethnicity and National Integration in West Africa," in van den Berghe, ed., pp. 472–482.
3. Richard S. Sklar, "The Contribution of Tribalism to Nationalism in Western Nigeria," pp. 407–415.
4. David R. Smock, *Conflict and Control in an African Trade Union* (Stanford: Stanford University Press for Hoover Institute, 1969); Mackintosh, pp. 290–317.
5. Barker, p. 170; Joan E. Vincent, "Status and Leadership in an African Community: A Case Study," unpub. diss. Columbia University, 1968; A. L. Epstein.

6. Geertz, p. 127, describes ethnic unions as having this effect in multi-ethnic cities.

7. Deutsch, *Nationalism and Social Communication,* pp. 86–105.

8. See, for example, Lawrence H. Fuchs, ed., *American Ethnic Politics* (New York: Harper and Row, 1968), p. 1.

9. Zolberg, "Patterns of National Integration," p. 451.

10. See, for example, Nathan Glazer and Daniel P. Moynihan, *Beyond the Melting Pot: The Negroes, Puerto-Ricans, Jews, Italians, and Irish of New York City* (Cambridge, Mass.: Massachusetts Institute of Technology Press, 1963); Milton M. Gordon, *Assimilation in American Life: The Role of Race, Religion, and National Origins* (New York: Oxford University Press, 1964); Wolfinger, "The Development and Persistence of Ethnic Voting," pp. 896–908.

11. Michael Parenti, "Ethnic Politics and the Persistence of Ethnic Identification," *American Political Science Review,* LXI (September 1967), p. 724.

12. Fuchs, p. 4.

13. Audrey C. Smock and David R. Smock, "Ethnicity and Attitudes Toward Development in Eastern Nigeria," *Journal of Developing Areas,* IV (July 1969), 499–512.

14. Mercier, p. 495; Zolberg, "Patterns of National Integration," p. 466; Geertz, p. 155.

15. Geertz, p. 110.

16. In 1962 the Action Group, the governing party in Western Nigeria, was in opposition on the federal level. When a few politicians became disorderly in the Western House of Assembly, the federal government declared a state of emergency in the Western Region, dissolved the Western government, and restricted most important Action Group politicians. Dissident Action Group politicians, who were willing to cooperate with the federal government, started a new party and recruited Action Group members of the Western House of Assembly through intimidation and bribery. In 1963 when the emergency was lifted, the new political party was able to form a government.

17. Myron Weiner, "India: Two Political Cultures," in Lucian W. Pye and Sidney Verba, eds., *Political Culture and Political Development* (Princeton: Princeton University Press, 1965), pp. 199–244.

NOTES TO CHAPTER XII

1. Gabriel A. Almond and G. Bingham Powell, Jrs., *Comparative Politics: A Developmental Approach* (Boston: Little Brown and Co., 1966), esp. pp. 50–72, 284–298. For the nature and components of political culture, see Pye and Verba, esp. pp. 3–26, 512–560; Gabriel A. Almond and Sidney Verba, *The Civic Culture* (Boston: Little Brown and Co., 1963).

2. For other definitions of integration, some of which stress objective factors such as the establishment of institutions linking the state territorially, see Myron Weiner, "Political Integration and Political Development," *The Annals of the American Academy of Political and Social Science,* 358 (March 1965), pp. 52–64.

3. Pye and Verba, esp. pp. 3–26.

4. Smock, "From Village to Trade Union."

5. Huntington, *Political Order,* pp. 74–78, 435–438.

6. Lloyd A. Free, *The Attitudes, Hopes, and Fears of Nigerians* (Princeton: Institute for International Social Research, 1964), p. 38.

7. Smock and Smock, "Ethnicity and Attitudes Toward Development."

8. John Mackintosh estimated that while the Calabar-Ogoja-Rivers area had only 35 percent of the population, it received 42 percent of the expenditures of the Ministry of Agriculture from 1957–1963 and 42 percent of the money loaned during that period for agricultural and industrial projects. Mackintosh, p. 525. It is likely that a similar distribution continued through 1966.

9. The existence of multiple centers in Mbaise made it similar to the structure of New Haven as described by Dahl in *Who Governs?*

10. Smock, "Changing Political Processes"; "From Village to Trade Union"; "Minutes of the Enugu Ezike Welfare Association, Home Branch," 1948–1951; "Minutes of the Enugu Ezike Improvement Union, Home Branch," 1953–1959; "Minutes of the Ihiala Progress Union, Enugu Branch," 1952–1955, 1957–1959; "Minutes of the Oghe Improvement Union, Enugu Branch," 1960–1961; Simon Ottenberg, "Improvement Associations among the Afikpo Ibo," *Africa,* XXV (January 1955), 1–23.

11. Richard N. Henderson, "Generalized Cultures and Evolutionary Adaptability: A Comparison of Urban Efik and Ibo in Nigeria," *Ethnology,* V (October 1966), 365–391.

12. Smock, "From Village to Trade Union," p. 350.

13. Pye, "Introduction," in Pye and Verba, p. 19.

14. Denis A. Goulet, "Development for What?" *Comparative Political Studies,* I (July 1968), 295–312.

15. Pye, "Introduction," in Pye and Verba, p. 19.

Bibliography

OFFICIAL SOURCES

"Annual Report, Owerri Province." Written by senior residents, 1931–1950. Archives, Enugu.

The Constitution of the Eastern Region of Nigeria. Lagos: Federal Ministry of Information, 1963.

The Constitution of the Federal Republic of Nigeria. Lagos: Federal Ministry of Information, 1963.

Dickenson, E. M. "Intelligence Report on the Ezennehitte Clan." Owerri Division, Owerri Province, 1931. Archives, Enugu.

Distribution of Amenities in Eastern Nigeria. Enugu: Government Printer, 1963, 1964, 1965.

Eastern Nigeria Development Plan, 1962–1968, Official Document No. 8. Enugu: Government Printer, 1962.

Eastern Nigeria, Local Government Estimates, 1963–1964, 1964–1965, 1965–1966. Enugu: Government Printer, n.d.

Federal Republic of Nigeria, Official Gazette. Lagos: Government Printer, 1966.

Jones, G. I. *Report on the Position, Status and Influence of Chiefs and Natural Rulers in the Eastern Region of Nigeria.* Enugu: Government Printer, 1956.

Mayne, C. J. "Intelligence Report on the Abam Clan and the Towns of Abiriba, Umuhu, and Nkporo." Bende Division, Owerri Province, 1933. Archives, Ibadan.

Memorandum and Estimates of Local Government Expenditures for 1963–1964. Enugu: Government Printer, n.d.

"Minutes of the Mbaise County Council," January 1955–January 1966. Owerri Divisional Office. Mimeographed.

Perkins, N. C. "Annual Report, Mbaise Council for Period from 1st April 1956 to 31st March 1957." Owerri Divisional Office.

259

Population Census in the Eastern Region of Nigeria, 1953. Lagos: Census Superintendent, 1954.

Population Census in the Eastern Region of Nigeria, 1963. Lagos: Census Superintendent, 1964.

Report of the Commission Appointed to Enquire into the Fears of the Minorities and the Means of Allaying Them. London: Her Majesty's Stationary Office, 1958.

Report of the Tribunal Appointed to Inquire into Allegations Reflecting on the Official Conduct of the Premier of, and Certain Persons Holding Ministerial and other Public Offices in the Eastern Region of Nigeria. London: Her Majesty's Stationary Office, 1957.

"Report on the Nguru Court Area with Regard to the Formation of New Native Courts at Obohia and Itu." Written by Assistant District Officer, 1929. Archives, Ibadan.

Weir, A. L. "Assessment Report, Bende Division," 1927. Archives, Ibadan.

DOCUMENTS AND PUBLICATIONS
OF THE IBO STATE UNION

"Ibo Day Celebration and Civic Reception for His Royal Highness, The Oba of Benin," Port Harcourt, December 7, 1963. Mimeographed.

The Ibo State Union Constitution. Port Harcourt: Ibioma Printing Press, n.d.

The Ibo State Union Memorandum to the Willink's Minority Commission. Port Harcourt: Nigerian Popular Printing Press, n.d.

"A Memorandum for Discussion Presented by a Delegation of the Ibo State Union to Alhaji Sir Abubakar Tafawa Balewa, Prime Minister of the Federal Republic of Nigeria, at Lagos on the 27th Day of August, 1965." Mimeographed.

"Nigerian Disunity: The Guilty Ones." Enugu, 1964.

Obi, Z. C. "Address to the Mammoth Assembly of the Ibo State Union Holding at Enugu, June 6, 1964." Mimeographed.

————. "Presidential Address to the 28th session of the Ibo State Union Assembly Holding at Port Harcourt, on the 12th and 13th of June, 1965." Mimeographed.

"One North or One Nigeria." Enugu, 1964.

Otuka, J. I. J. "Calling All Ibos: Ibo Day Celebrations 1965," Port Harcourt, November 1965. Mimeographed.

"Recommendations of an Ad Hoc Committee Adopted by the Ibo State Union Held at Aba on the 18th and 19th of September 1965." Mimeographed.

"The Resolution of the Ibo State Union Committee on the Award of National Honorary Chieftancy Titles Taken at the Meeting Held at Port Harcourt, 19 April 1965." Mimeographed.

DOCUMENTS, MINUTE BOOKS, AND PUBLICATIONS
OF THE ABIRIBA COMMUNAL IMPROVEMENT UNION

Abiriba Students Union (magazine). 1966.
Akuma, Ejim. "Annual Report of the Abiriba Improvement Union," 1941. Mimeographed.
———. "Financial Report of the Acting Administrative Secretary," February 1963–February 1965. Mimeographed.
———. "Annual Report of the Acting Administrative Secretary of the Abiriba Communal Improvement Union for the Year 1964." Mimeographed.
"Auditor's Report, Abiriba Communal Improvement Union: Income and Expenses, January 1961 to September 1962." Mimeographed.
"Constitution of the Board of Governors of Egwuena Girls' Secondary School." Mimeographed.
"Constitution of the Board of Governors, Enuda College." Mimeographed.
"Constitution of the Abiriba Communal Improvement Union." Mimeographed.
"Correspondence File of the Port Harcourt Branch of the Abiriba Communal Improvement Union," January 1945–April 1966.
"Memorandum Submitted to the ACIU Conference, September 1962, by the Abiriba Youth Movement." Mimeographed.
"Minutes of the Abiriba Youth League," 1939.
"Minutes of the General Meeting of the Abiriba Communal Improvement Union," January 1942–September 1965. Mimeographed.
"Minutes of the Joint Meeting of the Central Executive of the ACIU and the Board of Governors, Enuda College," September 2, 1964.
"Minutes of the Meetings of the Port Harcourt Branch of the Abiriba Communal Improvement Union." January 1945–April 1966.
Otisi, O. A. "Presidential Address to the General Meeting of the Abiriba Communal Improvement Union," August 1952. Mimeographed.
"Welcoming Address Presented to Chief Emole During His Visit to Port Harcourt and Diobu Branches of the Abiriba Communal Improvement Union," November 15, 1965.

DOCUMENTS, MINUTE BOOKS, AND PUBLICATIONS
OF UNIONS AND ORGANIZATIONS IN MBAISE

"Annual Report of the Secretary-General to the Conference of the Mbaise Federal Union, Nigeria," November 1953; December 1956, 1957, 1958, 1959.
"Constitution, Rules and Regulations of the Mbaise Federal Union," September 1952, July 1957. Mimeographed.
"Ezinihitte Newsletter," no. 1 (September/October 1965), no. 2 (December 1965/January 1966), no. 3 (March 1966). Mimeographed.

"Mbaise Spokesman," I (January 1964)–II (December 1965). Mimeographed.

"Minutes of the Ezinihitte Clan Union," January 1964–April 1966.

"Minutes of the Mbaise Federal Union," October 1951–August 1964. Mimeographed.

"Minutes of the Mbaise Youth Movement, Port Harcourt Branch," November 1954–April 1966.

"Minutes of a Select Committee of the Mbaise Federal Union." November 1956 (Future Plans for Mbaise Committee); April 22, 1957, and June 30, 1957 (Constitutional Committee); July 28, 1957 (Reception for Honorable Minister P. O. Nwoga).

Ogbonna, A. N. "Presidential Address to Annual General Meeting of the Mbaise Federal Union, Nigeria," December 1957, 1959, 1961.

Onu, Donatus. "Address to the Conference of Mbaise Leaders of Thought on Behalf of the Mbaise County Council," November 21, 1965. Mimeographed.

Onuoha, C. O. "Administrative Report to the Mbaise Federal Union," April 1955.

"Report of the Ways and Means Sub-Committee of the Mbaise Economic Committee, Mbaise Federal Union," September 21, 1963.

DOCUMENTS AND MINUTE BOOKS OF MISCELLANEOUS ORGANIZATIONS IN NIGERIA

"Constitution of the Bende Development Union," n.d.

"Constitution of the National Council of Nigeria and the Cameroons," 1944.

"Minutes of the Enugu Ezike Welfare Association," 1948–1951.

"Minutes of the Enugu Ezike Improvement Union," 1953–1959.

"Minutes of the Ihiala Progress Union, Enugu Branch," 1952–1955, 1957–1959.

"Minutes of the Oghe Improvement Union, Enugu Branch," 1950–1954, 1958–1961.

"Minutes of the Oghe Youth Association, Enugu Branch," 1960–1961.

GENERAL WORKS

Acquah, Ione. Accra Survey. London: University of London Press, 1958.

Akuma, Ejim. "History of Abiriba." Unpub. ms., n.d.

Almond, Gabriel A. "A Developmental Approach to Political Systems," World Politics, XVII (January 1965), 183–214.

———— and G. Bingham Powell, Jr. Comparative Politics: A Developmental Approach. Boston: Little Brown and Company, 1966.

———— and Sidney Verba. The Civic Culture. Boston: Little Brown and Company, 1963.

Apter, David E. The Politics of Modernization. Chicago: University of Chicago Press, 1965.

Ardener, Edwin. "Interim Report on a Social and Economic Survey of Mba-Ise." Unpub. ms., 1952.

————. "The Kinship Terminology of a Group of Southern Ibo," *Africa,* XXIV (April 1954), 85–98.

————. "Lineage and Locality among the Mba-Ise Ibo," *Africa,* XXIX (April 1959), 113–133.

Banfield, Edward C. *Political Influence.* New York: The Free Press of Glencoe, 1961.

Banton, Michael P. "Adaptation and Integration in the Social System of Temne Immigrants in Freetown," *Africa,* XXVI (October 1956), 354–367.

Barker, Jonathan S. "Local Politics and National Development: The Case of a Rural District in the Saloum Region of Senegal." Unpub. diss., University of California, 1967.

Bienen, Henry. *Tanzania: Party Transformation and Economic Development.* Princeton: Princeton University Press, 1967.

Brokensha, David. "Anthropological Enquiries and Political Science: A Case Study from Ghana." Presented at African Studies Association Annual Conference, 1965.

————. *Social Change at Larteh, Ghana.* London: Oxford University Press, 1966.

Burke, Fred G. *Local Government and Politics in Uganda.* Syracuse: Syracuse University Press, 1964.

Coleman, James S. *Nigeria: Background to Nationalism.* Berkeley and Los Angeles: University of California Press, 1958.

————. "The Role of Tribal Associations in Nigeria," *West African Institute of Social and Economic Research,* 1952 (first conference), pp. 61–66.

———— and Carl G. Rosberg, Jr., eds. *Political Parties and National Integration in Tropical Africa.* Berkeley and Los Angeles: University of California Press, 1964.

Cowan, L. Gray. *Local Government in West Africa.* New York: Columbia University Press, 1958.

Dahl, Robert A. *Who Governs? Democracy and Power in an American City.* New Haven: Yale University Press, 1961.

Deutsch, Karl W. *Nationalism and Social Communication: An Enquiry into the Foundations of Nationality,* 2nd ed. Cambridge, Mass.: Massachusetts Institute of Technology Press, 1966.

————. "Social Mobilization and Political Development," *American Political Science Review,* LV (September 1961), 493–514.

Dike, K. Onwuka. *Trade and Politics in the Niger Delta, 1830–1885.* London: Oxford University Press, 1956.

Durkheim, Emile. *The Division of Labor in Society.* Trans. George Simpson, New York: The Free Press of Glencoe, 1933.

Eisenstadt, S. N. "African Age Groups: A Comparative Study," *Africa,* XXIV (April 1954), 100–113.

————. "Primitive Political Systems: A Comparative Analysis," in William J.

Hanna, ed. *Independent Black Africa,* pp. 60–85. Chicago: Rand Mc-Nally and Company, 1964.

———. "Social Change and Modernization in Africa South of the Sahara," *Cahiers d'Etudes Africaines,* V (1963), 453–471.

Epstein, A. L. *Politics in an Urban African Community.* Manchester: Manchester University Press, 1958.

Fallers, Lloyd A. *Bantu Bureaucracy: A Century of Political Evolution among the Basoga of Uganda,* 2nd ed. Chicago: University of Chicago Press, 1965.

Forde, Daryll, and G. I. Jones. *The Ibo and Ibibio-Speaking Peoples of South-Eastern Nigeria.* London: Oxford University Press, 1950.

Free, Lloyd A. *The Attitudes, Hopes, and Fears of Nigerians.* Princeton: Institute of International Social Research, 1964.

Fried, Morton H. "On the Concepts of 'Tribe and Tribal Society,'" *Transactions of the New York Academy of Sciences,* XXVIII (February 1966), 527–540.

Fuchs, Lawrence H., ed. *American Ethnic Politics.* New York: Harper and Row, 1968.

Geertz, Clifford, ed. *Old Societies and New States: The Quest for Modernity in Asia and Africa.* New York: The Free Press of Glencoe, 1963.

Gerth, Hans H., and C. Wright Mills, eds. and trans. *From Max Weber: Essays in Sociology.* New York: Oxford University Press, 1946.

Glickman, Harvey. "Dialogues on the Theory of African Political Development," *Africa Report,* XII (May 1967), 38–39.

———. "Regionalism and Micropolitics," *Africa Report,* XII (June 1967), 31–32.

Glazer, Nathan, and Daniel P. Moynihan. *Beyond the Melting Pot: The Negroes, Puerto-Ricans, Jews, Italians, and Irish of New York City.* Cambridge, Mass.: Massachusetts Institute of Technology Press, 1963.

Gordon, Milton M. *Assimilation in American Life: The Role of Race, Religion, and National Origins.* New York: Oxford University Press, 1964.

Goulet, Denis A. "Development for What?" *Comparative Political Studies,* I (July 1968), 295–312.

Green, M. M. *Ibo Village Affairs,* 2nd ed. New York: Frederick A. Praeger, 1964.

Henderson, Richard N. "Generalized Cultures and Evolutionary Adaptability: A Comparison of Urban Efik and Ibo in Nigeria," *Ethnology,* V (October 1966), 365–391.

Hodgkin, Thomas. *African Political Parties.* Baltimore: Penguin Press, 1961.

———. *Nationalism in Colonial Africa.* New York: New York University Press, 1956.

Hunter, Floyd. *Community Power Structure.* Chapel Hill: University of North Carolina Press, 1953.

Huntington, Samuel P. "Political Development and Political Decay," *World Politics,* XVII (April 1965), 386–403.

———. *Political Order in Changing Societies.* New Haven: Yale University Press, 1968.

Jones, G. I. "From Direct to Indirect Rule in Eastern Nigeria," Seminar paper, Institute of African Studies, University of Ife, 1964.

————. "Ibo Age Organizations with Special Reference to the Cross River and the North-East Ibo," *Journal of the Royal Anthropological Institute,* XCII (1962), 191–211.

Kilson, Martin. *Political Change in a West African State: A Study of the Modernization Process in Sierra Leone.* Cambridge, Mass.: Harvard University Press, 1966.

Kornhauser, William. *The Politics of Mass Society.* New York: The Free Press of Glencoe, 1959.

Lemarchand, René. *Political Awakening in the Belgian Congo.* Berkeley and Los Angeles: University of California Press, 1964.

Lerner, Daniel. *The Passing of Traditional Society.* New York: The Free Press of Glencoe, 1958.

————. "Toward a Communications Theory of Modernization: A Set of Considerations," in Lucian W. Pye, ed. *Communications and Political Development,* pp. 327–250. Princeton: Princeton University Press, 1963.

Le Vine, Robert A. *Dreams and Deeds: Achievement Motivation in Nigeria.* Chicago: University of Chicago Press, 1966.

Leys, Colin. *Politicians and Policies: An Essay on Politics in Acholi, Uganda, 1963–1965.* Nairobi: East Africa Publishing House, 1967.

————. "What Is the Problem about Corruption," *Journal of Modern African Studies,* III (September 1965), 215–230.

Little, Kenneth. *West African Urbanization.* London: Cambridge University Press, 1965.

Lloyd, P. C., A. L. Mabogunje, and B. Awe. *The City of Ibadan.* London: Cambridge University Press, 1968.

Mackintosh, John P., ed. *Nigerian Government and Politics.* London: George Allen and Unwin, Ltd., 1966.

Maguire, Gene Andrew. "Toward Uhuru in Sukumaland: A Study of Micropolitics in Tanzania, 1945–1959." Unpub. diss., Harvard University, 1966.

Meek, C. K. *Law and Authority in a Nigerian Tribe.* London: Oxford University Press, 1937.

Mercier, Paul. "On the Meaning of Tribalism in Black Africa," in Pierre L. van den Berghe, ed. *Africa: Social Problems of Change and Conflict,* pp. 483–501. San Francisco: Chandler Publishing Company, 1965.

Merton, Robert K. *Social Theory and Social Structure.* Illinois: The Free Press of Glencoe, 1949.

Michels, Robert. *Political Parties: A Sociological Study of the Oligarchical Tendency of Modern Democracies,* trans. Paul and Cedar Eden. New York: Dover Press, 1915.

Miller, Norman W. "The Political Survival of Traditional Leaders," *Journal of Modern African Studies,* VI (August 1968), 183–203.

Morgenthau, Ruth Schachter. *Political Parties in French Speaking West Africa.* London: Oxford University Press, 1964.

Morrill, W. T. "Immigrants and Associations: The Ibo in Twentieth Century

Calabar," *Comparative Studies in Society and History,* V (July 1963), 424–448.

———. "Two Urban Cultures of Calabar, Nigeria." Unpub. diss., University of Chicago, 1961.

Ottenberg, Simon. "Ibo Oracles and Intergroup Relations," *Southwest Journal of Anthropology,* XIV (Fall 1958), 294–317.

———. "Ibo Receptivity to Change," in William R. Bascom and Melville J. Herskovits, eds. *Continuity and Change in African Cultures,* pp. 130–143. Chicago: University of Chicago Press, 1962.

———. "Improvement Associations among the Afikpo Ibo," *Africa,* XXV (January 1955), 1–23.

———. "Local Government and the Law in Southern Nigeria," *Journal of Asian and African Studies,* II (January and April 1967), 26–43.

Parenti, Michael. "Ethnic Politics and the Persistence of Ethnic Identification," *American Political Science Review,* LXI (September 1967), 716–726.

Plotnicov, Leonard. *Strangers to the City: Urban Man in Jos, Nigeria.* Pittsburgh: University of Pittsburgh Press, 1967.

Polsby, Nelson S. *Community Power and Political Theory.* New Haven: Yale University Press, 1964.

Pye, Lucian W., and Sidney Verba, eds. *Political Culture and Political Development.* Princeton: Princeton University Press, 1965.

Rotberg, Robert. "The Rise of Nationalism: The Case of East and Central Africa," *World Politics,* XV (October 1962), 75–90.

Rudolph, Lloyd I. "The Modernity of Tradition: The Democratic Incarnation of Caste in India," *American Political Science Review,* LIX (December 1965), 975–989.

——— and Suzanne H. Rudolph, "The Political Role of India's Caste Associations," *Pacific Affairs,* XXVIII (Spring 1955), 235–253.

Schacter, Ruth. "Single Party Systems in West Africa," *American Political Science Review,* LV (June 1961), 294–307.

Sklar, Richard L. *Nigerian Political Parties: Power in an Emergent African Nation.* Princeton: Princeton University Press, 1963.

———. "The Contributions of Tribalism to Nationalism in Western Nigeria," *Journal of Human Relations,* VIII (Spring, Summer 1960), 407–415.

Smith, M. G. "Historical and Cultural Conditions of Political Corruption among the Hausa," *Comparative Studies in Society and History,* VI (January 1964), 164–196.

Smock, Audrey C., and David R. Smock. "Ethnicity and Attitudes Toward Development in Eastern Nigeria," *Journal of Developing Areas,* III (July 1969), 499–512.

Smock, David R. "Changing Political Processes among the Abaja Ibo," *Africa,* XXXVIII (July 1969), 281–292.

———. *Conflict and Control in an African Trade Union.* Stanford: Stanford University Press for Hoover Institute, 1969.

———. "From Village to Trade Union in Africa: A Study of Power and

Decision-Making in the Nigerian Coal Miners' Union and in the Villages from which the Coal Miners Migrated." Unpub. diss, Cornell University, 1964.

Smythe, Hugh H., and Mabel M. Smythe. *The New Nigerian Elite*. Stanford: Stanford University Press, 1960.

Stevenson, Robert F. *Population and Political Systems*. New York: Columbia University Press, 1968.

Tonnies, Ferdinand. *Community and Society*, ed. and trans. Charles P. Loomis. New York: Harper and Row, 1957.

Uchendu, Victor C. *The Igbo of Southeast Nigeria*. New York: Holt, Rinehart and Winston, 1965.

Vincent, Joan E. "Status and Leadership in an African Community: A Case Study." Unpub. diss., Columbia University, 1968.

Wallerstein, Immanuel. "Ethnicity and National Integration in West Africa," in Pierre L. van den Berghe, ed. *Africa: Social Problems of Change and Conflict*, pp. 472–482. San Francisco: Chandler Publishing Company, 1965.

Weber, Max. *The Theory of Social and Economic Organizations*, ed. and trans. Talcott Parsons. New York: Oxford University Press, 1947.

Weiner, Myron. "Political Integration and Political Development," *The Annals of the American Academy of Political and Social Science*, 358 (March 1965), 52–64.

———. *Politics of Scarcity*. Chicago: University of Chicago Press, 1962.

Whitaker, C. S. "A Dysrhythmic Process of Political Change," *World Politics*, XIX (January 1967), 190–217.

Wolfinger, Raymond E. "The Development and Persistence of Ethnic Voting," *American Political Science Review*, LIX (December 1965), 896–908.

Wolpe, Howard E. "Port Harcourt, A Community of Strangers: The Politics of Urban Development in Eastern Nigeria." Unpub. diss., Massachusetts Institute of Technology, 1967.

———. "Port Harcourt: Ibo Politics in Microcosm." Presented at African Studies Association Annual Conference, 1968.

Wraith, Ronald, and Edgar Simpkins. *Corruption in Developing Countries*. New York: W. W. Norton and Company, 1964.

Young, Crawford. *Politics in the Congo: Decolonization and Independence*. Princeton: Princeton University Press, 1965.

Zolberg, Aristide A. *Creating Political Order: The Party States of West Africa*. Chicago: Rand McNally and Company, 1966.

———. "Mass Parties and National Integration: The Case of the Ivory Coast," *Journal of Politics*, XXV (February 1963), 36–48.

———. *One-Party Government in the Ivory Coast*. Princeton: Princeton University Press, 1964.

———. "Patterns of National Integration," *Journal of Modern African Studies*, V (December 1967), 449–468.

Index

Aba, 18, 34, 35, 37, 49, 123, 138, 163, 196

Abii, D. N., 80, 81, 84, 86, 91, 93, 94, 97, 105, 106, 107, 108, 114, 115, 149

Abiriba: location, 3, 21, 27; community, 21, 27, 30; compared with Mbaise, 22, 23, 69, 81, 82, 87, 88, 99, 102, 103, 105, 112, 173, 185, 186, 188, 193, 195, 199, 200, 201, 206, 211, 216, 222, 223, 224, 237; leadership in, 50–68, 230, 232, 233; residents from, in Port Harcourt, 119, 136, 146, 147; NCNC in, 160, 161–163, 166. *See also* Abiriba Communal Improvement Union; Agbaji; Amaogudu; Ameke

Abiriba Communal Improvement Union (ACIU), 21, 29, 69, 87, 119, 187, 189, 191, 193, 195, 206, 210, 218, 225, 227, 230; evolution of, 31–34; organization of, 34–39; central executive of, 35, 36, 37, 38, 48, 50–66, 232, 233; relations with local government council, 39–42, 185, 186, 199; functions of, 42–49; relations with NCNC, 161, 162, 163

Abiriba Communal Improvement Union, Diobu subbranch, 136, 141

Abiriba Communal Improvement Union, Port Harcourt branch, 22, 34, 35, 36, 54, 55, 56, 57, 60, 136–145, 147, 230

Abiriba Youth Movement, 54, 55, 57, 63

Aboh, 71, 82, 94, 95, 103, 210

Action Group, 12, 96, 101, 177, 178, 179, 256

Adaptability, 160, 184; definition, 161; of NCNC, 172–173; of local government councils, 185–188

Agbagha, O. M., 31, 52, 66

Agbaja: community in Mbaise, 71, 73, 74, 75, 76, 80, 82, 89, 93, 94, 105, 107, 206, 209, 210; community in Port Harcourt, 146

Agbaja Clan Union, 89, 209–210

Agbaji, 27, 28, 32, 48, 246

Age grades (sets): Ibo, 15, 222; in Abiriba, 28, 33, 44, 162, 190; role in ACIU, Port Harcourt branch, 137, 138, 143. *See also* Akahaba age grade; Egwuena age grade; Okezie age grade

Agwu, O., 52, 66, 67

Ahamba, S. M., 92, 107, 111, 114, 115

Ahiara: community in Mbaise, 71, 72, 73, 74, 75, 76, 78, 79, 80, 82, 84, 86, 89, 93, 94, 105, 108, 109, 111, 176, 210, 228; community in Port Harcourt, 147

Ahiara Clan Union: central union, 84, 92, 93, 99, 107, 110; Port Harcourt branch, 148

Ahoada, 132, 153

Akahaba age grade, 43, 46, 47, 65

Akahaba Joint Hospital, 46, 47, 65

Akintola, Samuel, 178

Akuma, Ejim, 29, 30, 31, 52, 66, 67, 68, 140, 247

Almond, Gabriel, 85, 86, 220

Amaogudu, 27, 28, 33, 148, 246

Ameke, 27, 28, 43, 48, 51, 52, 53, 246

Ardener, Edwin, 72, 250

Autonomy, 160, 184, 200; definition, 161; of NCNC, 175–177; of local government councils, 192–193

269